The Shadows of Hope

Modern Slavery in the Land of the Free

Contents

Part I: The Trap (The Mechanics of Acquisition)
How human beings are procured, groomed, and transported.

Chapter 1: The Digital Auction Block

When we try to visualize the sale of human beings, our collective imagination instinctively retreats to the sepia-toned horrors of the nineteenth century. We picture the humid squares of Charleston or New Orleans, the drone of the auctioneer's voice rising above the murmur of the crowd, the sharp crack of the gavel, and the physical inspection of bodies on a wooden platform. We imagine a spectacle of noise and public shame, a physical marketplace where the commodification of human life was visible, tangible, and loud. Because the Thirteenth Amendment dismantled those physical platforms in 1865, we comfort ourselves with the belief that the auction block has been relegated to the museum of history.

We are wrong. The auction block has not disappeared; it has merely gone digital. It has shed its physical bulk, its wooden planks, and its noisy crowds to become silent, frictionless, and infinitely more efficient. Today, the sale of human labor does not begin in a public square; it begins on a glowing screen in a darkened room in Honduras, in a crowded internet café in Chiapas, or on a smartphone held by a trembling hand in Guatemala City. The modern auction block fits in a pocket, and it operates twenty-four hours a day, seven days a week, connecting the desperate with the predatory at the speed of light.

The most dangerous misunderstanding about modern human trafficking is that it operates solely in the dark corners of the internet, hidden behind Tor browsers and encrypted walls accessible only to sophisticated criminal syndicates. The reality, as documented by the Polaris Project—the operator of the U.S. National Human Trafficking Hotline—is far more disturbing. The digital slave trade does not hide in the shadows; it thrives in the open, on the very same platforms that Americans use to share vacation photos and organize birthday parties. It operates on Facebook, Instagram, WhatsApp, and TikTok. It hides in plain sight, camouflaged by the banal architecture of social media.

This digital transformation has democratized the trade in human beings, lowering the barrier to entry for traffickers to virtually zero. In the antebellum South, becoming a slave trader required capital. One needed a ship, a holding pen, guards to prevent escape, and provisions to keep the "cargo" alive. It was a capital-intensive business with high overhead and significant risk.

Today's trafficker needs only a smartphone and a Wi-Fi connection. With these two tools, a single predator can cast a net over thousands of potential victims, identifying and grooming them with an efficiency that would have astonished the most ruthless trader of the 1850s.

The mechanism of this modern trade begins with the "ad." To the untrained eye, these advertisements look indistinguishable from legitimate opportunities. They appear in Facebook groups dedicated to "Visas for Work" or "Jobs in the USA." They feature stock photos of American agriculture—lush fields of tomatoes, clean rows of corn, or smiling workers holding baskets of fruit. The text is often simple, direct, and meticulously crafted to trigger the hope of the economically desperate. "Pickers needed in Florida," an ad might read. "$15.00 per hour. Housing provided. H-2A Visa processing included. Message for details."

For a father in rural El Salvador who earns five dollars a day and watches his children go to bed hungry, this digital flyer is not an advertisement; it is a lifeline. It represents the American Dream distilled into a jpeg. He does not see the trap; he sees the wage—a sum that could transform his family's future in a single season. He pauses his scrolling. He clicks "Like." He types a comment: "Info, please."

In that split second, the auction has begun.

The United Nations Office on Drugs and Crime (UNODC), in their landmark "Global Report on Trafficking in Persons," categorizes this digital engagement strategy into two distinct models: "fishing" and "hunting." The advertisement described above is "fishing." The trafficker baits the hook with promises of high wages and legal status, then waits for the victims to self-identify. By responding to the ad, the victim signals their desperation. They have raised their hand in the digital marketplace, marking themselves as ready for acquisition.

But the "hunting" model is even more insidious, leveraging the algorithmic power of social media platforms to identify vulnerability with surgical precision. Algorithms designed to maximize engagement function, in the hands of traffickers, as sophisticated scouting tools. When a user joins a group for "Single Mothers in Need of Aid" or posts about a recent job loss, the platform's underlying logic categorizes them. The trafficker can then browse these profiles, looking for the tell-tale markers of exploitability: recent migration, expressions of financial panic, or social isolation.

Just as the antebellum trader inspected the teeth and limbs of enslaved people to gauge their work capacity, the modern digital predator inspects the digital footprint of their target. They scroll through years of posts to understand the victim's psychology. Does this person have strong family ties in the United States who might intervene? Or are they alone? Do they have children they are desperate to support? Every shared photo, every status update, every check-in provides data that the trafficker uses to customize their pitch. The inspection is no longer physical; it is psychological, and it occurs without the victim ever knowing they are being assessed.

Once the target is identified—either through the fishing net of a fake ad or the hunting expedition through their profile—the transaction moves to the second phase: the migration to encryption. Almost invariably, the trafficker will direct the victim away from the public comments section and into a private messaging app, most commonly WhatsApp. "Send me a direct message," the recruiter types. "I can help you."

This shift from the public square of Facebook to the encrypted tunnel of WhatsApp is the digital equivalent of moving the captive from the auction block to the holding cell. It isolates the victim. It creates a private channel where the grooming can intensify, shielded from the oversight of platform moderators or law enforcement algorithms. In this encrypted space, the recruiter sheds the persona of a corporate hiring manager and adopts the role of a confidant and savior.

The Polaris Project has analyzed thousands of these interactions, revealing a standardized methodology that borders on industrial. The recruiter creates a sense of urgency and exclusivity. "We have only three spots left for the Florida crew," they might say. "I can save one for you, but I need to know today." They manufacture a scarcity that compels the victim to bypass their instincts and act on fear—the fear of missing out on salvation.

It is in this digital space that the first chains are applied, though they are forged not of iron but of data. To "process the visa," the recruiter demands personal information. "Send me a photo of your passport," they command. "Send me the birth certificates of your children, so we can register them for insurance." The victim, believing they are complying with bureaucratic requirements for a legitimate job, snaps the photos and hits send.

In doing so, they have unwittingly handed over the keys to their own coercion. The trafficker now possesses the victim's identity. They know where the victim lives, the names of their children, and the details of their citizenship. This data becomes collateral. Later, when the "job" turns out to be debt bondage and the "housing" turns out to be a squalid trailer, this information will be weaponized. "If you run," the trafficker will warn, "I know where your family lives. I have your passport. I will tell the authorities you are a criminal." The digital transfer of documents serves the same function as the physical branding of enslaved people: it marks the victim as property, bound to the will of the master.

The scale of this digital marketplace is staggering. Researchers analyzing recruitment patterns have found that recruitment occurs across every major social media platform. It is not limited to niche sites. On Instagram, the aesthetic of the "influencer" lifestyle is weaponized to lure young women into sex trafficking or domestic servitude, with promises of modeling careers or luxury travel. On LinkedIn, the veneer of professional networking provides cover for fraudulent visa scams that target educated workers, trapping them in debt bondage schemes disguised as white-collar employment.

The business model of the digital auction block is ruthlessly efficient because it leverages the infrastructure of legitimate commerce. The platforms themselves, designed to connect people and optimize advertising, have inadvertently created the perfect ecosystem for predation. The same tools that allow a small business to target customers in a specific zip code allow a trafficker to target vulnerable populations in specific regions of instability. The "Look-alike Audience" feature, a powerful marketing tool used by legitimate advertisers to find new customers who resemble their existing ones, can be theoretically reverse-engineered by criminal networks to find new victims who resemble those they have already enslaved.

Furthermore, the cost of customer acquisition for the modern trafficker is negligible. Posting an ad in a Facebook group costs nothing. Creating a fake profile costs nothing. WhatsApp messaging costs nothing. Compare this to the historical slave trade, where the cost of acquiring a human being was substantial. In 1860, a prime field hand might cost $1,800—the equivalent of tens of thousands of dollars today. This high capital cost meant that slave owners, however brutal, had a financial incentive to keep their "property" alive, at least long enough to recoup their investment.

In the digital era, the collapse of acquisition costs has led to a terrifying disposability of human life. Because it costs almost nothing to recruit a victim online, the modern trafficker faces little financial loss if a worker becomes sick, injured, or troublesome. They can simply discard the broken human being and return to the digital well to recruit another. The feed is endless. The supply is infinite. The digital auction block never runs out of inventory.

This disposable nature of the modern workforce is fueled by the anonymity the internet provides. The trafficker operates behind a veil of digital obfuscation. The profile picture is a stock photo. The name is a pseudonym. The phone number is a burner, easily discarded and replaced. When a victim finally realizes the trap has closed—perhaps standing in a muddy field in Georgia, thousands of miles from home—they often realize they do not even know the real name of the person who sold them. They have been trafficked by a ghost.

The complexity of this digital infrastructure poses a unique challenge for law enforcement. Jurisdiction becomes a fluid concept when the recruiter is in Mexico, the platform servers are in California, the victim is in Guatemala, and the exploitation occurs in Texas. The crime is distributed across borders and servers, fragmenting the evidence and diffusing responsibility. By the time investigators piece together the digital trail, the ad has been deleted, the profile deactivated, and the operation moved to a new URL.

Moreover, the sheer volume of content overwhelms traditional policing methods. Billions of posts are generated daily. Identifying the needle of trafficking in the haystack of legitimate commerce requires resources that most agencies lack. While automated moderation tools exist, the language of trafficking is slippery. Traffickers use emojis, slang, and coded language to evade detection. A post about "fresh meat" might refer to a barbecue—or it might refer to the sale of a child. Context is everything, and algorithms struggle with context.

We must also confront the uncomfortable reality of corporate complicity, whether through negligence or design. The tech giants that host these digital auction blocks generate revenue from the very engagement that facilitates trafficking. Every time a user clicks on a fake job ad, the platform's metrics tick upward. The data harvested from potential victims fuels the advertising models that power the tech economy. While these companies have policies against exploitation and work with law enforcement, the fundamental architecture of their platforms—designed for friction-less connection and targeted reach—is inherently suited to the needs of the predator.

The transition from the physical auction block to the digital one represents more than a change in technology; it represents a fundamental shift in the psychology of the market. The physical auction block was a spectacle that demanded the complicity of the crowd. To witness it was to participate in it. The digital auction block requires no such collective acknowledgement. It operates in the privacy of the inbox. It allows society to remain ignorant of the scale of the trade because the transaction is invisible to the public eye. The screams are silenced by the screen.

Consider the experience of the worker who has engaged with one of these ads. They believe they have secured a golden ticket. They show the WhatsApp messages to their family as proof of their good fortune. "Look," they say, pointing to the screen. "The recruiter says I will have a visa. He says there is a house waiting for me." They pack their bags. They borrow money to pay the "processing fees" demanded by the ghost in the machine. They board a bus, clutching their phone like a talisman, believing they are traveling toward freedom.

They do not know that they have already been sold.

They do not know that the "processing fee" is the first link in a chain of debt that will bind them for years. They do not know that the "visa" is either fake or, if real, will be used as a weapon to prevent them from leaving. They do not know that the friendly recruiter will vanish the moment they cross the border, replaced by a handler who views them not as a human being but as a commodity to be extracted.

The auction is over before the journey even begins. The digital gavel has already fallen. The modern slave trade does not require a physical platform or a screaming auctioneer. It requires only a desperate person, a predatory algorithm, and a "Send" button. And in the time it has taken you to read this chapter, thousands of new transactions have been initiated, thousands of new traps have been set, and thousands of human beings have entered the digital pipeline that leads to modern bondage. The auction block is open for business, and it is everywhere.

Chapter 2: The Psychology of the "Groomer"

If we were to cast the villain of a human trafficking story based on Hollywood tropes, we would look for a monster. We would imagine a scarred gangster, a shadowy figure in a tinted SUV, or a brute forcing a victim into the back of a van. We expect the mechanism of enslavement to be violent abduction, a sudden and terrifying rupture of reality where force is the primary instrument of control.

But in the modern landscape of labor exploitation, the villain rarely looks like a monster. More often, he looks like a savior. He appears as a benevolent uncle, a charming romantic partner, or a well-connected community leader offering a hand up to those who have fallen down. He does not break into the victim's life; he is invited in. He does not use handcuffs; he uses gratitude.

This figure is the "Groomer," and his role is the most psychologically sophisticated component of the trafficking supply chain. While the digital platforms discussed in the previous chapter provide the infrastructure for recruitment, the groomer provides the narrative. He is the architect of the trust that will eventually become the victim's prison.

The legal system struggles to grapple with this figure because his initial actions are rarely illegal. As I noted in my research, while the act of trafficking itself is criminalized, the methodical process that precedes it—what professionals call "grooming"—operates largely without legal consequence. This creates a dangerous paradox. We have outlawed the endpoint of the crime—the exploitation—but we leave the inception untouched, allowing predators to operate with impunity during the critical phase where the trap is being laid.

To understand the groomer, one must understand that he is not looking for a random victim; he is looking for a specific psychological profile. As the United Nations Office on Drugs and Crime has documented, traffickers do not simply identify vulnerable individuals; they build detailed psychological profiles based on freely shared personal information. The groomer studies his target with the intensity of a profiler. He looks for the fracture lines in a person's life—the recent divorce, the job loss, the sick parent, the rebellious child.

Once these fractures are identified, the groomer positions himself as the filler for those cracks. The manipulation is tailored with devastating specificity. If a target posts on social media about the difficulty of finding educational opportunities for their kids, the groomer does not just offer a job; he talks about the excellent public schools in the district where the "job" is located. If the target mentions chronic health issues or the crushing weight of medical debt, the groomer creates a fiction involving comprehensive health insurance and company doctors. If the target expresses homesickness or cultural isolation, the groomer speaks to them in their specific regional dialect, promising a community of compatriots waiting to welcome them.

This is not a sales pitch; it is a mirror. The groomer reflects the victim's deepest needs back to them, wrapped in a promise.

The process is slow, deliberate, and industrialized. It is not a crime of passion but a methodology refined over decades. Traffickers begin by identifying vulnerabilities, then systematically break down psychological resistance through calculated deception. They understand that trust is a currency, and they spend it lavishly in the early stages.

Consider the "Loverboy" model, a technique often associated with sex trafficking but increasingly prevalent in labor exploitation cases. The U.S. Department of State has documented how traffickers use promises of marriage or romantic relationships to lure victims. In these scenarios, the groomer plays the role of the perfect partner. He is attentive, protective, and seemingly wealthy. He spends weeks or months building a genuine emotional connection. They share stories, exchange photographs, and discuss a future life together.

For the victim, often lonely or socially isolated, this attention is intoxicating. It validates their worth. It creates a debt of emotional gratitude that is far harder to break than any financial debt. When the "partner" suggests moving to a new country or taking a specific job to build their future, the victim does not see a recruiter making a demand; they see a loved one making a plan. They believe they are making a free choice to travel, to trust, and to build a life. In reality, every option has been carefully crafted to lead to the same outcome: exploitation.

This psychological maneuvering serves a critical economic function: it lowers the cost of control. A victim who believes they are following a friend or a lover requires no guards. They will board the bus willingly. They will hand over their documents for "safekeeping" without protest. They will lie to border agents to protect their "benefactor." The groomer has effectively deputized the victim to police themselves.

The sophistication of this manipulation extends to the systematic isolation of the victim, a process that begins long before physical travel occurs. The groomer subtly drives wedges between the victim and their existing support network. "Your family doesn't want you to succeed," he might whisper. "They are jealous of this opportunity. You should keep our plans secret until everything is finalized." By framing secrecy as a necessary tactic to protect their good fortune, the groomer ensures that no skeptical third party can intervene.

This isolation is reinforced by the "debt of gratitude." In many labor trafficking cases, the groomer provides small amounts of financial assistance early in the relationship—money for medicine, a new phone, or help with rent. In the context of the victim's poverty, these gestures seem like miracles. But in the groomer's ledger, they are down payments on a soul. They create a psychological obligation that makes it difficult for the victim to ask questions or demand written contracts later. How can you doubt the motives of the man who paid for your mother's insulin?

Once the physical trap is sprung—once the victim is in the United States, in the field or the factory or the brothel—the groomer's mask slips, but it rarely falls off completely. Instead, the psychological manipulation shifts from seduction to gaslighting. The groomer reframes the exploitation as a shared struggle. "I am trying to help you," he will say as he deducts exorbitant fees from their paycheck. "But the lawyers are expensive. The rent is high. We are in this together."

Even when the relationship turns abusive, the groundwork laid during the grooming phase makes escape psychologically difficult. The victim is often far from home, stripped of identity documents, and controlled through debt. But more than that, they are paralyzed by the cognitive dissonance of realizing that their savior is their jailer. To admit the reality of their situation is to admit a devastating betrayal of trust.

In the digital age, the groomer's power extends even after the victim is enslaved. The Polaris Project has documented cases where traffickers actively monitor and control their victims' social media accounts. The groomer becomes a digital ventriloquist. He impersonates the victim online, posting photos of a happy life, sending reassuring messages to parents, and maintaining a digital façade that prevents anyone back home from raising the alarm.

This is the final cruelty of the groomer's art. He steals not just the victim's labor and liberty, but their voice. He wears their digital skin to reassure the world that everything is fine, while the human being underneath enters a nightmare of servitude.

Understanding the psychology of the groomer forces us to confront an uncomfortable truth: these are not crude operators. They are master manipulators who understand human psychology better than many therapists. They know exactly how to identify emotional needs and exploit them systematically. They operate in the gap between legal definition and moral reality, knowing that building a trap out of lies is not a crime until the door is locked.

By the time the law can intervene—when the exploitation is finally "proven"—the damage is irreversible. The trap has been sprung, and the victim's ability to escape has been systematically dismantled. The groomer has done his work. He has delivered a compliant, isolated, and indebted human being to the marketplace, and he is already returning to his screen, looking for the next fracture line in a stranger's life, ready to become whatever they need him to be.

Chapter 3: The Economics of the Smuggler

In the lexicon of the American border, the word "coyote" conjures a specific, dusty image: a lone operator in a battered pickup truck, navigating scrubland in the dark, guiding a handful of desperate people through a hole in a fence for cash. It is an image of disorganized criminality, a transaction of opportunity between a guide and a traveler.

This image is a fiction. It is a nostalgic relic that obscures the reality of a multi-billion-dollar logistics industry that rivals FedEx or DHL in its complexity, if not its legality. The modern smuggler is not a guide; he is a diversified financial services provider. He is a travel agent, a loan officer, and a commodities broker rolled into one. And the commodity he trades is debt.

To understand the trap that ensnares the modern slave, we must look away from the physical border and look instead at the ledger. The transformation of a free human being into an indentured servant is, at its core, a financial transaction. It begins with a price tag that defies the economic reality of the person paying it.

As documented by researchers at George Mason University's Terrorism, Transnational Crime and Corruption Center (TraCCC), the fees charged by these networks have skyrocketed. A journey that might have cost a few hundred dollars two decades ago now commands a price ranging from $5,000 to over $20,000. For a subsistence farmer in Guatemala or a displaced worker in Honduras, this sum is an abstraction—a number so large it might as well be infinity. It represents years, perhaps decades, of local wages.

The smuggler knows the victim cannot pay this cash upfront. In fact, the entire business model depends on their inability to pay. If the victim had $20,000, they would not need to be smuggled; they could likely qualify for legal visas or start a business at home. The poverty of the client is not an obstacle to the smuggler; it is the foundation of the contract.

This is where the economics of the smuggler diverge from legitimate commerce. In a normal transaction, if a customer cannot afford the product, the sale does not happen. In the smuggling economy, if the customer cannot afford the product, the smuggler becomes the financier. He offers a "package deal." He will cover the costs of the journey—the bribes to local police, the safe houses, the transport, the food—and, most seductively, the placement in a "guaranteed" job in the United States.

In exchange, the victim signs a contract. Sometimes this is a literal piece of paper, signed in a notary's office in their home village, disguised as a personal loan for "home improvements" or "medical expenses" to provide a veneer of legality. More often, it is a verbal contract enforced by the terrifying reputation of the smuggling network.

The collateral for this loan is everything the victim possesses. The smuggler requires the deed to the family's small plot of land. He demands the title to their home. He requires the signatures of parents or spouses as co-signers, explicitly tying their physical safety to the repayment of the debt. As the U.S. Department of State has noted in its trafficking assessments, this initial debt creation is the moment the trap snaps shut. Before the worker has taken a single step north, before they have crossed a single river, they have effectively mortgaged their entire existence.

This financial structure serves two ruthless purposes. First, it eliminates risk for the smuggler. If the worker gets cold feet in Mexico and tries to turn back, the smuggler forecloses on the family home. If the worker is deported by U.S. authorities, the debt remains. The smuggler gets paid whether the human cargo is delivered or not.

Second, and more importantly for the labor supply chain, this debt transforms the worker into a compliant asset. A person who owes $20,000 and knows their mother will lose her house if they miss a payment is a person who will not complain about wage theft. They will not report safety violations. They will not organize a union. They will work at whatever pace is demanded, for whatever wage is offered, for as long as it takes. The debt is the chain.

But the economic genius of the modern smuggler lies in what happens next. In many cases, the smuggler does not intend to collect these payments $50 at a time over the next five years. That would require a long-term accounts receivable department and the hassle of international collections. Instead, the smuggler often sells the debt.

This is the "asset transfer," the critical pivot point where the human being becomes a financial instrument traded between criminal entities. The smuggler in Central America coordinates with a labor broker—a "contractor"—in the United States. This U.S.-based broker needs workers for a poultry plant in Alabama or a construction site in Texas. The broker agrees to pay the smuggler a lump sum upon delivery of the workers—essentially paying off the "transportation fee" upfront.

Now, the worker owes the debt to the U.S. broker. The smuggler has his cash and returns to the village to recruit the next victim. The U.S. broker now "owns" the worker's debt. This transfer is seamless and invisible to the victim, who simply knows that upon arrival, they are told, "You work for me now. You owe me $15,000 for your travel. I will deduct it from your paycheck."

This structure mirrors the logic of the mortgage-backed security. The originator of the loan (the smuggler) sells the asset to an aggregator (the labor broker), who extracts the value over time. The human being is merely the collateral underlying the security.

The profitability of this trade is staggering. The International Labour Organization (ILO) estimates that forced labor generates $236 billion in illegal profits annually. A significant portion of this flows through these recruitment and transport networks. The smuggler's margin is protected by the illegality of the product. Because the worker cannot go to the police, the smuggler can charge monopoly prices. There is no competition law in the black market.

We must also dismantle the myth that the high fees reflect the high costs of evasion. While it is true that smuggling involves expenses—bribes to cartel gatekeepers, payoffs to corrupt officials, vehicle maintenance—the markup is exorbitant. A bus ticket from San Salvador to the U.S. border costs a few hundred dollars. The smuggler charges thousands. The difference is not "logistics"; it is the price of admission to the American economy. It is an access fee.

The smuggler justifies this fee by marketing himself as a premium service provider. He is not just selling a ride; he is selling a "guaranteed" outcome. The narrative is carefully crafted: "Do not trust the cheap coyotes," he warns. "They will leave you to die in the desert. I have connections. I have a lawyer in Texas. I have a job waiting for you."

This "premium" service often includes the provision of fraudulent documents, another profit center for the network. The TraCCC researchers have documented how fees are layered: a fee for the journey, a fee for the "crossing," a fee for the "safe house," and a separate fee for the "papers".

The smuggler operates like a low-budget airline, where the base price is just the beginning, and every necessity is an expensive add-on.

But unlike an airline, the passenger cannot opt out. Once the journey begins, the worker is a captive consumer. In the safe houses of Northern Mexico, the economics become predatory. The smuggler might delay the crossing for weeks, charging the migrants daily rent for the privilege of sleeping on a concrete floor. "The border is hot right now," they lie. "We must wait." Every day of waiting adds to the debt. The victim, cut off from home and terrified of the cartels outside the door, has no choice but to agree to the new charges.

This creates a terrifying form of "negative amortization." The victim is borrowing more money just to survive the journey to the place where they are supposed to start paying it back. By the time they see the Rio Grande, they are so deep in the hole that they are financially underwater. They arrive in the United States not as immigrants seeking opportunity, but as debtors fleeing ruin.

The financial entanglement is often reinforced by what the ILO calls "revenue generation strategies". The smuggler does not just move the body; he outfits it. He requires the worker to buy specific clothes for the crossing, to purchase a specific type of backpack, or to buy a "burner" phone for communication. These items are sold by the smuggler's associates at massive markups. It is the first iteration of the "company store" model that will define the worker's life in America: a closed economic loop where the boss sets the prices, and the worker has no choice but to pay.

There is a cold rationality to this system that is often missed when we focus only on the physical suffering of the journey. We see images of exhausted migrants and assume the chaos is a sign of incompetence. It is not. The deprivation is a cost-saving measure. Every dollar not spent on food or safe transport for the migrant is a dollar of profit for the smuggler. The callousness is an efficiency strategy.

Furthermore, the smuggler has diversified his risk through "volume." Like a venture capitalist who expects some startups to fail, the smuggling network expects some migrants to be caught. Because the debt is secured by assets in the home country, the apprehension of a migrant by Border Patrol is an inconvenience, not a financial disaster. The family back home still owes the money. The network still gets paid. The only one who loses is the human being who is deported with a $15,000 debt and no way to pay it.

This financial architecture explains why the flow of undocumented labor is so resilient. It is not driven solely by the "pull" of American jobs or the "push" of poverty. It is driven by the profit imperatives of the intermediaries. These networks have a financial incentive to actively recruit, to market their services, and to convince people who might otherwise stay home that migration is their only option. They are not merely fulfilling demand; they are manufacturing it to keep the loan books full.

The transfer of the worker from the smuggler to the U.S. labor broker is the final handshake in this illicit supply chain. It typically happens in border states—Texas, Arizona, California. The workers are moved from a stash house to a van owned by the contractor. No money may change hands visibly at this moment; the transaction has been settled digitally or through hawala-style networks that move money without moving cash.

As the van pulls away, heading toward a construction site in Dallas or a field in Florida, the smuggler's job is done. He has successfully monetized a human life. He has converted a desperate farmer into a securitized debt obligation. The worker looking out the window sees the landscape of America passing by, but he does not own his view. He does not own his time. He does not own his labor. He has been bought and paid for, and the ledger is open.

This is the economics of the smuggler. It is a business that relies not just on the violation of borders, but on the violation of the basic economic principle that a worker owns their own labor. In this market, labor is not hired; it is mortgaged. And the interest rate is a lifetime of servitude.

Chapter 4: The Debt Contract

The chains that bind the modern slave are not forged of iron; they are forged of arithmetic. In the physical reality of the American workplace—the construction site, the tomato field, the hotel laundry room—there are no shackles. The doors are often unlocked. The gates are sometimes open. To the casual observer, the workers appear free. They walk to the bus; they stand in line at the food truck; they check their phones.

But this freedom is an optical illusion maintained by a force more powerful than steel: debt. The true prison of the undocumented worker is constructed of compound interest, fraudulent fees, and a ledger that is rigged to ensuring the balance never reaches zero. This is the mechanism of "debt bondage," or *peonage*, a practice that Congress explicitly outlawed in 1867 but which thrives today in the shadow economy, protected by the silence of its victims and the indifference of the law.

To understand how a human being can be turned into a financial instrument, one must dissect the "contract." In the world of legitimate finance, a loan agreement is a regulated document with a fixed interest rate, a defined amortization schedule, and clear terms of repayment. Truth in Lending laws require transparency. If you borrow money to buy a car, you know exactly when that car will be yours.

In the world of labor trafficking, the contract is a weapon. As defined by the organization End Slavery Now, bonded labor occurs when individuals pledge their labor as security for a loan—often one with undefined terms that can be passed down to family members. The contract is rarely written down, for writing it would create evidence of a felony. Instead, it is spoken, usually in the back of a van crossing the border or in a crowded orientation room in a trailer park.

"You owe me," the labor broker says. The figure is rarely a round number. It is a specific, calculated weight: $12,500 for the journey, $500 for the "placement fee," $200 for the uniform, and $300 for the first month's rent. The worker accepts this debt because they have no choice; they are already here, thousands of miles from home, and the broker holds the keys to their survival.

This initial principal is merely the hook. The trap lies in the "service fees." As Respect International documented in their analysis of business models of exploitation, traffickers operate on a dual strategy: cost reduction (stealing wages) and revenue generation (inflating costs). The revenue generation strategy relies on imposing upfront fees for securing the job, followed by the systematic inflation of costs for transportation, housing, food, and necessary work equipment.

Consider the mathematics of a typical week for a trafficked agricultural worker. They might work 60 hours picking peppers. At a promised rate of $10 per hour—already below the legal minimum in many states—they should earn $600.

But payday operates according to the broker's arithmetic. First, the broker deducts taxes—not federal withholding sent to the IRS, but a "tax" that goes straight into the broker's pocket, justified by the lie that the worker is "independent." Then comes the housing deduction: $250 a week for a mattress in a trailer shared with six other men. Then the transportation fee: $10 a day for the ride in the broker's van to the fields, a service the worker is forbidden to refuse. Then the equipment fee: gloves, buckets, and shears sold at a 300 percent markup.

By the time the ledger is balanced, the $600 paycheck has dwindled to $50. The worker is handed a small envelope of cash, just enough to buy food from the broker's commissary, but not enough to pay down the principal of the debt. The $13,000 they owe remains $13,000. They have worked 60 hours for the privilege of staying exactly where they started.

This is "negative amortization" applied to human life. The worker is running on a treadmill that is programmed to move slightly faster than they can run.

The U.S. Department of State identifies this manipulation as a primary indicator of trafficking. In their definition of the crime, they note that traffickers manipulate debts *after* the economic relationship begins. The terms are fluid. If a worker works particularly hard and threatens to pay off the debt too quickly, the broker introduces a new fee. A "legal processing fee" appears on the ledger. A "medical surcharge" is added because another worker in the house got sick. The debt is not a fixed number to be repaid; it is a leash to be adjusted.

Historical parallels illuminate the durability of this model. Following the Civil War, when physical slavery was abolished, the South pivoted to peonage. As PBS documents in *Slavery by Another Name*, merchants and planters used credit to entrap workers. The sharecropper would buy seeds and tools from the plantation store on credit. At harvest time, the planter's fraudulent accounting would ensure the crop was worth slightly less than the debt. The worker was legally free, but economically bound to the land until the debt was cleared—a day that never came.

Today, the "company store" has returned, adapted for the gig economy. In Mexico during the Porfiriato period, *tiendas de raya* were symbols of exploitation where workers were forced to spend their wages. Modern labor trafficking replicates this closed loop. Wikipedia's analysis of labor trafficking notes that workers are often held in perpetual debt to crew leaders who impose mandatory communication fees—charging workers to use a phone to call their families—further indebting them.

This control over communication is critical. The debt contract relies on the isolation of the borrower. If the worker could check market prices for housing or transportation, they would realize they are being gouged. But they cannot shop around. They live in the broker's house, ride in the broker's van, and eat the broker's food. The broker is the landlord, the grocer, the bank, and the boss. There is no outside economy for the trafficked worker.

Why do they pay? Why not simply run?

The answer lies in the collateral. In a normal loan, the collateral is physical property—a house, a car. In a trafficking contract, the collateral is often flesh and blood. As End Slavery Now explains, bonded labor occurs when people give themselves into slavery as security for a loan, or even inherit a debt from a relative. The debt is often secured by the safety of the family back home.

"I know where your mother lives," the broker reminds the worker who questions a deduction. "I know which school your daughter attends." The verbal contract includes an implicit clause of violence. To run away is to default on the loan, and the penalty for default is visited upon those the worker loves most. This creates a psychological prison far more secure than any detention center. The worker stays not because they respect the debt, but because they love their family.

Furthermore, the illegality of the worker's status weaponizes the debt. In a legal dispute, a debtor can declare bankruptcy. A court can declare a contract unconscionable. But an undocumented worker cannot access the bankruptcy court. The broker holds the ultimate trump card: "If you complain about the debt, I will call ICE. You will be deported, but the debt will remain. And my associates in your village will collect it."

This duality—the threat of deportation combined with the threat of violence at home—makes the debt contract ironclad. It transforms the worker into an asset with a perpetual yield. For the trafficker, the worker is more valuable than a machine. A machine depreciates; it requires maintenance and eventually breaks down. A debt-bonded worker pays for their own maintenance, can be worked until exhaustion, and, if they break, can be replaced by another desperate borrower for the cost of a bus ticket.

The City of Hialeah, Florida—a community that has dealt extensively with the realities of immigrant exploitation—identifies coercion explicitly as including "debt bondage" alongside document confiscation. They recognize that the financial shackle is as binding as physical force. Yet, our national discourse often misses this nuance, focusing on "smuggling fees" rather than the ongoing, predatory extraction that occurs after arrival.

We must recognize the debt contract for what it is: a sophisticated financial crime that masquerades as an employment agreement. It is usury weaponized to strip human beings of their agency. It renders the Thirteenth Amendment null and void for millions of people, re-establishing the condition of involuntary servitude through the mechanism of the ledger.

The ledger does not bleed. It does not shout. It sits quietly in a notebook in a contractor's pocket, or on a spreadsheet in a laptop. But it is the most violent instrument in the trafficker's arsenal. It dictates who eats and who starves, who stays and who is cast out, who is free and who is owned. Until we tear up these contracts and criminalize the fraudulent debts that bind these workers, we are merely observers to a slavery that hides behind the math.

Chapter 5: The Journey as Conditioning

The journey from freedom to bondage is rarely instantaneous. It is a physical and psychological erosion, a grinding process that wears down the human spirit mile by mile until the victim arrives at their destination not only indebted and displaced, but fundamentally broken. We often conceive of the transportation phase of human trafficking merely as a logistical challenge—a question of how to move a body from Point A to Point B across guarded borders. This view misses the darker, more strategic function of the journey.

For the modern trafficker, the journey is not just transportation; it is conditioning. It is a brutal curriculum designed to teach the victim a single, devastating lesson: you have no control.

In the history of the Atlantic slave trade, this process was known as "seasoning." Captives who survived the Middle Passage were subjected to a period of acclimatization and breaking in the Caribbean before being sold to American plantations. The modern "Middle Passage" takes place on Greyhound buses, in the back of cramped vans, and along the terrifying corridors of the migratory routes, but its function remains remarkably similar. It strips the individual of agency, reduces them to a state of dependency, and uses physical exhaustion to ensure compliance.

The Polaris Project, in their analysis of trafficking logistics, has identified how traffickers weaponize the transportation industry to move victims while simultaneously isolating them. They do not always use clandestine smuggling routes. Often, they use the infrastructure of legitimate commerce—airlines, trains, and long-distance buses—to move victims in plain sight. Informal systems, such as the network of discount "Chinatown buses" operating along the East Coast, serve as ideal conduits because they often bypass the scrutiny of formal security checkpoints.

For the victim, this travel is defined by a terrifying information asymmetry. As they move further from home, their knowledge of the world shrinks. They do not know which state they are crossing. They do not know the laws of the towns they pass through. They are often forbidden from looking out the windows or speaking to fellow passengers. This enforced disorientation is the first step in the dismantling of the self. By the time they arrive, they are geographically unmoored, creating a reliance on the trafficker that borders on the infantile.

Consider the physical reality of this transit. Traffickers often crowd dozens of people into vehicles designed for a fraction of that number. Food is withheld or rationed to create a state of semi-starvation. Sleep is denied or interrupted. These are not merely cost-saving measures; they are interrogation techniques adapted for logistics. A sleep-deprived, hungry, and disoriented person is chemically incapable of complex resistance. They enter a survival mode where the higher cognitive functions required to plan an escape or question authority are shut down.

This physical degradation serves to lower the victim's expectations for their future existence. After weeks of sleeping on concrete floors in safe houses or sitting upright in a van for forty-eight hours straight, a mattress on the floor of a crowded trailer in a labor camp can feel like a luxury. The trafficker lowers the baseline of human dignity so profoundly during the journey that the exploitative conditions of the destination seem, by comparison, acceptable.

The State Department's 2024 report on the recruitment of vulnerable populations documents how this transition operates. Upon arrival at their destination, victims are often transported to large compounds where the final act of the journey—the stripping of identity—takes place. This is the moment when the physical trauma of the trip is cemented by legal erasure. Passports, visas, and identification documents are confiscated, ostensibly for "safekeeping" or "processing."

But the psychological groundwork for this confiscation was laid miles back on the highway. A victim who has spent days or weeks fully dependent on the trafficker for food, water, and safety has been conditioned to obey. They have learned that the trafficker is the only barrier between them and the chaos of the outside world. When the hand is extended for their passport, they surrender it not just out of fear, but out of a learned helplessness cultivated during every mile of the journey.

This dynamic creates a perverse psychological bond, similar to the "Stockholm Syndrome" observed in hostages. The trafficker, who is the source of the danger, also positions himself as the protector. During the journey, the migrants face threats from cartels, corrupt police, and rival gangs. The smuggler or trafficker steers them through these dangers. He becomes the pilot through hell. By the time they reach the United States, the victim views the trafficker with a complex mixture of fear and gratitude. He is the one who got them across. He is the one who fed them. This trauma bond makes the victim hesitant to report their exploiter to authorities, whom they have been taught to view as the ultimate threat.

The National Human Trafficking Hotline data reveals that "Recent Migration/Relocation" is the single most common vulnerability factor, present in 54 percent of all identified trafficking cases. This statistic confirms that the period of movement is the period of greatest risk. It is when the protective infrastructure of community and family is stripped away, leaving the individual exposed.

Furthermore, the journey introduces the victim to the specific economics of their enslavement. As noted in the discussion of debt contracts, the costs of this travel are often inflated and added to the victim's ledger. But the daily experience of the journey teaches the worker that everything has a price. A bottle of water costs a dollar. A bathroom break costs five. The "transportation fee" deducted from their future wages is made tangible by the misery of the ride. They learn, viscerally, that they are burning money with every mile, deepening the hole they must dig themselves out of.

For the trafficker, the journey is a screening process. Those who are too rebellious, too sick, or too psychologically resilient are often discarded along the route. The ones who arrive at the construction site in Texas or the farm in Florida are the ones who have survived the filtration. They are the ones who have proven they can endure suffering without breaking rank. They are pre-selected for compliance.

We must also recognize the gendered dimensions of this conditioning. For female victims, the journey often involves sexual violence, a horrific tool of control documented by the State Department. This violence serves a dual purpose: it is an act of domination that terrorizes the victim into silence, and it creates a shame that prevents them from seeking help. A woman who has been violated during her transit arrives carrying a burden of trauma that makes her feel unworthy of rescue. She has been "broken" in the most intimate sense, her autonomy shattered before she is ever asked to clean a hotel room or harvest a crop.

In this light, the bus ride or the van trip is not merely a bridge between the home country and the American workplace. It is a decompression chamber where a human being is converted into a unit of labor. It functions like the "boot camp" of the military, designed to break down individuality and build up obedience, but without the promise of honor or citizenship at the end.

When we see a van full of weary laborers on an American highway, we often assume they are merely commuting. We do not see the history contained in their exhaustion. We do not see that they have just emerged from a gauntlet designed to strip them of the will to resist. They have been conditioned by the road. They have learned that movement is dangerous, that authority is capricious, and that survival depends on silence.

By the time the door opens and their feet touch the soil of their new workplace, the transformation is complete. As I observed in my research, "In the span of a bus ride, a person moves from hope to captivity, from the promise of opportunity to the reality of servitude." They arrive stripped of dreams, stripped of documents, and stripped of the belief that they have any rights that this new world is bound to respect. The trap has not just been set; it has been internalized. The journey has done its work.

Chapter 6: Document Theft

The most devastating weapon in the modern slaver's arsenal weighs less than two ounces. It is made of paper, ink, and a laminated data page. It is the passport. In the architecture of human liberty, this small booklet serves as the cornerstone; it is the physical proof that a human being exists as a legal entity, that they belong to a nation, and that they possess the right to move.

When a trafficker takes a passport, he does not merely steal a document. He steals the victim's name. He steals their citizenship. He steals their ability to prove they are a human being with rights that any government is bound to respect. In that single, often quiet transaction, the worker ceases to be a person in the eyes of the administrative state and becomes a ghost—a "shadow person" who occupies physical space but possesses no legal weight.

The U.S. Department of State has identified the confiscation of passports, visas, and other identity documents as a primary method of coercion in human trafficking cases. It is almost always the first administrative act upon arrival at the destination. The moment marks the final transition from the "conditioning" of the journey to the "control" of the workplace. The worker steps off the bus or the van, exhausted and disoriented, and is met by the labor contractor or the "employer." The hand is extended. The demand is made. And the trap snaps shut.

The genius of this tactic lies in its banal presentation. Traffickers rarely snatch documents with violence. Violence is messy; it breeds resentment and leaves bruises that police can see. Instead, the theft is framed as a bureaucratic necessity or a benevolent service. "I need your passport to process your work visa," the contractor says. Or, "It is not safe to keep these in the trailer; things get stolen here. I will put it in the company safe for you."

The victim, who has likely been conditioned by the smuggler to view the U.S. legal system as a labyrinth they cannot navigate alone, complies. They hand over the booklet. They believe they are following the rules. In reality, they are surrendering their only exit strategy.

Once the document disappears into the contractor's safe—or, as is often the case, a locked drawer in a suburban kitchen or a glove compartment in a pickup truck—the power dynamic shifts irreversibly. The worker is now effectively a prisoner, yet there are no bars on the windows. They are contained not by walls, but by the terrifying reality of life in America without identification.

In the United States, a person without "papers" exists in a legal twilight zone. Without that document, the most basic functions of modern existence become impossible. You cannot open a bank account to store the few dollars you might earn. You cannot rent an apartment in your own name. You cannot board a domestic flight or a Greyhound bus without risking an interrogation that could lead to detention. You cannot enter a government building.

Most critically, you cannot approach law enforcement. This is the mechanism that silences the victim more effectively than any gag. A citizen who is abused by an employer can call 911. They can walk into a police station and file a report. An undocumented worker who has been stripped of their passport believes—often correctly—that walking into a police station is an act of suicide. To report a crime, they must first identify themselves. To identify themselves, they must reveal their lack of status.

The trafficker understands this calculus perfectly. They have weaponized the victim's lack of documentation, transforming the law from a shield into a sword held at the victim's throat. "Go ahead," the trafficker taunts. "Call the police. Tell them who you are. See who they arrest." The confiscated passport becomes the ultimate leverage. It is the proof that the trafficker holds the victim's identity hostage.

This practice creates a direct historical continuity with the "pass system" that controlled the movement of enslaved people in the antebellum South. In the 19th century, a slave could not leave their plantation without a written pass from their master. This scrap of paper was the difference between "traveling" and "escaping." Any white citizen could stop a Black person on the road and demand to see their pass. If they had none, they were presumed to be runaways and could be detained, whipped, and returned to bondage.

Today, the passport serves the identical function as the antebellum pass. It is the permission slip to exist in the public sphere. The trafficker who holds the passport acts as the master who controls the pass. He becomes the sole arbiter of the worker's movement. If the worker wants to leave—to go to the store, to visit a clinic, to return home—they must petition the holder of their identity for permission. The employer grants or withholds this permission based on his economic needs, not the worker's rights.

This control extends to the most intimate aspects of life. Victims of trafficking often refuse medical treatment even for severe injuries because they fear hospital administrators will ask for identification. They endure toothaches, broken bones, and infections in silence. The theft of the document essentially removes the worker from the healthcare system, the banking system, and the justice system, reducing them to a biological machine that labors but does not legally exist.

The Constitutional implications of this theft are profound. The Fourth Amendment guarantees "the right of the people to be secure in their persons, houses, papers, and effects". The Founding Fathers listed "papers" alongside "persons" and "houses" because they understood that in a free society, a person's documents are the repository of their privacy and their liberty. To be insecure in one's papers is to be insecure in one's person.

When a trafficker seizes a worker's documents, they are violating the spirit of the Thirteenth Amendment, which abolished involuntary servitude. While the trafficker may not claim legal ownership of the person, by claiming ownership of the *proof* of that person, they achieve the same result. They create a condition of involuntary servitude where the worker cannot quit, cannot run, and cannot negotiate, because they have been stripped of the legal capacity to do so.

In the digital age, this document theft has evolved to include the virtual self. Just as the trafficker takes the passport, they often confiscate the smartphone. Or, more insidiously, they demand the passwords. The Polaris Project has documented cases where traffickers actively monitor and control victims' social media accounts. This is the digital equivalent of the pass system. The trafficker controls who the victim talks to, what they see, and what the world sees of them. They might allow the victim to keep their phone to maintain the illusion of freedom, but with the understanding that every message is being read. The digital identity is hijacked just as the legal identity is locked away.

The recovery of these documents is often the primary obstacle to liberation. Even if a victim manages to physically escape the compound or the factory, where do they go? A person standing on a highway in rural

Nebraska with no money, no phone, and no passport is not free; they are merely loose. They are a "John Doe" or "Jane Doe" vulnerable to immediate arrest by immigration authorities who will view them not as a victim of a crime, but as a perpetrator of an immigration violation.

This reality forces many victims to return to their exploiters. The gravitational pull of the passport is immense. The victim knows that without that booklet, they can never go home. They can never see their children again. The trafficker holds the key to their past and their future. "Finish the contract," the trafficker says, "and I will give it back." Of course, the contract is never finished, and the document is rarely returned voluntarily.

In the legal battles against trafficking, the "safekeeping" defense is a common tactic used by defense attorneys. They argue that the employer was merely protecting the documents for the workers, who lived in communal housing where theft was common. They frame the confiscation as an act of benevolence. But the context reveals the lie. A bank protects your money, but it allows you to withdraw it at will. A landlord might hold a key, but they cannot prevent you from leaving. When the "safekeeping" is accompanied by debt, threats, and restricted movement, it is not protection; it is possession.

We must understand document theft not as a minor administrative infraction, but as a violent act of erasure. It is a kidnapping of the legal self. It transforms a subject of rights into an object of labor. When we look at the supply chains of American agriculture, construction, and hospitality, we must look past the products to the people, and ask: who holds their papers? In the answer to that question lies the difference between employment and slavery.

Chapter 7: The "Welcome" Orientation

The journey ends not with a handshake, but with the unlocking of a door. The van that has carried its human cargo across state lines, often moving by night to avoid highway interdiction, finally slows to a halt. The passengers, stiff from days of travel and vibrating with a mixture of exhaustion and adrenaline, peer out the windows expecting to see the skyline of opportunity. Instead, they usually see a dirt road, a row of dilapidated trailers, or the peeling paint of a repurposed motel on the edge of an industrial park.

This is the moment of arrival. In the timeline of trafficking, it marks the shift from the logistical phase to the operational phase. The first twenty-four hours in the United States are critical for the trafficker; this is the period where the "welcome" orientation takes place. It is not an introduction to the job, but an introduction to the cage.

The environment is designed to shock the senses into submission. As documented by researchers, modern slave quarters have been replaced by overcrowding that defies fire codes and basic sanitation standards. The "housing" provided is rarely the clean dormitory promised in the WhatsApp messages. Instead, workers often find themselves herded into rusted trailers or crammed apartments where entire families—or groups of strangers—huddle in perpetual fear.

The tour of these facilities serves a specific psychological function: it demonstrates the total degradation of standard of living. Workers may find themselves in spaces lacking basic amenities like running water or functioning toilets. By forcing human beings to live in squalor immediately upon arrival, the trafficker signals that the social contract has been suspended. There will be no privacy here. There will be no comfort.

But the most insidious aspect of this housing is not its filth; it is its cost. In the orientation meeting—often held standing up in a kitchen or outside a bunkhouse—the financial terms of existence are laid out. The trafficker explains that rent is mandatory and will be deducted directly from wages.

The arithmetic of this "rent" reveals the predatory brilliance of the scheme. A labor broker might rent a dilapidated trailer for two hundred dollars a month. By cramming a dozen workers inside and charging each of them three hundred dollars a month for "lodging," the broker transforms a liability into a two-thousand-dollar monthly profit center. The housing is not a benefit provided to employees; it is a revenue stream extracted from captives. The worker pays premium prices for the privilege of living in conditions that would be illegal for livestock.

This arrangement creates what sociologists call "total dependency". Because the employer controls the housing, losing the job means losing the roof over one's head. In the orientation, this threat is made explicit. "If you don't work," the contractor explains, "you don't stay." For a person thousands of miles from home with no vehicle and no knowledge of the local geography, eviction is tantamount to a death sentence.

Following the housing assignment comes the establishment of the "rules of the compound." These rules are arbitrary, rigid, and designed to enforce isolation. Curfews are common. Visitors are strictly prohibited. The U.S. Department of State has noted that victims are often transported to large compounds where physical and sexual violence can occur with impunity because the space is privately controlled.

The orientation speech often includes a ban on external commerce. Workers are told they cannot go to the local Walmart or 7-Eleven. "It's too dangerous," the trafficker lies. "Immigration is everywhere in this town. If you leave the compound, they will take you."

Instead, the workers are introduced to the internal economy of the camp. This is the modern resurrection of the company store. The trafficker explains that he will provide for all their needs. Do they need work boots? He sells them. Do they need food? He has a commissary. Do they need water for the fields? He provides it.

But nothing is free. The orientation makes clear that every necessity comes with a markup. As noted in investigations of labor abuses, traffickers inflate costs for food, clothes, and necessary work equipment. In some extreme cases documented in agricultural settings, workers are even prohibited from bringing their own water to the fields, forcing them to purchase hydration from the employer during shifts in the scorching heat. The "welcome" orientation is where the worker learns that their biological needs—thirst, hunger, shelter—have been monetized.

The final component of the orientation is the establishment of hierarchy. The labor contractor introduces the "straw bosses" or supervisors. These are often men from the workers' own country, perhaps even their own region, who have been promoted to positions of petty authority. This tactic mirrors the "driver" system of the antebellum plantation. By elevating a few workers and giving them minor privileges—a better bed, a slightly higher wage—the trafficker fractures the solidarity of the workforce. The new arrivals learn immediately that they are being watched not just by the owner, but by their peers.

The orientation concludes with the integration of the debt. The costs of the journey, the new "rent" for the trailer, the price of the boots and the water—all are tallied up. The worker is told their starting balance. It is always negative.

In this first twenty-four hours, the psychological shift is seismic. The immigrant who crossed the border believing themselves to be a traveler seeking fortune realizes they are an inmate accumulating debt. The "welcome" is a closing of the perimeter. They have arrived in the land of the free, only to find themselves in a zip code where the Constitution does not apply. The journey is over. The work—and the paying—is about to begin.

Part II: The Legal Shackles (Systemic Complicity)

How American laws and courts enable the system.

Chapter 8: *Hoffman Plastic Compounds v. NLRB*

On the morning of March 27, 2002, inside the marble columns of the United States Supreme Court, a decision was handed down that would silently rewrite the economic logic of the American workplace. The case was *Hoffman Plastic Compounds, Inc. v. NLRB*, and while it lacked the immediate cultural explosive power of *Roe v. Wade* or *Brown v. Board of Education*, its impact on the labor market was arguably just as profound. In a 5-4 ruling, the Court effectively hung a "Open for Exploitation" sign on the door of every sweatshop, slaughterhouse, and construction site in America.

The story began not in Washington, but on a factory floor in California. Jose Castro, a production worker at Hoffman Plastic Compounds, had done something dangerous: he had handed out union authorization cards to his coworkers. He believed, as the National Labor Relations Act (NLRA) had promised American workers since 1935, that he had a federally protected right to organize for better wages and working conditions. His employer disagreed. In a blatant violation of labor law, the company fired him for his union activities.

Under normal circumstances, the legal remedy for such a retaliatory firing is straightforward. The National Labor Relations Board (NLRB) orders the employer to cease the illegal activity and, crucially, to pay the worker "back pay"—the wages they would have earned between the time of the illegal firing and the resolution of the case. This financial penalty serves as the primary deterrent against union-busting. It ensures that breaking the law costs the employer money.

But during the administrative hearing, a fact emerged that would derail the entire machinery of justice: Jose Castro was an undocumented immigrant.

The company's lawyers seized on this revelation with the precision of chess grandmasters. They argued that because Castro had no legal right to be in the United States, he had no legal right to work. Therefore, they contended, he had no right to be paid for work he had not performed, even if the reason he hadn't performed it was an illegal firing. They pitted the Immigration Reform and Control Act of 1986 (IRCA), which prohibits the employment of undocumented aliens, against the NLRA, which protects "employees" regardless of status.

The question before the Supreme Court was stark: When labor law collides with immigration law, which statute prevails? Does the government prioritize the protection of workers from exploitation, or does it prioritize the punishment of undocumented status?

The Court's conservative majority chose the latter. Chief Justice Rehnquist, writing for the five-justice majority, argued that awarding back pay to an undocumented worker would "condone" and "encourage" violations of immigration law. The Court held that allowing the NLRB to award back pay would trivialize the immigration laws and encourage future illegal migration.

The legal reasoning created a paradox that would have been familiar to any observer of antebellum jurisprudence. Just as the *Dred Scott* decision of 1857 declared that Black Americans could be physically present but legally invisible, possessing "no rights which the white man was bound to respect", the *Hoffman* ruling created a class of workers who were "employees" in name but specters in practice. The Court acknowledged that undocumented workers were indeed covered by the NLRA—they were technically "employees"—yet it stripped them of the only remedy that gave that designation any teeth.

The dissenters on the Court, and labor advocates across the country, immediately recognized the catastrophic economic signal this decision sent to employers. By denying back pay, the Court had inadvertently created a perverse financial incentive—a "moral hazard" of the highest order.

Consider the calculus of a ruthless employer in the post-*Hoffman* era. If this employer hires a U.S. citizen and then illegally fires them for complaining about safety or organizing a union, they face a substantial financial penalty: they must pay that worker all the wages they missed. The risk of breaking labor law is high.

However, if that same employer hires an undocumented worker and treats them exactly the same way—firing them for organizing or complaining—the financial penalty is zero. The employer keeps the money. They face no back pay liability. The Supreme Court had essentially ruled that the punishment for firing an undocumented worker illegally is nothing.

The decision did not discourage illegal immigration, as the majority claimed it would. Instead, it incentivized the hiring of undocumented workers by making them cheaper to abuse than American citizens. It effectively created a discount on labor law violations. An employer who wanted to bust a union or cut corners on safety now had a powerful economic reason to prefer undocumented labor: these workers came with a built-in liability shield.

The *Hoffman* decision gave employers a green light to retaliate. It signaled that employers need not fear violating labor laws when their workforce lacks immigration status. If a worker tried to organize, the employer could simply fire them. If the worker filed a complaint, the employer could bring up their immigration status during the legal proceedings, knowing that doing so would likely end the case and potentially trigger the worker's deportation.

The fallout was immediate and devastating. Lower courts seized on the *Hoffman* reasoning to limit remedies in cases far beyond union organizing. The logic proved infinitely expandable: if immigration policy concerns trumped labor protections in the context of union busting, why not in cases of wage theft, workplace safety, or discrimination?.

In case after case, defendants began to inquire into plaintiffs' immigration status during discovery, claiming it was relevant to potential damages. This tactic had a predictable chilling effect. Workers who had been cheated out of wages or injured on the job dropped their lawsuits rather than risk revealing their status. The mere threat of a *Hoffman* defense became enough to silence entire workforces.

The decision created a "legal black hole" where constitutional protections evaporated. Within this void, human beings could be reduced to units of production with minimal risk to those who profited from their misery. It solidified the legal architecture of the modern plantation. Just as the slave codes of the South prohibited literacy to keep the enslaved ignorant of their power, the *Hoffman* decision stripped the undocumented of the financial remedies that allow power to be exercised.

The irony of the Court's reasoning is bitter. The majority claimed that awarding back pay would "encourage" illegal immigration. Yet, by making undocumented workers the most attractive hires for unscrupulous employers—because they carry the least legal risk—the Court guaranteed that the demand for such labor would skyrocket. The decision fueled the very magnet of employment it claimed to be dismantling.

Twenty years later, the *Hoffman* decision stands as the cornerstone of the exploitation economy. It is the judicial seal of approval on a two-tier labor market. It separated the American workforce into two castes: those who can enforce their rights, and those who cannot. And in doing so, it ensured that the "cheaper" caste—the one stripped of protection by the highest court in the land—would drag down the wages and conditions of everyone else.

The employer in *Hoffman* had violated the law just as surely as Jose Castro had. The company had knowingly hired an unauthorized worker and then illegally fired him. Yet the Court's decision punished only the worker. The employer walked away with a slap on the wrist, their profits intact, their power absolute. The message to corporate America was clear: Immigration law is a sword to be used against workers, not a shield to protect the border. And labor law applies only to those who can afford the price of citizenship.

Chapter 9: The H-2A Loophole

In the American imagination, the antidote to illegal immigration is the "line." We constantly hear the refrain that immigrants should "get in line" and enter the country the "right way." We presume that this legal pathway represents a gold standard of order, fairness, and liberty. We assume that a worker who enters with a visa, stamped by the State Department and approved by the Department of Labor, steps into the full protection of American law.

But when we examine the H-2A agricultural visa—the primary "legal" mechanism for importing farm labor—we discover that the "right way" is merely a bureaucratic reinvention of the oldest wrong way in American history: indentured servitude.

The H-2A program is not an immigration channel; it is a labor supply chain management tool designed to provide growers with a workforce that is legally present but structurally unfree. Its defining feature, the mechanism that transforms a worker from a free agent into a captive asset, is the "tying" provision. Under the terms of the visa, a guest worker is not authorized to work in the United States generally; they are authorized to work *only* for the specific employer who petitioned for them.

This seemingly bureaucratic stipulation creates a power imbalance so profound that it corrupts the very definition of employment. In a free labor market, the worker's ultimate power is the ability to say, "I quit." It is the right to walk away from an abusive boss, a dangerous field, or a stolen paycheck and find a better job down the road. This mobility is the engine of competition; it forces employers to offer decent wages and safe conditions to retain staff.

The H-2A worker possesses no such right. Their legal status is inextricably bound to their employment. If they are fired, or if they quit, they lose their visa status immediately. They become deportable. This means that an H-2A worker faces a binary choice every morning: accept whatever conditions the employer imposes, or become a fugitive.

As I noted in my analysis of guest worker programs, this arrangement transforms the worker from a free participant in the economy into a "bound servant". The employer holds the visa like a leash. The threat need not be spoken; it is written into the federal code. A worker who complains about pesticide exposure, unpaid overtime, or sexual harassment knows that the employer can simply terminate the contract. The result is not just job loss—it is exile.

This legal architecture creates a captive workforce that is actually *more* desirable to predatory employers than undocumented labor. An undocumented worker, though vulnerable, can technically walk off a job site and disappear into the shadows to find work elsewhere. They have mobility, however risky. The H-2A worker has none. They are tracked, registered, and tied to a single plot of land. They are the perfect realization of the "company man," where the company owns the man.

The historical echoes are deafening. The H-2A program is the direct descendant of the *Bracero* program, the mid-century agreement between the U.S. and Mexico that brought millions of Mexican men to harvest American crops. The *Bracero* program was eventually terminated in 1964 after activists exposed it as "legalized slavery," rife with abuse, wage theft, and squalid living conditions.

Yet, the H-2A program resurrected the core mechanic of *Bracero*: the single-employer restriction. It effectively recreated the conditions of colonial indenture, where a servant's passage was paid in exchange for a fixed term of labor during which they had no liberty to change masters. The modern iteration simply swapped the trans-Atlantic ship for a charter bus and the parchment contract for a biometric visa.

The abuse enabled by this loophole is not hypothetical; it is endemic. In 2021, the Department of Justice unsealed an indictment for what they termed "Operation Blooming Onion," a massive federal investigation into a multi-state criminal syndicate operating within the H-2A program. The conspirators were accused of trafficking foreign nationals from Mexico and Central America into the United States under the guise of agricultural guest workers.

Once these "legal" workers arrived in Georgia, their passports were confiscated—a tactic I identified earlier as a hallmark of trafficking, but here practiced on workers with valid visas. They were held in cramped, unsanitary work camps surrounded by electric fences. They were forced to dig onions with their bare hands for pennies a bucket. When they complained, they were threatened with gun violence. At least two workers died due to workplace conditions.

The shocking reality of Operation Blooming Onion was not that criminals were smuggling people; it was that the federal government had stamped the paperwork. The traffickers had used the H-2A program exactly as it was designed: to procure a large volume of workers who could not leave. The government had processed the petitions, approved the housing, and issued the visas. The "right way" had led directly to a modern plantation.

While Operation Blooming Onion represents an extreme, the mundane, daily operation of the H-2A program involves a systematic extraction of wealth that is perfectly legal. Employers are required to pay a minimum wage known as the Adverse Effect Wage Rate (AEWR), designed to prevent the depression of wages for U.S. workers. However, through a complex system of "productivity quotas," employers often drive the effective hourly wage far below this floor.

A worker might be told they must pick a certain number of buckets per hour to keep their job. If they fail to meet the quota, they are fired and effectively deported. To meet the quota, workers skip breaks, run through the fields, and work off the clock. The employer gets hyper-productivity for a fixed price, while the worker destroys their body to avoid the "termination for cause" that would end their legal status.

Furthermore, the "benefits" mandated by the H-2A program often function as tools of control. Employers are required to provide housing and transportation. On paper, this sounds like a perk. In practice, it creates total dependency. The employer is the landlord and the bus driver.

The housing provided is often isolated, miles from the nearest town, with no access to public transit. Workers live in barracks or trailers located on the employer's property. This geographic isolation ensures that workers cannot access legal aid, religious services, or community support without the employer's facilitation. They are cut off from American society, living in an archipelago of labor camps where the only authority figure is the foreman.

If a worker is fired, they are instantly evicted. Imagine the leverage this gives a supervisor. A female H-2A worker who faces sexual advances from a crew leader knows that rejecting him means not just losing her paycheck, but losing her bed and being stranded in a foreign country in the middle of the night. The "benefit" of housing becomes the mechanism of coercion.

The recruitment process for H-2A workers also reveals the fiction of the "fee-free" model. By law, H-2A workers are not supposed to pay recruitment fees. The employer is supposed to cover the cost of transportation and visas. However, investigations by groups like Centro de los Derechos del Migrante (CDM) consistently find that workers pay thousands of dollars in illegal kickbacks to recruiters in their home countries to secure these coveted spots.

Because the demand for U.S. wages is so high in rural Mexico or Guatemala, local recruiters act as gatekeepers. They charge "lists fees" or "pre-processing fees" that are invisible to the U.S. Department of Labor but very real to the worker. The worker arrives in the U.S. carrying a significant debt—often $3,000 to $5,000—owed to the recruiter's network back home.

This debt acts as a secondary lock on the H-2A trap. Even if a worker wanted to quit and return home to escape abuse, they cannot. They must work to pay off the recruiter, or face violence or financial ruin in their home village. The U.S. employer may claim ignorance of these fees, but the system relies on this pre-screened, indebted compliance. The employer gets a worker who *cannot* afford to be fired.

The government's oversight of this program is largely performative. The Department of Labor's Wage and Hour Division is tasked with inspecting H-2A housing and auditing payrolls. But as noted in the discussion of enforcement resources, the agency is critically underfunded. Inspections are often announced in advance, giving employers time to clean up the barracks and coach the workers.

Moreover, the legal structure of the program creates a "catch-22" for whistleblowers. If an H-2A worker reports a violation, and the employer is subsequently banned from the program, the worker loses their job and their visa. The remedy for the crime punishes the victim. There is no automatic "portability" that allows a whistleblower to simply transfer their visa to a law-abiding farm down the road. The system is designed to protect the continuity of the harvest, not the rights of the harvester.

Defenders of the program argue that H-2A is essential for American food security, claiming that without these workers, crops would rot in the fields because "Americans won't do these jobs." This argument mirrors the

antebellum insistence that cotton could not be harvested without slave labor
. It posits that the agricultural economy is chemically dependent on a class of workers who lack full rights.

But the reality is that Americans won't do these jobs *under these conditions*. They won't accept being tied to a single employer, living in employer-controlled barracks, and facing deportation for failing to meet a quota. The H-2A program artificially depresses the labor market by introducing a supply of workers who are legally prevented from bargaining. It shields the agricultural industry from the need to modernize, mechanize, or improve working conditions to attract free labor.

The H-2A visa is ostensibly a "guest worker" program. But the term "guest" implies a relationship of hospitality and voluntary association. A guest is free to leave. A guest is not threatened with arrest if they walk out the front door. A guest does not have to pay a bribe to be invited.

What we have in the H-2A program is a state-sponsored lease of human beings. It is a system that rents the muscles of the global poor to American corporations while stripping the people attached to those muscles of their civil liberties. It provides the employer with all the benefits of owning a workforce—total control, fixed costs, zero mobility—without the moral stigma of chattel slavery.

By maintaining the "tying" provision, the federal government acts as the enforcer for the employer. Immigration and Customs Enforcement (ICE) becomes the company's private security firm, standing ready to remove any worker who asserts their independence. The "loophole" of the H-2A visa is not an error in the law; it is the entire point of the law. It creates a labor force that is legally present but structurally enslaved, proving that in the American economy, legal status is no guarantee of liberty if the law itself is designed to bind.

Chapter 10: The Independent Contractor Sham

On a bustling construction site in downtown Denver or the sprawling suburbs of Phoenix, the morning ritual appears indistinguishable from any other workplace in the industrialized world. Men arrive in boots and vests, carrying tools and lunch coolers. They gather around a foreman who barks orders, assigns tasks, and sets the schedule for the day. They are told when to start, when to break, and when to go home. They are supervised, corrected, and directed in every movement they make. By every common-sense definition, and by the strict criteria of the Internal Revenue Service, these men are employees.

But in the payroll ledger of the company that hired them, they are something else entirely. They are listed as "independent contractors."

This designation is the single most pervasive legal fiction in the American economy. It is a bureaucratic sleight of hand that transforms a dependent laborer into a "business owner" for the sole purpose of stripping them of rights. To the casual observer, it looks like a tax classification issue—a boring dispute for accountants to settle. In reality, it is a mechanism of dispossession that rivals the debt contract in its power to subjugate. It is the legal shell game that allows billion-dollar construction firms to operate with the liability exposure of a lemonade stand.

To understand the magnitude of this sham, one must first understand what an independent contractor is supposed to be. In a functioning market, an independent contractor is a plumber with his own van, a lawyer with her own practice, or a freelance graphic designer who sets their own rates. They have multiple clients. They negotiate their fees. They determine the means and methods of their work. They take risks, and in exchange, they capture the profit.

The undocumented worker hanging drywall in a Las Vegas high-rise possesses none of these freedoms. He cannot negotiate his rate; he takes what is offered. He cannot work for multiple clients; he is expected to be on this site, and only this site, for the duration of the project. He does not determine how the wall is built; he follows the blueprints provided by the developer. He is an employee in every sense except the one that matters: the paycheck.

By misclassifying this worker as an independent contractor—often by forcing him to sign a 1099 tax form he cannot read, or by paying him in cash with no tax withholding at all—the employer achieves an immediate and massive reduction in labor costs. The savings are not generated by efficiency; they are generated by evasion.

When a company hires a W-2 employee, they are legally responsible for a suite of costs that form the American social safety net. They must pay the employer's share of Social Security and Medicare taxes (7.65 percent). They must pay unemployment insurance premiums. They must carry workers' compensation insurance to cover medical bills if the worker falls off a ladder. They must withhold income taxes. They must comply with overtime laws.

When that same company designates the worker as a "1099," all these obligations vanish. The 7.65 percent tax burden is shifted entirely to the worker (who, being undocumented, likely cannot file taxes to pay it). Unemployment insurance is nonexistent. Workers' compensation premiums—often the most expensive line item in construction—drop to zero because "contractors" are expected to insure themselves.

The arithmetic is compelling for the unscrupulous. By simply changing a worker's tax status, a construction firm can slash its labor costs by 30 percent or more. This is not a marginal saving; it is a decisive competitive advantage. As the Center for Construction Research and Training (CPWR) noted in their analysis of the industry, the economic exploitation of undocumented workers through such mechanisms has become a "cornerstone" of the non-union construction industry's business strategy. It is the structural foundation upon which the low-bid economy rests.

This system creates a race to the bottom that destroys the market for honest business. Consider two framing companies bidding on a housing development. Company A classifies its carpenters as employees, pays workers' comp, and follows safety regulations. Company B classifies its crew as independent contractors. Company B's bid comes in 30 percent lower. The developer, driven by profit and shielded by layers of subcontracting, chooses Company B. Company A goes bankrupt, or, as is increasingly common, fires its employees and "re-hires" them as independent contractors to survive. The sham becomes the industry standard.

For the undocumented worker, this classification is a catastrophe. It removes the floor beneath their feet. Because they are not "employees," they are often told they have no right to the minimum wage. If they work 60 hours a week, they are told they are not entitled to overtime pay because "business owners" don't get overtime. The misclassification serves as a preemptive legal defense against wage theft claims. "I didn't steal his wages," the employer argues. "He failed to fulfill the terms of our commercial contract."

The University of Michigan, in a comprehensive study of the industry, found that this vast subcontracting structure allows a large portion of the workforce to be paid as independent contractors in cash. The impact on earnings is measurable and severe: U.S.-born construction workers, who are more likely to be properly classified, earn an average of $3.12 more per hour than their undocumented counterparts for the same work. That wage gap is the price of the sham.

But the most dangerous consequence of misclassification is not financial; it is physical. The "independent contractor" label is a get-out-of-jail-free card for workplace safety. Under OSHA regulations, employers are responsible for providing a safe workplace and safety training. But if the worker is an "independent business," the general contractor can argue that safety is the "business owner's" responsibility.

This logic is lethal. The University of Michigan study revealed a chilling statistic: an estimated 73 percent of undocumented construction workers have never received basic safety training. Why would a contractor spend money training a worker they claim not to employ? Why invest in safety harnesses or respirators for a "vendor"?

When an undocumented "independent contractor" falls from a roof or is crushed by a palette of bricks, the sham reveals its true cruelty. In a normal employment relationship, workers' compensation would pay for the ambulance, the surgery, and the rehabilitation. It is a no-fault system designed to keep injured workers from destitution.

For the misclassified worker, there is no such safety net. The ambulance ride is a financial crisis. The surgery is an impossibility. The hospital absorbs the cost as uncompensated care—shifting the burden to the taxpayer—while the worker is sent home disabled and destitute. The employer, who saved thousands in insurance premiums, bears no cost for the body broken in his service. He simply hires a new "contractor" the next morning.

The mechanisms used to enforce this sham have become increasingly sophisticated. It is no longer just a matter of handing out cash envelopes. In many states, labor brokers have industrialized the creation of shell companies. They herd groups of undocumented workers into offices where notaries help them register Limited Liability Companies (LLCs).

Suddenly, a bricklayer who speaks no English and owns no assets is the CEO of "Jose Construction LLC." The labor broker then "contracts" with this LLC. It gives the arrangement a veneer of corporate legitimacy. "We don't hire illegal aliens," the big developer can claim. "We do business with minority-owned small businesses." It is a diversity washing of exploitation. The worker, of course, has no idea what an LLC is, nor do they understand that by signing those papers, they have legally absolved the general contractor of all responsibility for their life and limb.

This creates a "ghost workforce." These workers are present on the job site, building the skylines of Miami and Houston, but they are absent from the books. They do not appear on payroll rolls. They do not appear in safety logs. They are invisible to the state until a tragedy occurs, at which point the paper trail leads nowhere.

The psychological impact of this arrangement reinforces the control of the trafficker. By forcing the worker to participate in the fraud—by signing the false tax forms or agreeing to the cash payments—the employer makes the worker complicit. "You are getting paid under the table," the boss reminds them. "If you complain, the IRS will come for you, not me." The misclassification becomes another layer of blackmail.

Furthermore, this system destroys the possibility of collective bargaining. You cannot organize a union of independent contractors; that would be an antitrust violation, a conspiracy to fix prices. By atomizing the workforce into thousands of competing "businesses of one," the industry ensures that workers can never combine their strength to demand better terms. They are kept in a state of permanent competition with each other, driving wages down to the subsistence level.

The defense offered by the construction lobby is that this flexibility is necessary for the cyclical nature of building. They argue that "Americans won't do these jobs" at the prices consumers want to pay. But as a Texas contractor candidly admitted to *Newsweek* when immigration raids frightened his workforce away, the reality is strictly economic: "We are forced to hire inexperienced laborers at higher rates to replace our employees".

This admission is the smoking gun. When the supply of misclassified, exploitable labor dries up, the market corrects. Wages rise. Employers are forced to hire legal workers at "higher rates"—meaning, legal market rates. The "necessity" of the independent contractor model is a lie; it is simply a preference for an artificially cheap labor supply subsidized by tax evasion and human suffering.

The independent contractor sham is the mechanism that connects the modern economy to the logic of the plantation. On the plantation, the owner bore the cost of maintaining the slave—food, housing, medical care— because the slave was a capital asset. In the modern gig economy of construction and agriculture, the employer has achieved a darker efficiency: he extracts the labor but outsources the maintenance.

He rents the human being for the productive hours of the day and takes no responsibility for their survival during the rest. If they starve, it is a business failure of their "independent company." If they are injured, it is an occupational hazard of their "entrepreneurship."

This is not liberty. It is the ultimate neoliberal perversion of freedom: the freedom to starve, the freedom to fall, the freedom to be discarded. It is a system that allows capital to move freely while labor is trapped in a legal fiction. Until we pierce the corporate veil of the "independent contractor" and recognize that control implies employment, we will continue to have a labor market where the only thing being built is a monument to fraud.

Chapter 11: The Subcontracting Shield

If you walk into the headquarters of a major American homebuilder, a multinational hotel chain, or a global fashion brand, you will likely find a framed document on the wall of the lobby. It is usually titled "Vendor Code of Conduct" or "Commitment to Ethical Sourcing." It is printed on heavy stock, perhaps in an elegant serif font, and it pledges that the corporation holds itself to the highest standards of human rights. It strictly forbids child labor, forced labor, and wage theft. It is a beautiful promise.

It is also, in legal and practical terms, a wall.

This document is not designed to protect workers; it is designed to protect the corporation *from* the workers. It is the cornerstone of the most effective liability shield in the modern economy: the subcontracting chain.

In the antebellum South, the ownership of human beings was direct. The planter's name was on the deed; the slave lived on the planter's land. Liability and profit were concentrated in the same hands. If a slave was starved or murdered, the community knew exactly who was responsible, even if the law rarely punished them.

The modern economy has innovated beyond this crude directness. Today, the entities that profit most from cheap labor—the brands we buy, the hotels where we sleep, the developers who build our homes—have severed the legal link between themselves and the people who do their work. They have created a "fissured workplace," a term coined by former Department of Labor administrator David Weil, where the company that holds the power sheds the responsibility.

The structure resembles a pyramid scheme of accountability. At the top sits the Brand. The Brand does not hire workers; it hires a General Contractor. The General Contractor does not hire carpenters or cleaners; he hires "specialized" Subcontractors. The Subcontractor, facing tight margins, hires a Labor Broker. And the Labor Broker hires the crew leader who picks up undocumented men on a street corner.

By the time we reach the bottom of this chain—where the actual work of pouring concrete, scrubbing toilets, or sewing seams takes place—we are four or five removes away from the logo on the building.

This distance is not accidental; it is architectural. It allows the flow of money to move upward while the flow of risk moves downward. When the

Department of Labor uncovers a sweatshop in Los Angeles or a crew of unpaid roofers in Dallas, the investigation climbs the ladder only to hit the firewall of the subcontract.

"We had no idea," the Brand's spokesperson will say, pointing to the framed Code of Conduct in the lobby. "Our contract explicitly requires all vendors to follow the law. We are shocked—shocked!—that this subcontractor violated our trust."

They terminate the contract with the offending middleman, issue a press release reaffirming their values, and hire a new subcontractor who operates under the exact same economic constraints that caused the violation in the first place. The Brand remains pristine. The stock price holds. The system resets.

The mechanism that drives this inevitable exploitation is the "reverse auction." When a major retailer or developer puts a project out for bid, they hold immense market power. They demand a price that is often mathematically incompatible with legal wages. As Wikipedia's analysis of labor trafficking notes, the limited number of contracts often go to the cheapest subcontractor. Since human labor is the largest variable cost in industries like construction and agriculture, the subcontractor who wins the bid is almost invariably the one who has found a way to cheat.

Consider the math of a janitorial contract for a large supermarket chain. If honest labor costs—including minimum wage, payroll taxes, and insurance—dictate that cleaning a store costs $1,000 a night, but the chain demands it be done for $700, they have effectively mandated wage theft without ever saying the words. The winning bidder *must* hire undocumented workers, pay them in cash below minimum wage, and skip the insurance. There is no other way to make the numbers work.

The corporation at the top knows this. They employ sophisticated analysts who know the cost of labor down to the penny. When they accept a bid that is 30 percent below market rate, they are consciously purchasing a crime. But because they have purchased it through an intermediary, they have purchased "plausible deniability" along with the clean floors.

This dynamic creates a "race to the bottom" where ethical businesses are priced out of existence. The subcontractor who insists on following the law loses the contract. The one who is willing to exploit survives. Over time, entire industries—housekeeping, landscaping, residential construction—become dominated by shadow operators because the pricing structure set by the corporate giants leaves no room for legality.

To maintain the illusion of oversight, corporations engage in what labor experts call "compliance theater." They hire third-party auditing firms to inspect their supply chains. On the surface, this looks like rigorous self-policing. In reality, it is often a game of cat and mouse where the cat has been paid to be blind.

Audits are frequently announced in advance. This gives the subcontractor time to "clean the house." When the auditors arrive at a garment factory or a farm, the underage workers are sent out the back door. The undocumented workers are told to stay home. The "double books"—one set for the payroll, one set for the auditors—are swapped. Workers are coached on what to say, often under threat of firing. "Tell them you work eight hours," the foreman warns. "Tell them you get water breaks."

Even when violations are found, the consequences are rarely structural. A fine is paid; a corrective action plan is signed; business continues. The auditing industry itself is conflicted—the auditors are paid by the corporations they are inspecting. A reputation for being "too difficult" or finding "too many problems" can lose an auditing firm its clients. It is a system designed to produce certificates of compliance, not compliant conditions.

The legal system facilitates this shielding. In many jurisdictions, establishing "joint employer" status—proving that the Brand is legally responsible for the Subcontractor's employees—is notoriously difficult. Corporate lawyers have mastered the art of writing contracts that dictate every detail of the work—the uniform, the schedule, the specific chemicals to use—while disclaiming any control over the workers themselves. They want the control of an employer with the liability of a customer.

This structure allows for the ultimate diffusion of moral responsibility. In the 1800s, the plantation owner could not deny he owned the slave. Today, the CEO of a fast-fashion brand can honestly say, "I do not employ those children." He employs a Vice President of Sourcing, who hires a Global Logistics Firm, which contracts with a factory in Bangladesh, which subcontracts to a workshop in a basement. The CEO's hands are clean because he has paid three other people to do the dirty work.

But the money trail tells the truth. The profits generated by that basement workshop flow ultimately to the shareholders of the Brand. The low cost of the goods on the shelf is subsidized by the stolen wages and safety shortcuts at the bottom of the chain.

For the worker, the subcontracting shield is a labyrinth that makes justice impossible. If a worker on a construction site is injured or cheated, whom do they sue? The crew leader who hired them often has no assets—he is just a guy with a truck. The Labor Broker is a shell company that can dissolve and reappear under a new name tomorrow. The General Contractor points to the indemnification clause in his contract. And the Developer is legally untouchable.

The worker is left chasing ghosts. They are injured in the service of a billion-dollar project, but legally, they were employed by a phantom.

This system is not a failure of corporate governance; it is a success of corporate engineering. It allows the American economy to have it both ways: to enjoy the cheap prices and high stock valuations driven by exploitation, while maintaining a self-image of legal and ethical propriety. We look at the framed Code of Conduct in the lobby and believe it. We do not see the walls of the maze that have been built behind it.

Until we pierce this veil—until we pass laws that establish "chain of commerce" liability, making the lead company responsible for labor violations anywhere in its supply chain—we are fighting a hydra. We cut off one head—shutting down one abusive subcontractor—and the Brand simply grows another, awarding the contract to the next bidder willing to do the impossible for the price of the illegal. The shield remains intact, and the exploitation continues, protected by the very contracts that claim to forbid it.

Chapter 12: The Failure of OSHA

On December 29, 1970, President Richard Nixon signed the Occupational Safety and Health Act into law. It was a moment of rare bipartisan consensus, born of a radical yet simple premise: that in the wealthiest nation on earth, economic profit should never require the sacrifice of human flesh. The legislation promised that every man and woman in the United States would work under "safe and healthful working conditions." It established a federal administration, OSHA, charged with the sacred duty of turning that promise into a reality on every factory floor, construction site, and farm across the continent.

Half a century later, for the millions of undocumented workers who form the backbone of the American industrial and agricultural economy, that promise is not just broken; it is a dead letter. It is a statute that exists in the library of Congress but evaporates the moment one crosses the threshold of a slaughterhouse in Nebraska or a roofing site in Texas.

The failure of OSHA to protect this specific, vulnerable sector of the workforce is not merely a story of bureaucratic incompetence or the lack of effort by individual inspectors. It is a story of structural design and geometric impossibility. We have constructed a regulatory system that is mathematically incapable of fulfilling its mandate, creating a vacuum of oversight that predatory employers have learned to inhabit with comfortable impunity.

To understand the magnitude of this failure, one must first confront the arithmetic of inspection. The Occupational Safety and Health Administration is tasked with regulating approximately eight million worksites in the United States. To perform this Herculean task, the federal agency and its state partners employ roughly 1,850 inspectors.

The math is unforgiving. If OSHA attempted to inspect every workplace under its jurisdiction just once, it would take, by current estimates from the AFL-CIO's "Death on the Job" report, over 160 years to complete a single cycle. This is not oversight; it is a lottery. The probability of a specific employer seeing a federal inspector in any given year is statistically indistinguishable from zero.

This scarcity forces the agency to operate on a triage basis that effectively abandons prevention in favor of autopsy. OSHA cannot be a "beat cop" walking the factory floor, deterring bad behavior by its mere presence.

Instead, it has been forced into the role of a coroner, arriving at the scene only after the disaster has occurred. The agency prioritizes investigations into fatalities, catastrophes, and amputations because it simply lacks the manpower to conduct the kind of proactive, randomized surveillance that actually prevents accidents before they happen.

For the exploitative employer, this reality creates a rational expectation of immunity. A contractor who decides to skip buying safety harnesses or shoring up a trench knows he is not gambling against the house; he is gambling against a ghost. Unless a worker dies or is maimed so publicly that it makes the evening news, the regulatory apparatus will remain invisible.

This immunity is compounded by the specific legal architecture that surrounds the industries where undocumented labor is concentrated. As we saw in the discussion of the "Subcontracting Shield," the modern economy has fractured the workplace. But this fragmentation does more than shield liability; it actively blinds the inspector.

Federal appropriations riders—provisions attached to budget bills—often restrict OSHA from conducting programmed safety inspections of small businesses with ten or fewer employees in certain industries. While high-hazard sectors like construction are technically open to inspection, the sheer volume and transience of small subcontractors make them elusive targets.

Consider the logistics of inspecting a residential housing development. A general contractor oversees the project, but the actual work is performed by dozens of small, independent crews: framers, roofers, drywallers, painters. A crew of five undocumented framers working for a shell LLC exists below the radar. They arrive in a van at 6:00 AM, work until dusk, and move to a different site the next day. They have no fixed address, no permanent office, and often no paper trail.

By the time an OSHA inspector could theoretically schedule a visit, the crew is gone. They dissolve and reform like smoke. This creates a regulatory blind spot where the most dangerous work is performed. It results in a safety apartheid: on large, unionized commercial sites, safety protocols are rigorous because the general contractor fears liability and the union demands protection. On the residential sites and light commercial projects where undocumented labor predominates, safety is an optional expense.

The consequences of this deregulation are visible in the injury statistics. As the University of Michigan found in its comprehensive study of the industry, an estimated 73 percent of undocumented construction workers have never received basic safety training. They are handed pneumatic nail guns, sent up ladders without harnesses, and ordered into un-shored trenches not because the technology to protect them doesn't exist, but because the regulatory threat that compels its use is absent.

The situation is equally dire, and perhaps more scientifically calculated, in the meat and poultry industries. Here, the hazards are built into the physics of the production line. As the U.S. Department of Agriculture's own studies have noted, poultry workers are required to perform repetitive, forceful motions up to 30,000 times per day. The relentless pace of the line creates a breeding ground for musculoskeletal disorders, chemical burns from sanitation fluids, and traumatic amputations from saws and blades.

In a functional regulatory environment, OSHA would set strict standards on line speeds to prevent these injuries. But the agency has no specific standard for line speed ergonomics. Instead, it relies on the "General Duty Clause," a catch-all provision that requires employers to provide a workplace free from recognized hazards. Proving a violation of this clause is legally burdensome and time-consuming.

Consequently, the industry operates with a green light to push the human body to its mechanical limit. The undocumented workforce in these plants is often composed of those least able to demand a slowdown. They absorb the cost of the speed in their tendons and joints, knowing that the federal government has effectively ceded the floor to the foreman.

But the most fatal flaw in the OSHA system regarding undocumented workers is its reliance on the "complaint-based" model. In the absence of enough inspectors to patrol the beat, the agency relies on workers to be its eyes and ears. The theory is that if a hazard exists—a locked fire exit, an unguarded machine, a toxic leak—the worker will call the OSHA hotline, triggering an inspection.

This theory collapses completely in the face of the deportation regime. It assumes a workforce that feels secure enough to speak up. For undocumented workers, this assumption is a cruel fiction. To file a complaint is to invite government agents into the workplace. For a worker living in terror of "La Migra," there is no meaningful distinction between a Department of Labor inspector and an Immigration and Customs Enforcement agent. They are both the federal government. They both represent the power that wants to expel them.

Employers weaponize this confusion with ruthless efficiency. A foreman does not need to know the nuances of administrative law to control his crew. He simply needs to say, "If you call OSHA, they will come with badges and check everyone's papers." The threat is existential. A report about a slippery floor could lead to family separation. A complaint about a lack of gloves could lead to exile.

This dynamic creates a zone of silence around the most egregious violations. Hazards go unreported. Chemical spills are mopped up by workers holding their breath. Injuries are treated with first aid kits in the breakroom rather than at the hospital. The official statistics on workplace injuries become a work of fiction, undercounting the carnage because the victims are too afraid to be counted.

The medical management of these injuries reveals the depth of the collusion between profit and neglect. Many large processing plants maintain on-site infirmaries or "wellness centers." To the outsider, this looks like a perk. In practice, it is a triage unit designed to keep injuries off the OSHA logs.

Federal regulations require employers to report injuries that require medical treatment beyond first aid. Therefore, the "company doctor" or nurse is often under explicit or implicit pressure to categorize every injury as minor. A worker with a laceration that requires stitches is treated with butterfly closures and glue—"first aid." A worker with a rotator cuff tear is given a bag of ice and ibuprofen—"first aid." A worker with chemical burns is given ointment.

By keeping these treatments within the definition of first aid, the plant avoids creating a "recordable incident." This keeps their injury rates artificially low, which in turn lowers the likelihood of a targeted OSHA inspection. The worker is sent back to the line, injured and untreated, while the company wins safety awards based on fraudulent data.

The failure extends to environmental hazards that leave no immediate mark but kill slowly. The Occupational Safety and Health Act was supposed to protect workers from toxic substances. Yet, in the cleanup of disasters—the work performed by the "storm chasers" discussed in later chapters—undocumented workers are routinely exposed to asbestos, lead, and mold without respiratory protection. OSHA's presence in disaster zones is often advisory rather than enforcement-oriented. They hand out pamphlets on heat stress while workers collapse from dehydration.

The issue of heat stress illustrates the paralysis of the agency. Despite rising global temperatures and the clear danger to agricultural and construction workers, there is no federal OSHA standard for heat exposure. Inspectors must rely on the cumbersome General Duty Clause to issue citations, a process so difficult that few heat-related violations are ever penalized. In the tomato fields of Florida and the melon fields of California, workers die of heat stroke with disturbing regularity, and the regulatory response is often a posthumous fine that amounts to a rounding error on the company's ledger.

When penalties *are* issued, the amounts are often insultingly low. The structure of OSHA fines is set by Congress and has not kept pace with inflation or corporate profits. A "serious" violation—one that could cause death or serious physical harm—carries a maximum penalty of roughly $16,000. For a multi-billion dollar construction firm or a massive agribusiness, this is not a deterrent; it is a petty cash expense. It is cheaper to pay the fine than to buy the scaffolding.

Even in cases of death, the consequences are minimal. Criminal prosecution under the OSH Act is limited to cases where a willful violation causes a fatality, and even then, it is only a misdemeanor punishable by a maximum of six months in jail. You can spend more time in prison for harassing a protected owl than for killing a worker through negligence.

This lack of teeth signals to the market that the lives of workers are commodities of low value. It teaches the unscrupulous employer that safety is a discretionary budget item.

The failure of OSHA is not an accident of history; it is the result of a political choice. We have chosen to prioritize the policing of borders over the policing of labor conditions. We have built a surveillance state to track the movement of immigrants, utilizing drones, sensors, and databases, but we rely on the honor system to ensure their safety at work.

By starving the agency of resources and maintaining a legal framework that silences the whistleblowers, we have created a two-tiered system of safety. There is the protected tier, inhabited by citizens in unionized or high-visibility jobs, where the law has force. And there is the disposable tier, inhabited by the undocumented, where the law is a ghost.

The OSH Act of 1970 was a promise that work would not be a death sentence. But until the agency is empowered to make inspection a certainty rather than a rarity, and until the firewall between labor enforcement and immigration enforcement is made absolute so that workers can report hazards without fear, that promise will remain a lie. The law says the workplace must be safe. The economy, operating in the vacuum of enforcement, says that safety is for citizens, and risk is for the rest.

Chapter 13: Local Law Enforcement as Enforcers

In a functioning society, the number 911 represents a universal covenant. It is the digital embodiment of the social contract: in moments of supreme crisis—when a fire starts, when a heart stops, or when violence erupts—the state promises to send help. Implicit in this promise is the assumption that the state's primary interest is the preservation of life and the restoration of order.

For millions of undocumented workers in the United States, however, dialing those three digits is not an act of seeking safety; it is a game of Russian roulette.

The transformation of local law enforcement into the frontline infantry of federal deportation policy is one of the most effective, and destructive, force multipliers in the machinery of modern exploitation. It effectively deputizes every beat cop, every sheriff's deputy, and every highway patrolman as a potential immigration agent. This blurring of lines has created a catastrophic "chilling effect" that insulates criminals, empowers abusive employers, and creates a sub-class of residents who are functionally excluded from the protection of the police.

To understand how this mechanism operates, we must look beyond the federal agency of Immigration and Customs Enforcement (ICE). ICE, despite its formidable budget, has finite resources. It cannot be on every street corner. It cannot pull over every car with a broken taillight. To achieve "total enforcement," the federal government needed to leverage the manpower of local municipalities.

The primary vehicle for this leverage is the 287(g) program, a section of the Immigration and Nationality Act that allows the Department of Homeland Security to enter into agreements with state and local law enforcement agencies. Under these agreements, designated local officers are trained and authorized to perform the functions of federal immigration agents. They can interview individuals about their immigration status, check federal databases, and issue detainers to hold people for ICE.

The expansion of this program, alongside similar initiatives like "Secure Communities," has fundamentally altered the relationship between the police and the community. In jurisdictions that have aggressively embraced these partnerships, a traffic stop is no longer just a traffic stop. For an undocumented worker driving to a construction site, failing to signal a lane change can lead directly to deportation.

This reality creates a powerful tool of control for those who profit from exploitable labor. The employer need not hire private security to keep workers in line; the local police department does it for free.

Consider the dynamic on a construction site where wage theft is occurring. If a dispute arises and tensions flare, the employer has a nuclear option. "Get back to work," he can say, "or I will call the police and tell them you are trespassing." In a sanctuary city, this threat might ring hollow. But in a county with a 287(g) agreement, the threat is existential. The police will arrive. They will ask for identification. Finding none, or finding foreign documents, they may arrest the worker for the alleged trespassing. Once booked into the county jail, the worker's fingerprints are shared with federal databases. An ICE detainer is lodged. The wage theft dispute is over because the victim is being processed for removal.

The employer, conversely, faces no such risk. The police do not ask for his payroll records. They do not investigate whether he is violating labor laws. They are there to enforce property rights and public order, definitions which, in practice, protect the owner and punish the undocumented.

This dynamic creates what criminologists call the "perfect victim." Criminals—both white-collar wage thieves and violent street predators—understand this vulnerability perfectly. They know that undocumented immigrants are "walking ATMs." They are often paid in cash because they cannot open bank accounts, and they carry that cash on their bodies. A robber knows he can put a gun to the head of a day laborer, take his week's wages, and walk away with near-total impunity. The victim will not call 911. The victim *cannot* call 911.

The Major Cities Chiefs Association, an organization representing police executives from the largest cities in the United States and Canada, has long warned against this entanglement. They argue that when local police enforce immigration law, it destroys the trust required for community policing. Witnesses stop coming forward. Information dries up. Crimes go unsolved. A community that fears the police is a community where criminality festers.

Yet, in many rural and suburban jurisdictions—precisely where agricultural and meatpacking industries are concentrated—local sheriffs have embraced this role enthusiastically. The political incentives often align with the economic ones. A "tough on illegal immigration" stance wins local elections, while the local industries quietly benefit from a workforce that is terrified of leaving their homes for anything other than work.

This terror restricts the mobility of the workforce, creating a form of geographic containment that mirrors the "pass system" of the antebellum South. In the 1850s, slave patrols roamed the roads, stopping Black individuals to demand proof of their right to travel. Today, the pretextual traffic stop serves the same function.

An undocumented worker in a rural county knows exactly which roads are patrolled by deputies who "look for" immigrants. They learn to navigate a narrow corridor between home and work. They do not drive to the next town for a better job because the risk of interdiction is too high. They do not drive to the cinema or the park. They are effectively confined to a geographic radius determined by the enforcement priorities of the local sheriff. This immobility suppresses wages by reducing competition; the worker cannot seek better opportunities, so they must accept whatever the local employer offers.

The gendered impact of this enforcement model is particularly horrific. Domestic violence shelters and advocates report a disturbing pattern: abusers weaponize the police to maintain control over undocumented partners. "If you leave me," the abuser threatens, "I will call the cops and tell them you hit me. When they run your prints, you will be deported, and I will keep the children."

This is not an idle threat. In "dual arrest" situations, where police arrest both parties to sort it out later, the citizen partner might spend a night in jail. The undocumented partner faces permanent exile. The fear of police prevents women from seeking restraining orders or reporting abuse, trapping them in violent homes just as effectively as it traps workers in abusive jobs.

The legal architecture of 287(g) and Secure Communities creates a dragnet that captures people regardless of their criminal history. While proponents argue these programs target "criminal aliens," the data reveals a different story. A vast number of those detained through local cooperation are arrested for minor non-violent offenses—traffic violations, driving without a license, or civil ordinances. The system is efficient at removing workers, not necessarily criminals.

By offloading the costs of detection and initial detention onto local taxpayers, the federal government achieves a massive subsidy for its enforcement goals. But the local community pays a steep price. The cost is not just in police overtime or jail beds; it is in the erosion of the rule of law itself.

When a significant portion of the population believes that the legal system is a threat to their survival, the legitimacy of the law collapses. Workers stop cooperating with investigations into workplace accidents. They stop reporting housing code violations. They withdraw into a shadow society where problems are solved through informal, often predatory, mechanisms rather than through public institutions.

This environment creates a breeding ground for corruption. In some jurisdictions, predatory tow-truck companies and bail bondsmen work in tandem with aggressive enforcement strategies, extracting wealth from immigrant families who are desperate to keep a breadwinner out of the system that leads to ICE. The traffic stop becomes a revenue generation event for the local apparatus, stripping the worker of the capital they have managed to accumulate.

Historically, the Fugitive Slave Act of 1850 required local officials and citizens to assist in the capture of runaway slaves. It federalized the enforcement of bondage, overriding local sentiments or laws that might have offered sanctuary. Today's debates over "sanctuary cities" versus federal enforcement are a direct constitutional echo of that conflict.

The federal government effectively creates a mandate: local police must prioritize the property rights of the employer (by enforcing trespassing or theft laws) and the regulatory priorities of the immigration service, over the human rights of the worker. When a local police department acts as a funnel to deportation, it is making a choice. It is choosing to be the enforcer for a system of labor exploitation.

The police officer who pulls over a van full of workers because of a "suspected window tint violation" is not making the roads safer. He is participating in the maintenance of a caste system. He is reminding the workers that their presence is conditional, that their mobility is restricted, and that their bodies can be seized by the state at any moment.

For the employer, this is the ultimate convenience. They get the labor of the worker, but the state provides the discipline. The threat of the badge keeps the workforce compliant, cheap, and quiet. The worker knows that in a confrontation with the boss, the police will never be on their side. And so, 911 remains the number they never dial, and the crime of exploitation proceeds in a silence purchased by the public's tax dollars.

Chapter 14: The Impossibility of Civil Court

In the American civic religion, the courthouse occupies a sacred space. It is the architectural embodiment of the promise that, when all else fails—when the boss cheats you, when the landlord locks you out, when the corporation poisons your water—you can file a complaint, stand before a judge, and demand redress. We are a litigious nation because we believe in the power of the lawsuit to equalize the powerless against the powerful. The threat "I'll see you in court" is the ultimate check on tyranny in the private sector.

For the eleven million undocumented people living in the United States, however, the courthouse is not a sanctuary. It is a trap.

To understand why the civil justice system has effectively collapsed for the bottom tier of the American workforce, one must look beyond the statutes and examine the brutal mechanics of litigation itself. The barrier is not just that the laws are weak; it is that the process of enforcing them requires a level of visibility that is suicidal for someone hiding from the state.

The transformation of the civil court system from a venue of justice into a tool of deportation begins with a legal procedure known as "discovery." In theory, discovery is the truth-seeking phase of a lawsuit, where both sides exchange evidence and answer questions under oath to prevent trial by ambush. In practice, defense attorneys for exploitative employers have weaponized this process into an instrument of terror.

Imagine a worker—let's call him Mateo—who has been cheated out of $5,000 in overtime pay by a construction firm. He finds a brave attorney willing to take his case. They file a complaint. The employer's lawyers respond not with a settlement check, but with a notice of deposition.

Mateo must sit in a conference room, under the fluorescent lights, with a court reporter typing every word. The defense attorney slides a piece of paper across the table. It is not about his hours worked. It is not about the quality of his carpentry. It is a question about his life: "Please state your social security number." "Where were you born?" "What name did you use to enter the country?" "Have you ever used a false document to obtain employment?"

This is the "credibility trap." If Mateo answers truthfully, he admits to federal crimes—illegal entry, document fraud—on the record. He creates a sworn transcript that can be handed directly to Immigration and Customs

Enforcement (ICE). If he lies to protect himself, he commits perjury, destroying his credibility and potentially facing criminal charges. If he refuses to answer, the defense attorney moves to dismiss the case for failure to cooperate.

The employer's lawyer knows exactly what they are doing. They are not looking for relevant evidence; they are looking for the "kill switch." As we saw in Chapter 8, the Supreme Court's decision in *Hoffman Plastic Compounds, Inc. v. NLRB* fundamentally altered the landscape of labor litigation. While *Hoffman* specifically addressed back pay in union-busting cases, corporate defense attorneys have aggressively expanded its logic to infect every corner of employment law.

Leveraging the precedent established in *Hoffman*, defendants now routinely argue that a plaintiff's immigration status is relevant to "credibility" or "potential damages" in almost any civil dispute. If a worker sues for unpaid wages, the defense argues that their status matters because they were never legally entitled to the job. If a worker sues for a workplace injury, the defense argues that their "future lost wages" should be calculated based on the economy of their home village in Honduras, not the economy of the United States.

This legal maneuvering has a devastating chilling effect. It sends a clear message to the plaintiff: *If you pursue this $5,000 claim, you will lose your life in America.*

Courts are supposed to protect plaintiffs from irrelevant and harassing questions. In many jurisdictions, enlightened judges have ruled that immigration status is not relevant to whether a worker is owed wages—work is work, regardless of status. But getting to that ruling requires fighting a "protective order" battle that is expensive, time-consuming, and uncertain. Many workers, terrified by the mere question, drop the lawsuit immediately. They walk away from their stolen wages because the price of admission to the courtroom is too high.

This dynamic creates a zone of immunity for employers. They know that the civil justice system operates on a cost-benefit analysis. For the undocumented worker, the cost is existential—the risk of family separation and exile. The benefit is merely monetary. No rational actor trades their survival for a paycheck they have already lost.

But the impossibility of civil court extends beyond the terror of discovery. It is also a matter of economics. The American legal system for civil disputes is largely privatized; you get the justice you can pay for. Wealthy corporations pay hourly rates to defense firms. Indigent workers rely on the "contingency fee" model, where a plaintiff's attorney takes a case for free in exchange for a percentage of the winnings, usually 30 to 40 percent.

This model depends on the existence of a "pot of gold" at the end of the rainbow. Attorneys take risks on cases where the potential damages are high enough to justify hundreds of hours of work. But for undocumented workers, the pot has been systematically smashed.

The "calcification of damages" that flowed from *Hoffman* destroys the economic incentive for private attorneys to take these cases. Why would a lawyer spend $50,000 in time and resources to litigate a case where the maximum recovery is capped at a few thousand dollars because the plaintiff has no legal right to work? The risk-reward ratio is broken. Consequently, undocumented workers struggle to find representation. They are priced out of the market for justice.

There is, of course, the public safety net: Legal Aid. But here, too, the trap is set. The Legal Services Corporation (LSC), the primary funder of civil legal aid in the United States, operates under strict congressional restrictions. Since 1996, LSC-funded organizations are largely prohibited from representing undocumented immigrants. The very lawyers who are dedicated to helping the poor are legally barred from helping the poorest and most vulnerable among them.

This leaves a handful of non-LSC non-profits and boutique firms to handle a tidal wave of exploitation. They are overwhelmed, underfunded, and outgunned. For every one case they take, thousands of violations go unchallenged.

The final lock on the courthouse door is the rise of forced arbitration. Over the last two decades, American corporations have aggressively inserted mandatory arbitration clauses into employment contracts—even the informal ones signed by low-wage workers. These clauses strip workers of their right to sue in court, forcing them instead into private tribunals.

In arbitration, there is no jury. The proceedings are secret. The arbitrator is often a corporate lawyer chosen by the employer. Class actions—the only mechanism that allows workers with small individual claims to band together and afford high-quality counsel—are frequently banned.

For an undocumented worker, arbitration is a black box. The secrecy might seem appealing at first, offering a shield from public exposure. But without the threat of public accountability or a jury verdict, the employer holds all the cards. The "repeat player" effect ensures that arbitrators who rule too often for workers find themselves unemployed. The system is privatized justice, designed by corporate architects to ensure that claims die in quiet rooms rather than result in loud verdicts.

Furthermore, the physical presence required by the legal system poses a logistical nightmare. Civil trials require the plaintiff to be present. But what if the worker has already been deported? Traffickers and abusive employers often use the deportation system to "cleanse" their liability. If a worker threatens to sue, the employer calls ICE. Once the worker is removed to Guatemala, the lawsuit effectively dies. It is nearly impossible to litigate a complex wage theft case from a rural village in Central America. The employer succeeds in deporting the evidence.

This creates a perverse incentive for employers to hire undocumented workers specifically because they are "deportation-ready." It is a form of liability insurance. If the worker gets injured or complains, the employer pulls the rip cord, and the problem vanishes across the border.

Even in the rare instances where a worker wins—where they brave the discovery process, find a lawyer, survive the arbitration trap, and secure a judgment—collection is a separate hell. Small contractors who rely on undocumented labor often operate as shell companies. They have no assets. When a judgment is entered against "Sunshine Construction LLC," the owner simply dissolves the LLC, declares bankruptcy, and opens "Moonlight Construction LLC" the next day. The worker is left with a piece of paper that says they won, but a wallet that remains empty.

This reality has created a culture of impunity that pervades the labor market. Employers know that the civil court system is a paper tiger. They calculate the risk of a lawsuit not as a probability, but as a remote possibility akin to a meteor strike.

The result is that the law, for millions of people, is a fiction. We teach in civics classes that the courts are open to all, that justice is blind, that the law is the great leveler. But for the dishwasher in the back of the kitchen, for the roofer on the scorching shingle, for the maid in the hotel room, the courthouse is a fortress built to keep them out.

When we strip a population of their standing in civil court, we do not just deny them money; we deny them their personhood. We tell them that their injuries do not matter, that their contracts are unenforceable, and that their time has no value that the state is willing to defend. We relegate them to a pre-legal state of nature, where the only law is the law of the strong.

The impossibility of civil court is the final nail in the coffin of the worker's autonomy. It ensures that the exploitation documented in the fields and factories cannot be challenged by the victims themselves. It forces the worker to accept the abuse, not because they are weak, but because they are rational. They look at the courthouse, they look at the risks, and they realize that in America, justice is a luxury they cannot afford to buy.

Part III: The Plantation (Industry Deep Dives)

Specific industries. No generalizations—specific environments.

Chapter 15: The Tomato Fields (Florida)

To understand the architecture of the modern plantation, one must first understand the geography of Immokalee, Florida. Located just thirty miles inland from the pristine beaches and multi-million-dollar estates of Naples, Immokalee exists in a separate universe. It is a town carved out of the swamp, a grid of concrete and dust where the humidity hangs so heavy it feels like a physical weight. In the indigenous language of the region, the name means "My Home," but for the thousands of workers who sleep in its crowded trailers and board the buses before dawn, it is less a home than a holding pen.

This is the epicenter of America's winter tomato production. It is here, in the vast, flat fields that stretch toward the Everglades, that the theoretical concepts of labor exploitation become tangible, sweaty, and toxic reality.

The tomato is a demanding master. Unlike corn or wheat, which can be harvested by massive combines guided by GPS, the fresh-market tomato requires the human hand. It is fragile. It must be picked at a specific stage of "mature green"—hard enough to survive transport, but developed enough to eventually turn red when gassed with ethylene. No machine has yet been invented that can judge this ripeness or pluck the fruit without bruising it as efficiently as a human being.

Consequently, the industry relies on a workforce that functions as a biological machine. The unit of measurement in Immokalee is not the hour; it is the bucket. This plastic bucket holds thirty-two pounds of tomatoes. For decades, the piece rate for this bucket hovered around fifty cents. To earn the federal minimum wage, a worker had to pick, carry, and hoist nearly two and a half tons of tomatoes in a single day.

This arithmetic dictates the pace of life in the fields. There is no time to rest. There is no time to stretch. There is certainly no time to complain. The worker runs—literally runs—with the full bucket to the waiting truck, tosses it up to the "dumper," takes a token, and runs back to the row. The "piece rate" system transforms the worker into their own overseer. If they stop to wipe the sweat from their eyes, they are docking their own pay.

But the pace is only one component of the brutality. The primary adversary in Florida is the sun. The fields are open, shadeless expanses where temperatures frequently exceed ninety degrees, with humidity pushing the heat index well over one hundred. In these conditions, the human body begins to fail. Heat stress is not merely uncomfortable; it is a physiological crisis. The heart pumps furiously to send blood to the skin for cooling, depriving the muscles and brain of oxygen. Confusion sets in. Kidneys begin to shut down.

In a regulated workplace, heat stress is managed with mandatory water breaks, shade tents, and acclimatization protocols. In the tomato fields of the recent past—and in those operations that still operate outside the reforms I will discuss later—water was a privilege, not a right. Workers have reported being prohibited from bringing their own water into the rows to prevent "contamination" or simply to keep their hands free for picking. They were forced to buy sodas or water from the crew leader's truck at inflated prices, returning a portion of their meager wages to the company store before the sweat on their brow had even dried.

This environment created a medical crisis that went largely unrecorded. Workers collapsed in the rows and were told to sit in the bus until they recovered or died. Chronic dehydration led to a prevalence of kidney disease among young men that puzzled epidemiologists until they looked at the working conditions. The heat was not an act of God; it was a condition of employment.

Then there is the chemical assault. To keep the tomatoes perfect, to prevent the blight and the bugs in the tropical humidity, growers wage a chemical war. The fields are sprayed with a cocktail of fungicides, herbicides, and pesticides. Many of these chemicals are neurotoxins.

Workers tell stories of the "green mist." They recount being in the fields when the crop dusters flew over, or when the tractors spraying the adjacent rows turned with the wind. They describe the stinging in their eyes, the rashes that bloom on their skin, the nausea that grips their stomachs. Pregnant women working in these fields have given birth to children with profound deformities, a tragedy that the industry consistently attributes to bad luck or genetics rather than the toxic soup in which the mothers labored.

The vulnerability of this workforce is absolute. They are overwhelmingly immigrants, many undocumented, many indigenous people from Southern Mexico and Guatemala who speak Spanish as a second language or not at all. They are geographically isolated in Immokalee, miles from legal aid or media scrutiny. They are the perfect victims.

It was this perfect storm of isolation, desperation, and lack of regulation that led federal prosecutors to give Immokalee a chilling designation. In a series of high-profile prosecutions in the 1990s and early 2000s, the Department of Justice exposed operations that went far beyond wage theft and safety violations. They found chains. They found box trucks where workers were locked in at night to prevent escape. They found beatings for those who did not work fast enough.

Douglas Molloy, the chief assistant U.S. attorney in Fort Myers who prosecuted these cases, did not mince words. He called these fields "ground zero for modern-day slavery".

This was not hyperbole. It was a legal finding. In *United States v. Ramos*, prosecutors detailed how crew leaders threatened workers with death if they tried to leave. In *United States v. Navarrete*, a family of labor contractors was convicted of holding workers in debt bondage, slashing them with knives, and chaining them to posts. These were not events from 1860. They happened in the age of the internet, a short drive from golf courses where tourists paid hundreds of dollars for a round.

The slavery cases revealed the ultimate logic of the plantation model. When you strip a worker of legal status, isolate them geographically, and pay them piece rates that require superhuman exertion to survive, you create a gravity well that pulls inevitably toward bondage. The "bad apple" contractors who locked workers in trucks were not anomalies; they were simply the ones who took the prevailing logic of the industry to its extreme conclusion. They realized that if you can treat a worker like a machine, you might as well lock them up like one.

The economic structure of the tomato industry incentivized this race to the bottom. For decades, the large buyers—the fast-food giants and supermarket chains—demanded ever-lower prices for tomatoes. They leveraged their massive purchasing power to squeeze the growers. The growers, facing fixed costs for land, fertilizer, and equipment, squeezed the only variable they could control: labor.

The pressure moved downward, from the corporate boardroom to the packing house to the grower to the crew leader, until it landed on the back of the picker. The crew leader, paid by volume, had every incentive to drive his crew to exhaustion. If he could steal a few dollars from each worker's pay envelope, or charge them for a ride to the fields, or force them to work off the clock, his margin increased. The system was designed to extract value from the bottom to subsidize the cheap prices at the top.

This was the reality that gave birth to the Coalition of Immokalee Workers (CIW). They did not start as a powerful NGO with slick lobbyists. They started as a group of workers meeting in a church, realizing that no one was coming to save them. They understood that the law enforcement model—waiting for a slavery case to break and then prosecuting the offender—was insufficient. It punished the slaver after the crime, but it did nothing to change the conditions that allowed slavery to take root.

The CIW's analysis was radical in its simplicity. They realized that the growers were merely the middle managers of exploitation. The real power lay with the brands. The tomato on the burger at Wendy's or Taco Bell connected the consumer directly to the field. If they could force the brands to take responsibility for the conditions in their supply chain, they could bypass the gridlock of government enforcement.

Their struggle was epic. It involved hunger strikes that lasted for weeks. It involved marches across the state of Florida. It involved facing down multi-billion-dollar corporations that insisted they had no role in labor relations. "We buy tomatoes," the CEOs would say. "We don't hire pickers." It was the same subcontracting shield I described in Chapter 11, the same denial of responsibility that allowed Northern textile mills to profit from Southern cotton.

But the CIW persisted. They exposed the reality of the fields to the American public. They connected the "ground zero" of slavery to the "value menu" of the fast-food chain. And slowly, crack by crack, the wall of denial began to break.

The story of the CIW's eventual victory—the creation of the Fair Food Program—is a subject for a later chapter on solutions. But here, in the mud and heat of the fields, we must linger on the reality that necessitated it. We must recognize that for generations, the Florida tomato was a fruit of poison. It was produced by a system that consumed human bodies with the same indifference that a tractor consumes diesel.

Even today, outside the protected sphere of the Fair Food Program, in the fields that still operate in the "old way," the risks remain. The heat is still deadly. The pesticides still drift. The piece rate still demands a punishing pace. And the shadow of the overseer still falls across the rows.

The tomato fields of Florida serve as the clearest possible example of the "plantation" model of modern industry. They demonstrate that when we allow agriculture to operate as a zone of exception—exempt from overtime laws, hidden from public view, reliant on a disenfranchised workforce—we recreate the conditions of the past. We build a food system that feeds the nation by eating its workers.

When you hold a tomato in your hand, you are holding a product that carries a heavy history. It is red not just by nature, but by the blood and heat invested in its harvest. The lesson of Immokalee is that the market will not correct this moral failure on its own. Left to its own devices, the market will drive the price of the tomato down and the cost of human suffering up, until the breaking point is reached. The fields of Florida broke, and from that fracture, a new model began to emerge. But we must never forget what the ground looked like before the change, because that ground—the ground of exploitation—is the default state of the shadow economy.

Chapter 16: The Dairy Barns (Vermont & Wisconsin)

If the tomato fields of Florida represent the inferno of American agriculture—a landscape of scorching heat, open skies, and vast, visible crews—the dairy farms of the North are its silent, frozen oubliette.

In the American imagination, the dairy farm occupies a sacred space. It is the visual shorthand for wholesomeness: the red gambrel roof against a green hillside in Vermont, the black-and-white Holsteins grazing in a Wisconsin pasture, the family patriarch in a plaid jacket checking the morning frost. We see the milk carton and think of calcium, strong bones, and the Protestant work ethic. It is an industry marketed on the aesthetic of purity.

But if you drive past those picturesque barns in the dead of winter, when the temperature plunges to twenty below zero and the snowdrifts pile against the siding, you will not see the reality inside. You will not see the workforce that actually keeps the milk flowing. They are hidden behind the sliding doors, ankle-deep in manure, working a shift that effectively never ends.

The dairy industry has undergone a quiet demographic revolution over the last three decades. As young Americans fled rural areas for the cities and the children of farmers chose college over the herd, the labor supply collapsed. The cows, however, remained. And the cow is a biological machine that cannot be paused. She must be milked two or three times a day, every day, without exception. She does not know it is Christmas. She does not care if the milker has the flu. If she is not milked, she develops mastitis; she suffers; she stops producing.

This biological imperative creates a relentless, 24/7 rhythm that few domestic workers are willing to sustain. To fill the void, the dairy industry turned to the only population desperate enough to accept the isolation and the grind: undocumented immigrants, primarily from Mexico and Central America.

Unlike the seasonal harvest of vegetables, where workers might travel in large groups following the ripening crops, dairy work is year-round and static. This creates a unique form of captivity. The dairy worker does not migrate; they disappear. They vanish into the rural hollows of Upstate New York, the Northeast Kingdom of Vermont, and the vast counties of Wisconsin, often finding themselves the only Spanish speakers for fifty miles.

The isolation is the primary mechanism of control. In Immokalee, a worker can walk to a grocery store or a church. On a dairy farm in rural Vermont, the nearest town might be ten miles away, and there is no public transit. Without a driver's license—which undocumented immigrants are barred from obtaining in many states—the worker is totally dependent on the employer for mobility. They cannot drive to the doctor. They cannot drive to Western Union to send money home. They cannot leave the property to buy food.

This dependency creates a "company town" dynamic on a micro scale. The farmer becomes the sole conduit to the outside world. He buys the groceries. He cashes the checks (often for a fee). He drives the worker to the clinic if an injury is severe enough to threaten production, and decides when an injury is minor enough to ignore. The worker is not just an employee; they are a ward of the farm.

The work itself is a study in repetitive trauma. Modern milking is an industrial process. In a "parlor" system, cows are herded into stanchions, their udders cleaned, machines attached, and then detached, hundreds of times per shift. The worker stands in a "pit" below the cows, reaching up to clean and attach the units.

This motion—reaching up, scrubbing, twisting, attaching—is repeated thousands of times a day. The human body is not designed for this. The result is a constellation of chronic injuries so specific they have their own nomenclature. "Milker's knee" is a degradation of the joint caused by constant squatting and pivoting on concrete floors. Rotator cuffs shred from the repetitive overhead motion. Wrists develop carpal tunnel syndrome that turns hands into claws.

Then there is the danger of the animal itself. A Holstein weighs 1,500 pounds. In the confined space of the milking parlor or the holding pen, the cow is a lethal weapon. Workers are kicked, crushed against gates, and trampled. The floors are perpetually slick with a mixture of water, milk, and manure, creating a slip-and-fall hazard that exists in every single shift. In the winter, the water freezes, turning the barn into an ice rink.

Yet, OSHA inspections on dairy farms are vanishingly rare. A "small farm" exemption often shields operations with fewer than eleven employees from programmed safety inspections. Since many dairy farms operate with a skeleton crew of five or six workers managing hundreds of cows, they exist in a regulatory blind spot. The injuries happen in the dark. A crushed hand is wrapped in duct tape. A twisted knee is treated with ibuprofen. The work continues because the cows are waiting.

The housing situation on these farms adds another layer to the indignity. Because the farms are so remote and the shifts are split—often requiring workers to be in the barn at 3:00 AM for the first milking and again at 4:00 PM for the second—commutes are impractical. The solution is on-site housing.

Sometimes, this is a trailer down the road. Frequently, it is a room built directly into the barn, above the milking parlor or next to the machinery room. Workers live, sleep, and eat inside the industrial facility. The smell of manure is omnipresent. The noise of the vacuum pumps and the lowing of cattle never ceases. There is no psychological separation between "home" and "work." The worker is simply stored on-site, like a piece of equipment, powered down for a few hours before being rebooted for the next shift.

Surveys by migrant justice organizations like Migrant Justice in Vermont have documented the squalor of this housing: lack of heat in sub-zero winters, vermin infestations, overcrowding, and unsafe drinking water. Yet, because the housing is tied to the job, complaining carries the risk of immediate homelessness in a climate where being outside can kill you.

The geography of the northern border adds a specific, terrifying dimension to this isolation. The U.S. Border Patrol has jurisdiction within 100 miles of any external boundary. This zone encompasses the entirety of states like Maine and Florida, but in the dairy belts of New York, Vermont, and Washington state, the enforcement is particularly aggressive.

Undocumented dairy workers in these zones live in what they describe as a "prison without walls." They know that Border Patrol agents cruise the rural highways. They know that a trip to the Walmart or the laundromat could end in detention. As a result, many workers essentially sentence themselves to house arrest. They do not leave the farm for months, sometimes years, at a time.

I have interviewed workers in Vermont who have not seen the town five miles away in two years. They rely on the "patron" (the farmer) to bring them bags of rice and beans. Their world shrinks to the path between the bed and the barn. The psychological toll of this confinement is profound. Depression, anxiety, and substance abuse are rampant, fueled by the crushing loneliness of looking out a window at a white landscape you are forbidden to traverse.

This immobility destroys the labor market's natural corrective mechanisms. In a free market, if a farm offers terrible wages or abusive conditions, the worker leaves and goes to the farm down the road. In the northern border zone, leaving the farm requires a vehicle and a risk tolerance that most workers lack. The bad actor faces no competition for labor because his workforce is captive. He can suppress wages, ignore safety, and increase hours with impunity.

The legal architecture of the visa system has historically compounded this trap. For decades, the H-2A visa program—the primary legal channel for agricultural workers—was restricted to "seasonal or temporary" work. This fit the rhythms of fruit and vegetable harvesting. It did not fit dairy. Cows are not seasonal. Milk production is year-round.

This meant that for decades, there was literally no legal way for a dairy farmer to hire a foreign worker for a permanent position. The law demanded a workforce that did not exist (Americans willing to milk cows at 3:00 AM for $10 an hour) and forbade the workforce that was available.

The result was the criminalization of an entire industry. Farmers, squeezed by the consolidation of the milk market and the plummeting price of their product, turned to undocumented labor not as a way to cheat, but as the only way to operate. The "family farm" survived by becoming a sanctuary for the undocumented, a relationship built on mutual necessity and mutual legal vulnerability.

But this relationship is not symmetrical. The farmer risks a fine; the worker risks their life. The economic pressure on the dairy industry—where the price of milk is set by global commodities markets often below the cost of production—is transferred directly onto the backs of the workers. When the price of milk drops, the farmer cannot pay the feed company less. He cannot pay the bank less. The only variable he can squeeze is labor.

This squeeze manifests in "speed-ups." A parlor designed for one milker to handle roughly fifty cows an hour is pushed to sixty, then seventy. The worker runs from udder to udder. Breaks are eliminated. The twelve-hour shift stretches to fourteen. The "milker's knee" grinds bone on bone.

The invisibility of this workforce allows the consumer to maintain the pastoral fantasy. When we buy a pint of premium ice cream featuring a cartoon cow and a story about "values-led sourcing," we are buying a story that ends at the barn door. We do not see the Guatemalan teenager working the night shift in the sub-zero Vermont winter, sending money home to a family he hasn't seen in five years, trapped on a farm he cannot leave.

There is a supreme irony in the fact that many of these workers come from agrarian backgrounds in Mexico and Central America. They know animals. They know the land. They are skilled laborers in every sense of the word. Yet the system treats them as disposable unskilled inputs. Their knowledge is extracted, but their humanity is denied.

In recent years, worker-led movements like the "Milk with Dignity" campaign have begun to challenge this silence, pressuring major corporate buyers to take responsibility for the conditions in their supply chains. They are demanding that the brands we trust look inside the barns we romanticize. They are exposing the fact that the "wholesome" dairy industry is built on a foundation of fear and isolation that rivals any sweatshop.

Until the structural issues are addressed—the exclusion from legal status, the geographic isolation, the exemption from safety oversight—the dairy barn will remain a cold prison. The milk will continue to flow, white and pure, but the hands that draw it will remain in the shadows, bruised, frozen, and unseen. The pastoral ideal is a façade; the reality is an industrial engine fueled by the burning of human lives in the cold.

Chapter 17: The Poultry Line (The South)

In the rural counties of Alabama, Arkansas, and Georgia, the landscape tells a story of succession. Where cotton fields once stretched to the horizon, white monoliths now rise from the red clay. These are not plantation houses; they are windowless, metal-clad fortresses surrounded by chain-link fences and guard shacks. They are poultry processing plants, the industrial engines that have replaced King Cotton as the dominant economic force of the rural South.

To the consumer, the chicken is a symbol of affordable protein, the twenty-cent nugget, the family bucket. To the economist, it is a triumph of vertical integration and efficiency. But to the worker standing inside those metal walls, the chicken is an adversary in a relentless physical war—a war fought in near-freezing temperatures, amidst a fog of chemical spray, against a clock that ticks in milliseconds.

The modern poultry plant is not a farm. It is a disassembly line. It operates on a principle of reverse manufacturing: a complex biological organism enters at one end and is reduced to standardized, plastic-wrapped parts at the other. The speed at which this reduction occurs is the single most defining characteristic of the industry. It is the variable that determines profit, and it is the weapon that destroys the human body.

The process begins in the "hanging" room. Here, the environment is dark, lit only by red bulbs to keep the birds calm. The air is thick with dust, feathers, and the smell of ammonia. Workers stand in a pit as a conveyor belt carrying metal shackles rushes past their faces at eye level. Their job is to grab a live bird—weighing five or six pounds, often thrashing and scratching—by the legs and slam it into the shackles.

The physical demand of this task defies comprehension. A hanger must lift a struggling weight, twist their wrists, and lock the bird into the metal clamp, repeating the motion every two seconds. In a single shift, a worker might lift tens of thousands of pounds of living weight. Their hands become claws, frozen in a permanent grip. Their shoulders burn with the lactic acid of continuous exertion. And the line never stops.

From there, the birds move to the "kill line," then the scalder, and the plucker. But the true labor intensity—and the site of the most profound exploitation—is found in the "evisceration" and "deboning" departments.

This is the "cold room." To prevent bacterial growth, the temperature is kept at a constant, bone-chilling forty degrees Fahrenheit.

In this refrigerated twilight, workers stand shoulder to shoulder, packed so tightly that a slip of a knife can—and frequently does—stab the person next to them. The floor is a slick treacherous surface coated in a mixture of water, fat, and blood. As the Texas Department of Insurance notes in its safety advisories for the industry, workers in these environments face constant dangers from slippery floors, sharp equipment, and loud machinery that makes verbal communication impossible.

But the primary hazard is the motion itself. As the U.S. Department of Agriculture's Food Safety and Inspection Service (FSIS) documented in their "PULSE Poultry Study," processing workers perform thousands of repetitive, forceful motions per shift. Some tasks require a specific cut or pull every ten seconds or less. The study found that a single worker might execute up to 30,000 repetitions in a single workday.

Try to visualize the mechanics of this. Imagine holding a pair of scissors. Now, imagine cutting through a piece of tough gristle. Now, do it thirty thousand times. Do it while your hands are numb from the cold. Do it while standing on a concrete floor for eight to eleven hours. Do it knowing that if you miss a cut, the supervisor screaming in your ear will write you up, and three write-ups mean you are fired.

The human body is an engineering marvel, but it has mechanical limits. It is not designed for 30,000 forceful repetitions a day. The connective tissues—the tendons, the ligaments, the cartilage—begin to fray. Inflammation sets in. The result is a pandemic of musculoskeletal disorders that is endemic to the industry. Carpal tunnel syndrome is not an anomaly here; it is an inevitability. Rotator cuffs disintegrate. Discs in the spine compress and rupture.

Researchers like J.L. Harmse have documented the "ergonomic stress" and "exposure to cold" that define these shifts. The cold is a force multiplier for injury. It restricts blood flow to the extremities just as the muscles demand oxygen. It stiffens the tissues just as they need to be pliable. The worker leaves the plant at the end of the shift unable to straighten their fingers, their hands shaped into the grip of the knife they have held for ten hours.

Yet, the industry's response to this physical toll has been to demand *more* speed. For decades, the maximum line speed for evisceration was capped at 140 birds per minute—a pace already blindingly fast. In recent years, major poultry corporations have lobbied aggressively for "line speed waivers" to increase this to 175 birds per minute. They argue that automation allows for faster processing.

But machines do not debone the thigh. Machines do not cut the wing. People do. When the line speeds up, the human component must accelerate to match it. The worker who was making 40 cuts a minute must now make 50. The margin for error vanishes. The knife slips. The tendon snaps.

This relentless pressure creates an environment where basic biological functions become liabilities. The most degrading secret of the poultry line is the battle for the bathroom. Because the line runs continuously, a worker cannot simply step away to use the restroom. They must wait for a "relief worker" to take their spot. But relief workers are expensive, so plants often understaff them.

Reports from organizations like Oxfam have documented the horrific consequences: workers denied bathroom breaks for hours, mocked by supervisors for asking, or told to "hold it" until lunch. In a humid, cold environment where the body naturally needs to expel fluid, this is torture. To keep their jobs, workers resort to the ultimate indignity: they wear adult diapers on the line. They urinate on themselves while cutting meat destined for American dinner tables, because the cost of stopping the line is higher than the cost of their dignity.

This is the modern plantation. It is a place where the human being is reduced to a biological appendage of the machine, where the right to use a toilet is negotiable, and where the body is consumed as a raw material.

Who accepts these conditions? Who stays in a job where they must wear a diaper to avoid being fired?

For decades, this work was performed by African Americans in the rural South. But as the Civil Rights movement opened other doors and the brutality of the plants became widely known, the local labor supply dried up. The industry needed a new workforce—one that was more vulnerable, more desperate, and less likely to organize.

They found it in the shadows. Today, the poultry workforce is heavily comprised of undocumented immigrants from Mexico and Central America, alongside refugees resettled from Burma, Somalia, and the Marshall Islands. These groups share a common trait: a lack of political power.

The undocumented worker in a poultry plant lives in a state of double captivity. They are captive to the line speed because they need the job, and they are captive to the employer because they fear deportation. Supervisors weaponize this fear. If a worker complains about the pain in their wrist, they are told, "There are ten people waiting outside for your job." If they threaten to report a safety violation to OSHA, the threat of ICE is engaged.

The industry has structured itself to absorb the "churn." They know the work breaks people. They expect high turnover. In many plants, turnover rates exceed 100 percent annually. This means the entire workforce effectively replaces itself every year. This is not a failure of management; it is a feature of the business model.

A high-turnover workforce is a compliant workforce. New workers do not know their rights. They do not know that the pain in their shoulder is a permanent injury in the making. They do not have the social capital to organize a union. By the time they realize the trap they are in, they are injured and discarded, replaced by the next busload of recruits.

The hazards extend beyond the orthopedic. The air in these plants is a toxic soup. To kill bacteria like Salmonella and Campylobacter, the carcasses are bathed in antimicrobial chemicals, most notably peracetic acid (PAA). This chemical is sprayed into the air and onto the meat.

As the Texas Department of Insurance warns, workers are exposed to these "airborne contaminants" and "harmful chemicals" for their entire shift. PAA is a strong irritant. Workers report burning eyes, nosebleeds, and chronic respiratory issues. They develop a "poultry cough" that never goes away. In the enclosed environment of the plant, where ventilation is often inadequate to keep the "cold room" temperature stable, the gas concentrates.

Recently, a new biological threat has entered the plants: avian influenza. As noted by safety regulators, workers face the risk of exposure to viruses carried by the birds. When a flock is infected, it must be depopulated and processed. The workers on the line are the first responders to a zoonotic disease, often provided with inadequate personal protective equipment. They are the biological buffer between the pandemic and the public.

The medical system in these company towns is often complicit in the exploitation. Many plants maintain on-site "infirmaries" or first-aid stations. When a worker is injured—a cut, a strain, a fall on the slippery floor—they are sent to the company nurse. The goal of this internal medicine is often not to heal, but to keep the injury off the OSHA logs.

If an injury is treated with "first aid" only, it does not have to be reported to the federal government. So, workers with repetitive motion injuries are given ibuprofen and ice packs and sent back to the line. Workers with lacerations are glued shut rather than stitched. They are discouraged from seeing outside doctors. This manipulation of medical data allows the industry to claim that injury rates are falling, even as the bodies of the workers tell a different story.

The "point system" used for attendance reinforces this cruelty. In many plants, missing a shift results in a "point." Accumulate too many points, and you are fired. If a worker wakes up with hands so swollen they cannot hold a toothbrush, they must decide: stay home and get a point, or go to work and permanently damage the nerve. For the undocumented worker living paycheck to paycheck, there is no choice. They take the pills, wrap their hands, and go to the line.

The poultry industry in the South is a testament to the efficiency of modern capitalism when stripped of moral or legal constraint. It has engineered a system where the animal is grown to maturity in six weeks, processed in minutes, and sold for pennies. It is a miracle of logistics.

But the true cost of that twenty-cent nugget is not found on the menu board. It is hidden in the disability checks of rural counties. It is hidden in the emergency rooms where uninsured workers finally collapse. It is hidden in the crowded trailer parks where families live in the shadow of the processing plant.

The chicken on the American table is subsidized by the destruction of the human body. The line speed is the dictatorial force that governs the life of the worker, a mechanical tyrant that demands 30,000 tributes a day. In the South, where the specter of the plantation has never fully faded, the poultry plant stands as its modern industrial incarnation—a place where the work is hard, the pay is low, the bodies are brown, and the exit is barred by fear.

Chapter 18: The Slaughterhouse (Beef & Pork)

If the poultry plant is a factory of repetition, defined by the relentless speed of light objects, the beef and pork slaughterhouse is a factory of mass and violence. Here, the adversary is not a five-pound bird but a twelve-hundred-pound steer or a three-hundred-pound hog. The physics of the kill floor are different; the danger is not just repetitive stress, but catastrophic impact. In these facilities, the industrialization of biology reaches its most terrifying scale, and the exploitation of the workforce reaches its most dangerous intensity.

To enter a modern beef packing plant is to enter a world designed to dismantle giants. The architecture is vast, a labyrinth of steel catwalks, humming conveyor belts, and hydraulic lifts capable of hoisting a sedan. The noise is a physical assault—a cacophony of grinding gears, hissing steam, and the bellowing of animals in the holding pens. It is an environment so hostile to human senses that survival requires a shutting down of the self, a narrowing of focus to the single, repetitive task at hand.

The process begins with the "knock." In the stunning chute, a worker—often one of the few positions still held by a U.S. citizen due to the skill required—uses a captive bolt pistol to render the animal unconscious. But biology is resilient. If the stun is imperfect, the animal thrashes. A kick from a steer can shatter a human femur; a crush against the steel gate can collapse a lung. The workers in the stunning area live in the splash zone of this violence, managing the transition from living creature to raw material.

From there, the animal is hoisted by a hind leg, bleeding out as it moves down the "disassembly" line. This is where the undocumented workforce is concentrated, in the fabrication rooms where the carcass is broken down into primals and sub-primals. Unlike the poultry line, where a pair of scissors is the primary tool, the beef line requires band saws, circular saws, and twelve-inch breaking knives.

The danger here is calibrated in torque and horsepower. A band saw used to split a brisket does not distinguish between bone and safety gloves. The speed of the line—which dictates profit margins in an industry where pennies per pound matter—forces workers to make cuts with a velocity that invites disaster. A slip on a floor slick with tallow does not result in a stumble; it results in a fall into a moving blade or a conveyor belt.

As noted in investigations of the industry, meatpacking workers face some of the most dangerous conditions in American commerce, including slippery floors, sharp equipment, and loud machinery. But in beef and pork, the specific nature of the injury shifts from the ergonomic to the traumatic. While poultry workers suffer from carpal tunnel, slaughterhouse workers suffer from amputations. Fingers, hands, and arms are the tithes paid to the speed of the line.

The industry has long argued that these accidents are the result of "worker error." They blame the victim for losing focus. But focus is a finite resource, and after eight hours of wrestling heavy carcasses in near-freezing temperatures, the mind wanders. The physical exhaustion of manipulating heavy meat—pulling loins, throwing ribs—drains the body of the reserves needed to be careful.

Yet, the day shift, for all its horrors, operates under a veneer of scrutiny. USDA inspectors are present to ensure food safety. Management walks the floor. There is light.

The true heart of darkness in the slaughterhouse beats at night.

When the "second shift" ends and the production line halts, the "third shift" begins. This is the sanitation crew. In the industry, they are the ghosts. They arrive when the community is asleep and leave before the sun rises. Their job is to scrub the facility clean of the blood, fat, and bone amassed during sixteen hours of slaughter, resetting the stage for the next day's kill.

The sanitation shift is the most dangerous job in the American food system. It combines the hazards of heavy industrial machinery with the dangers of chemical warfare. To cut through the animal fat that coats every surface, the crews use high-pressure hoses spraying water heated to 180 degrees, mixed with caustic chemicals like chlorine and quaternary ammonium.

These chemicals are not household cleaners; they are industrial solvents capable of dissolving organic matter. When sprayed into the air, they form a toxic mist. Workers report chemical burns on their skin, eyes that sting perpetually, and respiratory issues that mimic chronic asthma. The "sanitation cough" is a badge of the trade, a sign that the lungs have been scorched by the very air they breathe.

But the chemicals are secondary to the machines. To clean a band saw or a grinder, the machine must often be running, or at least disassembled while parts are still mobile. The protocol known as "lockout/tagout"—which ensures machines are powered down and cannot be turned on while a worker is inside them—is the golden rule of industrial safety. But on the third shift, under the pressure to finish before the morning kill begins, these protocols are often bypassed.

Workers climb inside massive blenders to scrub the blades. They reach into augers to pull out stuck gristle. If a sensor trips, or if a coworker in the control room makes a mistake, the machine activates. The results are gruesome beyond description—workers crushed, ground, or severed in the gears of the plant.

This night workforce is overwhelmingly composed of undocumented immigrants. They are the "subcontracted of the subcontracted." Major meatpacking corporations rarely employ their own sanitation crews. Instead, they hire specialized cleaning companies, like Packers Sanitation Services Inc. (PSSI), to handle the night shift. This layering of liability—the same "Subcontracting Shield" discussed in Chapter 11—allows the plant owner to disclaim responsibility for the atrocities that happen in the dark.

It is within this shadowy layer of the industry that the most disturbing trend has re-emerged: child labor. Recent investigations by the Department of Labor have uncovered hundreds of children—some as young as thirteen—working the overnight sanitation shifts in slaughterhouses across the Midwest. These are not teenagers bagging groceries; they are children cleaning bone saws with corrosive chemicals at 3:00 AM.

These children are often unaccompanied minors who arrived at the border and were released to sponsors, only to find themselves pressed into debt bondage to pay for their journey. They use false documents to secure jobs with the sanitation contractors. The contractors, driven by the labor shortage and the need for compliant bodies, turn a blind eye to the obvious youth of their workforce. The meatpacking giants claim ignorance, pointing to their contracts that forbid child labor, while profiting from the clean machines that greet them every morning.

The presence of children on the slaughterhouse floor is the ultimate indictment of the system. It represents a regression to the industrial conditions of the 19th century, a Dickensonian nightmare resurrected in the 21st. It proves that the "market" will not police itself; if labor is scarce and enforcement is weak, the market will consume children.

The physical toll of the slaughterhouse extends to the biological. The concentration of animals and people creates a petri dish for zoonotic disease. As safety regulators have warned, workers face the risk of exposure to viruses and bacteria carried by the animals. In pork plants, the risk of MRSA (methicillin-resistant Staphylococcus aureus) is elevated. During the COVID-19 pandemic, meatpacking plants became vectors of mass infection, with employers betting that the "essential" nature of the work would shield them from liability for the deaths of their disposable workforce.

The "essential worker" designation during the pandemic revealed the cynical core of the industry's view of its labor. Workers were ordered to stay on the line as infection rates skyrocketed. They were given commemorative t-shirts and "hero pay"—a few dollars extra an hour—while the companies lobbied for liability shields to prevent lawsuits from the families of the dead. The message was clear: the meat matters more than the man.

The pace of the beef and pork lines creates a culture of "toughness" that silences complaints. The environment is hyper-masculine and aggressive. A worker who complains about pain is seen as weak. A worker who reports a safety hazard is seen as a snitch. This culture is reinforced by the presence of the "company doctor" or nurse, whose primary role, as in the poultry industry, is to keep injuries off the official OSHA logs.

If a worker slices their hand on a beef hook, the nurse glues it shut and wraps it. If a worker strains their back, they are given a heating pad and sent back to the line. By keeping these treatments at the "first aid" level, the plant avoids reporting a "recordable injury." This statistical manipulation allows the industry to boast of declining injury rates while the bodies of the workers tell a different story.

The pork industry, in particular, has aggressively pushed for the "modernization" of inspection systems, which effectively privatizes quality control and removes limits on line speeds. Faster lines mean more hogs processed, more profit, and more injuries. The worker standing at the conveyor belt, knife in hand, must synchronize their movements with a machine that has been accelerated by deregulation.

For the undocumented worker, the slaughterhouse is a paradox. It offers wages that are often higher than those in agriculture or hospitality—sometimes $15 or $20 an hour. But this "hazard pay" comes with a mortgage on the body. The career expectancy of a line worker is short. The joints give out. The hearing goes. The chemical sensitivity becomes chronic.

After five or ten years, the slaughterhouse worker is often physically spent, discarded by the industry to join the ranks of the disabled. But because they are undocumented, they cannot access Social Security Disability Insurance. They are left to rely on the charity of their families or the emergency room, transferring the long-term cost of their exploitation to the public.

The beef and pork that arrive in American supermarkets, neatly packaged in Styrofoam and plastic, bear no trace of this violence. The blood has been washed away by the night shift. The bone dust has been scrubbed. The screaming of the saws is silenced. But every steak and every chop is a product of this industrial combat zone.

The slaughterhouse stands as the fortress of the exploitation economy. It is where the sheer physical weight of the animal meets the legal weightlessness of the worker. It is where the American appetite for cheap meat is satisfied by a workforce that eats pain in the dark. To look inside is to see the true cost of the barbecue, a cost paid in severed fingers, burned lungs, and the stolen childhoods of the night shift.

Chapter 19: Residential Construction

The American Dream has a specific architectural form. It is the single-family home, detached and sovereign, sitting on a quarter-acre of manicured lawn in a subdivision with a name like "Oak Creek" or "Whispering Pines." This structure is the primary repository of middle-class wealth, the setting for family life, and the ultimate symbol of stability. Yet, if you were to peel back the vinyl siding or lift the asphalt shingles of these monuments to domestic tranquility, you would find that the foundations are poured, the frames are raised, and the roofs are laid by a workforce that possesses none of the stability the home represents.

Residential construction is the wild west of the American labor market. Unlike the massive commercial projects—the skyscrapers and stadiums where union presence is strong and safety protocols are rigidly enforced—the residential sector operates in a regulatory shadow land. Here, the scale is smaller, the crews are transient, and the oversight is non-existent. It is an industry built on the speed of the nail gun and the silence of the worker.

The mechanism of employment in this sector often begins not with an application or an interview, but on the "cash corner." In almost every major American city, there are specific intersections, parking lots of home improvement stores, or gasoline stations that serve as open-air hiring halls. These are the *esquinas*, the corners where the law of supply and demand operates in its rawest, most brutal form.

At 6:00 AM, men gather in clusters, waiting. They are visibly anxious, scanning the traffic for the slowing pickup truck or the white van that signals work. When a vehicle pulls over, the dynamic is primal. The driver does not ask for resumes. He looks at the physical build of the men. He points. "You, you, and you. Roofing. Cash. Get in."

This transaction is the ultimate commodification of the human body. The worker's name is often never asked. His experience is secondary to his willingness to get in the truck immediately. The wage is negotiated in seconds, often under the pressure of competing workers willing to take less. There is no paperwork, no insurance, no record that the worker ever stepped foot on the job site. If he is injured at 10:00 AM, the driver can push him out of the truck at 10:15 AM and claim he never saw him before.

This day-labor system is the lifeblood of residential construction because the industry is defined by volatility. A framing crew is needed for three days; a roofing crew for two. The "just-in-time" delivery model applied to human beings allows small contractors to operate with zero overhead. They own the truck and the tools; they rent the muscles by the day.

Once inside the van, the destination is often the roof. Roofing is widely acknowledged as one of the most punishing jobs in the economy. It combines the dangers of extreme heat, heavy lifting, and gravity. On a summer day, the surface temperature of a black asphalt roof can exceed 150 degrees Fahrenheit. The radiant heat is inescapable; it rises through the soles of the boots and reflects off the shingles into the face.

In this environment, the worker is a beast of burden. Bundles of shingles weigh roughly seventy pounds. They must be carried up ladders, balanced on shoulders, and deposited on a pitched surface. The physical strain of the ascent is compounded by the precariousness of the footing. A "12/12 pitch"—a steep roof rising 12 inches for every 12 inches of horizontal run— is essentially a cliff face.

In a regulated workplace, the primary defense against gravity is the fall arrest system: a harness, a lanyard, and an anchor point bolted into the roof. OSHA regulations are unambiguous: any work over six feet requires fall protection. Yet, drive through any active subdivision in Texas, Florida, or Arizona, and look up. You will see silhouettes moving along the ridge lines, untethered, balancing on toe-boards, defying death with every step.

The absence of harnesses is not an oversight; it is a calculation. Safety gear costs money. Properly installing anchors takes time. Wearing a harness restricts movement and slows the pace of work. In an industry where profit margins are razor-thin and contracts are awarded to the lowest bidder, speed is the only currency.

The Center for Construction Research and Training (CPWR) has documented that falls are the leading cause of death in construction, accounting for roughly one-third of all fatalities. The data reveals a grim disparity: Hispanic workers, who make up a disproportionate share of the residential workforce and the undocumented population, die from falls at significantly higher rates than their white counterparts. They are falling because they are unprotected, and they are unprotected because they are disposable.

The pressure to work without safety gear is enforced by the "piece rate" system. In many residential crews, workers are not paid by the hour, but by the "square" (a 10-by-10-foot area of roofing) or the "board foot" of framing. This compensation model incentivizes risk. Every minute spent tying off a lanyard is a minute not nailing shingles. Every break for water is money lost. The worker is forced to gamble their life against their paycheck.

This gamble is rigged by the complete lack of training. As the University of Michigan study noted in Chapter 10, nearly three-quarters of undocumented construction workers have never received basic safety training. They are handed a pneumatic nail gun—a weapon capable of firing a three-inch spike at 1,400 feet per second—and told to shoot. They are sent up ladders without learning the "three points of contact" rule. They are thrust into environments where a single misstep means paralysis or death, armed only with their desperation.

The residential construction site is also a landscape of chemical exposure. Framers work with pressure-treated lumber soaked in arsenic and copper compounds. Painters spray lacquers and solvents in unventilated rooms. Insulation installers breathe glass fibers. In a compliant workplace, these hazards are mitigated by respirators, ventilation fans, and protective suits. On the undocumented job site, the only filter is the worker's lungs.

The silica dust generated by cutting concrete backer board or dry-cutting tile is a particularly insidious killer. Inhaling this dust causes silicosis, an incurable lung disease that suffocates the victim from the inside. OSHA strictly regulates silica exposure, requiring water saws and vacuum attachments. But on a small renovation project or a tract home build, these expensive tools are rare. The undocumented worker cuts the tile in a cloud of white dust, coating their clothes and their alveoli in a substance that will kill them ten years later, long after the house is sold and the contractor has moved on.

When gravity eventually wins—when the boot slips on the shingle, or the ladder slides on the pavement—the true savagery of the system is revealed. In a legitimate employment relationship, a fall triggers a standardized protocol: 911 is called, workers' compensation insurance is notified, and an investigation begins.

On the shadow work site, a fall triggers a cover-up.

Investigative reports from news organizations like McClatchy and NPR have documented the "dump and run" tactic used by unscrupulous contractors. When a worker falls, the foreman does not call an ambulance to the site, because an ambulance brings police and questions. Instead, the injured worker is dragged into a private vehicle. They are driven to the emergency room and dropped off at the curb, or told to walk in and lie about where the accident happened.

"Tell them you fell off a ladder at your house," the foreman commands. "If you say it happened at work, the police will come, and ICE will deport you."

The worker, writhing in pain from a shattered pelvis or a broken spine, complies. They lie to the triage nurse. This lie severs the link between the injury and the employer. It shifts the financial burden of the catastrophic injury from the contractor's insurance (which likely doesn't exist) to the public safety net. The hospital treats the worker as an indigent charity case. The taxpayer absorbs the cost of the surgery. The contractor drives back to the cash corner to pick up a replacement.

The consequences for the worker are total ruin. Without workers' compensation, there is no wage replacement during recovery. There is no payment for permanent disability. An undocumented roofer who loses the ability to walk loses the ability to feed his family. He is transformed from a breadwinner into a burden, discarded by the industry that consumed his body.

Who is responsible for this? The legal structure of residential construction is designed to ensure the answer is "no one." The "Subcontracting Shield" discussed in Chapter 11 is deployed here with fractal complexity. The large national homebuilder who puts their sign on the front lawn hires a "construction manager," who hires a "shell contractor" for the frame, who hires a "labor broker," who hires the van driver.

The homebuilder can honestly say they check the papers of their direct employees. But they have no direct employees swinging hammers. They have "partners." When OSHA attempts to fine a builder for a fall fatality, the builder points to the contract requiring the subcontractor to follow all safety laws. The subcontractor points to the labor broker. The labor broker dissolves his LLC and disappears. The liability dissipates like mist.

But the ultimate driver of this system is the American consumer's demand for affordability. We have cultural expectations about what a house should cost. We want granite countertops, hardwood floors, and intricate rooflines, and we want them at a price point that defies the rising cost of materials.

The only elastic variable in the cost of a new home is labor. Lumber prices are set by global markets. Concrete has a fixed cost. Land is expensive. To hit the price target that the market demands, the labor cost must be suppressed. The undocumented worker is the subsidy that makes the American housing market function.

The honest contractor who attempts to compete in this market faces an impossible math problem. If he pays a living wage, carries insurance, and buys safety gear, his bid for a framing job might be $50,000. The competitor who uses a crew of misclassified, uninsured, undocumented workers bids $35,000. The homeowner or developer, looking only at the bottom line, chooses the lower bid. They do not ask why it is lower. They do not want to know.

This dynamic has decimated the unionized residential construction sector in many parts of the country. In the mid-20th century, building homes was a middle-class career. A carpenter could support a family, own a home, and retire with a pension. Today, in the non-union residential sector, carpentry is a poverty-wage job with a high probability of disability. We have de-skilled the trade and de-valued the tradesman, replacing the craftsman with the casual laborer.

The physical quality of the housing stock suffers as well. A worker who is untrained, exhausted, and paid by the piece has no incentive to ensure a wall is plumb or a flashing is watertight. They are incentivized to cover the ground as fast as possible. The epidemic of construction defect lawsuits in new developments is a symptom of a workforce that is churned and burned rather than trained and retained.

The residential construction site is a microcosm of the broader exploitation economy. It is a place where the finished product—the home—

is a symbol of security, while the process of its creation is defined by profound insecurity. The roof that keeps the rain off a suburban family was likely laid by a man who cannot afford a roof of his own, who has no health insurance to treat the burns on his skin, and who knows that if he slips, he will fall alone.

We drive past these sites every day. We hear the pop-pop-pop of the nail guns and see the frames rising against the sky. We see the progress. We do not see the lack of harnesses. We do not see the cash changing hands in the parking lot. We do not see the fear in the eyes of the man on the ridge line. We see only the house, clean and new, and we do not ask who paid the price for its existence.

Chapter 20: Disaster Recovery

When the wind stops howling and the floodwaters recede, or when the last ember of a wildfire is finally extinguished, a predictable silence descends on the devastated landscape. It is the silence of shock. Homeowners stand in the ruins of their living rooms, staring at waterlines that reach the ceiling or foundations stripped bare by flame. Municipal leaders survey the debris—millions of cubic yards of shattered timber, twisted metal, and soggy drywall—and issue the same urgent command: "We will rebuild."

This command triggers one of the largest and least regulated migrations of labor in the American economy. Before the Federal Emergency Management Agency (FEMA) trucks even arrive, a different fleet is already on the highway. They travel in beat-up vans and convoys of pickup trucks, racing toward the catastrophe. These are the disaster chasers, the "resilience force" that America relies on to clean up its messes.

To the residents of a hurricane-ravaged town in Florida or Louisiana, these workers appear as a godsend. They are the men who show up when the power is out and the streets are impassable, armed with chainsaws and pry bars, willing to do the filthy, dangerous work of "mucking out" flooded homes. They strip the moldy insulation, haul the waterlogged carpets, and patch the roofs before the next rain comes.

But if you look closely at who is doing this work, you will see the same faces that populate the tomato fields and the slaughterhouses. The disaster recovery industry has become the emergency room of the exploitation economy. It is a sector defined by extreme urgency, total chaos, and a suspension of normal rules—conditions that create a perfect laboratory for labor abuse.

The mechanics of this mobilization are distinct from standard construction. In traditional building, a project is planned for months. In disaster recovery, the demand for labor spikes from zero to infinite overnight. A town that usually employs five hundred construction workers suddenly needs five thousand. The local labor market cannot meet this demand, so the vacuum is filled by a mobile workforce of migrant laborers, many of them undocumented, who follow the weather across the map.

They are recruited through the digital networks discussed in Chapter 1—WhatsApp groups pinging with messages: "Hurricane work in Houston. $18 an hour. Cash. Leave tonight." Or they are picked up on the day-labor corners of Atlanta, Dallas, and Miami by brokers who promise high wages and lodging. They pack their bags, expecting a few weeks of hard but lucrative work.

What they find upon arrival is a landscape where the rule of law has been washed away along with the roads.

The work itself is a descent into toxicity. "Mucking out" a flooded home is not just heavy lifting; it is a hazardous materials operation. Floodwaters are not just rain; they are a toxic soup of sewage, industrial runoff, gasoline, and pesticides. Once the water recedes, it leaves behind a coating of sludge that immediately begins to bloom with black mold.

In a regulated environment, dealing with black mold or asbestos (which is often disturbed during demolition of older homes) requires Tyvek suits, respirators, and decontamination showers. But in the disaster zone, speed is the only metric. The "storm chaser" contractors who descend on these towns operate on thin margins and high volume. Safety gear is expensive and slows down the work.

Consequently, workers are sent into rotting houses wearing t-shirts and sneakers. They breathe in spores that colonize their lungs. They handle insulation fiberglass with bare hands. They wade through standing water that hides nails, broken glass, and live wires. The injury rate in disaster recovery is astronomical, yet rarely recorded. When a worker steps on a rusty nail in a gut-renovated house in New Orleans, there is no school nurse or company doctor. There is just a rag to wrap the foot and a demand to keep moving.

The "Katrina Cough" became a famous medical phenomenon after 2005—a persistent, debilitating respiratory illness affecting those who cleaned up New Orleans. It was caused by the inhalation of mold spores and the "toxic dust" of dried sediment. Today, every major disaster produces its own cohort of victims with the same symptoms, a disposable army of workers who sacrifice their long-term health to restore American cities, only to be discarded when the coughing starts.

But the physical danger is only half the trap. The financial architecture of disaster recovery is designed to facilitate theft on a massive scale.

The chain of command in a disaster zone is a masterclass in the "Subcontracting Shield" . At the top is often the federal government or a major insurance company. FEMA awards multi-million dollar contracts to large engineering firms to manage debris removal. These firms subcontract to regional construction companies. The regional companies subcontract to local "storm chasers." And the storm chasers hire the "man in the van"—the labor broker who actually brings the workers.

By the time the money trickles down to the worker, it has passed through four or five sets of hands, each taking a cut. The margin for the actual labor is razor-thin. This creates an immense incentive for the lowest-level contractor to cheat.

The theft often happens in the chaos of demobilization. A crew will work for two weeks, gutting houses from dawn until dusk. They are promised payment at the end of the job. They sleep in the unfinished houses or in tents in a parking lot, dependent on the contractor for food and water. When the job is done, or when the contractor decides to move to the next town, he simply vanishes.

This is the "phantom contractor" phenomenon. The worker stands in the parking lot of a Home Depot, waiting for a white pickup truck that never returns. The contractor has changed his phone number. He has dissolved his LLC. He has driven back to Texas or Georgia with the payroll in his pocket.

The worker is left stranded in a devastated city, often with no money to get home. Because they are undocumented, they cannot go to the police. Even if they did, the local police are overwhelmed with looting and traffic control; a wage dispute is the last priority. The theft is perfect because the victim has no voice and the crime scene is a disaster zone where records essentially do not exist.

Following Hurricane Harvey in Houston, surveys of day laborers involved in the recovery found that more than a quarter had experienced wage theft. In some cases, workers were paid with bad checks. In others, they were paid, but then "charged" exorbitant fees for the food and lodging they had been forced to accept, leaving them with pennies.

The role of the federal government in this exploitation is complex and damning. In the wake of major disasters, it is common for the executive branch to suspend the Davis-Bacon Act, a law that requires contractors on federal projects to pay "prevailing wages." The logic is that suspending the law lowers costs and speeds up reconstruction.

In practice, the suspension of Davis-Bacon acts as a signal to the market: *all bets are off*. It removes the floor for wages. It tells contractors that the government is prioritizing speed and cheapness over labor standards. When the government itself signals that wage protections are an impediment to recovery, it emboldens every predator in the supply chain.

Furthermore, the "essential" nature of the work is used to bypass safety regulations. During the cleanup of the California wildfires, crews were sent into zones where the air quality was hazardous to clean up toxic ash containing heavy metals. They were often not provided with N95 masks, even as residents were warned to stay indoors. The logic of the "essential worker" is perverted here to mean "expendable worker." The work is essential; the human being performing it is not.

The housing situation for these mobile crews adds another layer of vulnerability. Because the housing stock in the disaster zone has been destroyed, there is literally nowhere to stay. Hotels are full of displaced residents and insurance adjusters. The workers are forced to live in the conditions they are remediating.

They sleep on the floors of mold-infested houses. They camp in parks. They crowd into trailers with no electricity. This creates a total dependency on the employer for basic survival. If the contractor provides the only generator and the only clean water, the worker cannot negotiate. They cannot quit. They are trapped by the very destruction they are there to fix.

This industry is growing. As climate change accelerates the frequency and intensity of hurricanes, floods, and wildfires, the demand for this "resilience force" is exploding. We are entering an era of perpetual reconstruction. The "hundred-year flood" now happens every five years. The fire season is now year-round.

This means that the migrant workforce is becoming a permanent fixture of the American landscape, a nomadic tribe of fixers who move from one tragedy to the next. They are the "climate refugees" of the labor market, displaced not just by conditions in their home countries but by the environmental instability of their new one.

There is a profound irony in this dynamic. The people rebuilding the homes of the American middle class—restoring the assets of the insured and the wealthy—are themselves homeless and uninsured. They are saving the American Dream for others while living in a nightmare of instability.

Consider the roofer in Florida after a Category 4 hurricane. He is up on a slick, damaged roof in ninety-degree heat, repairing the damage so the homeowner can return. He has no harness. He has no health insurance. If he falls, he is broken. If he finishes the job, he might not get paid. And when the work is done, the community often wants him gone.

This is the final insult of the disaster recovery model: the "cleanup" often includes cleaning up the workers. Once the heavy lifting is done, local law enforcement often shifts from a posture of tolerance to one of enforcement. The workers who were heroes when the streets were blocked become "vagrants" and "illegals" once the lights are back on. Immigration raids often follow the recovery phase, sweeping up the very people who made the recovery possible.

The "storm chaser" model is the ultimate expression of the gig economy's predatory nature. It is short-term, high-risk, and zero-liability. It relies on a workforce that can be mobilized instantly and discarded instantly. It is a system that views human beings as just another form of equipment— necessary for the job, but liable to be left behind if the cost of transport is too high.

We see the shiny new roofs and the freshly painted drywall and we call it "resilience." We celebrate the spirit of a community that "came back." We do not see the stolen wages, the scarred lungs, and the broken bodies that form the foundation of that return. We have outsourced the suffering of recovery to a shadow workforce, allowing us to rebuild our lives on the backs of those who are not allowed to have a life of their own.

Until we mandate that every federal dollar spent on disaster relief comes with rigorous labor enforcement—until we ensure that the people cleaning up the toxic sludge are protected by the same gear as the engineers supervising them—our recovery will always be a secondary disaster. We are rebuilding our cities, yes. But we are burying our values in the rubble.

Chapter 21: The Hospitality Underbelly

The American service economy is built on a specific, carefully curated aesthetic: the aesthetic of effortlessness. When a guest walks into the lobby of a luxury hotel, the floors gleam with a shine that suggests they have never been trodden upon. When a diner sits at a white tablecloth in a high-end bistro, the water glass is filled before they realize they are thirsty. The entire experience is designed to simulate a world where needs are anticipated and messes vanish by magic.

But there is no magic. There is only the "back of the house."

In the architecture of the hospitality industry, the swinging door that separates the kitchen from the dining room, or the service elevator that separates the lobby from the laundry, is a portal between two distinct legal and economic universes. On one side lies the "Front of House," a world of tips, smiles, and customer service. On the other lies the "Back of House," a subterranean engine room of steam, heat, and chemical fumes where the illusion of luxury is manufactured by a workforce that is overwhelmingly undocumented and rigorously invisible.

The restaurant industry, which positions itself as the nation's dining room, is in reality the single largest violator of labor laws in the American economy. According to data from the Department of Labor's Wage and Hour Division, restaurants consistently account for more wage and hour violations than any other sector. This is not because restaurant owners are uniquely villainous; it is because the industry's profit margins are razor-thin, and the variable that is easiest to compress is the wages of the non-tipped staff.

At the bottom of this hierarchy stands the dishwasher. In the culinary world, the "dish pit" is often romanticized as the entry point for the aspiring chef—the place where the hard work begins. In reality, for the undocumented worker, the dish pit is not a stepping stone; it is a terminus.

The environment is a physical assault. The commercial dishwasher is a roaring beast that generates clouds of steam, raising the ambient temperature of the pit to over a hundred degrees. The worker stands on a rubber mat, soaked to the skin, handling plates that are scorching hot one second and handling broken glass the next. The chemicals used to strip grease—industrial degreasers and bleach—are inhaled continuously.

But the true hazard of the dish pit is not the heat; it is the clock.

In the restaurant industry, wage theft has been digitized. Modern point-of-sale systems allow managers to edit time clocks with a few keystrokes. This practice, known as "time shaving," is endemic. A dishwasher might clock in at 10:00 AM to begin prep work. At the end of the week, he looks at his pay stub and sees that his start time was adjusted to 11:00 AM every day. Five hours of pay have vanished.

Or, the theft happens at the other end of the shift. The restaurant closes at 10:00 PM, and the servers clock out. But the kitchen must be scrubbed. The fryers must be filtered; the floors must be mopped. The manager says, "Clock out now, but finish the close." The worker, knowing that there are ten other men waiting for his job, clocks out and works for another hour for free.

This theft is practically invisible. There is no gun, no robbery. It is a silent deletion of time. Because the worker is undocumented, he has no recourse. He cannot go to the labor board without risking exposure. He cannot quit and demand his back pay. He is trapped in a cycle where he is paid for forty hours but works fifty, effectively driving his hourly wage far below the legal minimum.

The tipping system adds another layer of opacity. By law, tips belong to the service staff. However, in many establishments, owners engage in illegal tip pooling, taking a cut of the gratuities to pay the back-of-house staff—or simply to keep for themselves. The undocumented dishwasher sees none of this money, yet his low wages are often justified by the "team" nature of the restaurant. He subsidizes the front of the house with his sweat, while the front of the house subsidizes the owner with their tips.

If the restaurant kitchen is a sweatshop, the modern hotel is a factory of repetitive trauma disguised as a bedroom.

The housekeeping department is the financial heart of the hotel industry. Room revenue drives profit. But to the housekeeper—often an immigrant woman, frequently undocumented—the room is a battlefield.

Over the last two decades, the hotel industry has engaged in a "luxury arms race." Beds have become bigger and heavier. Mattresses are now "pillow-top" monsters weighing over a hundred pounds. Duvets are thicker. Amenities are more numerous.

To the guest, this is comfort. To the housekeeper, it is pain. To make a "Heavenly Bed," a worker must lift the mattress corner to tuck the sheets—a motion that requires significant torque on the lower back. She must do this four times per bed, often with two beds per room. If her quota is sixteen rooms a day, she is lifting thousands of pounds of mattress every shift.

A study published in the American Journal of Industrial Medicine found that hotel housekeepers have higher rates of bodily pain and injury than workers in the coal mining industry. They suffer from debilitating back injuries, rotator cuff tears, and severe repetitive strain injuries.

Yet, the quota system remains rigid. Hotel management calculates the "minutes per room" (MPR) with industrial precision—typically giving a worker 20 to 30 minutes to strip the bed, scrub the bathroom, vacuum the floor, and restock the amenities.

This quota creates a perverse incentive structure. If a room is particularly trashed—after a bachelor party or a family with small children—it might take 45 minutes to clean. That puts the housekeeper behind schedule. To catch up, she must skip her lunch break. She must run between rooms. Or, most commonly, she must work off the clock after her shift ends to finish her assignment.

"If you don't finish your board," the supervisor warns, "don't come back tomorrow."

This is the definition of "speed-up," a tactic used on the assembly line to squeeze more productivity out of the same labor hours. But unlike an assembly line, the hotel room is a private space. The worker is alone. This isolation breeds a specific type of vulnerability: sexual harassment.

The hospitality industry has one of the highest rates of sexual harassment of any sector. Housekeepers are routinely exposed to guests who answer the door naked, who make lewd comments, or who attempt to grope them. For the undocumented housekeeper, this is a terrifying predicament. Reporting a guest means bringing police into the hotel. It means "causing trouble."

In recent years, unions have fought for "panic buttons"—small GPS devices that housekeepers can press to summon security. But for the non-union, undocumented workforce that cleans the budget motels and the subcontracted resorts, there are no panic buttons. There is only the instruction to "be polite" and the knowledge that the customer is always right, even when the customer is a predator.

The structural invisibility of this workforce is reinforced by the "staffing agency" model. Major hotel chains increasingly do not employ their own housekeepers. Instead, they contract with third-party agencies. This is the same liability shield seen in agriculture and construction, applied to the hospitality sector.

The housekeeper wears a uniform with the hotel's logo, but her paycheck comes from "Quality Staffing LLC." If she is injured or cheated, the hotel claims they are not her employer. The staffing agency, often operating on thin margins, disappears or claims bankruptcy. The worker is left with a broken back and no workers' compensation.

This subcontracting model also destroys the possibility of advancement. In the past, a housekeeper might hope to become a supervisor, then a manager. Today, the housekeeper is not even an employee of the hotel. She is a vendor. There is no ladder to climb; there is only a floor to scrub.

The chemicals used to achieve the "sparkling clean" standard add a toxic dimension to the work. To clean a bathroom in minutes, workers use powerful solvents and bleaches. In unventilated bathrooms, they breathe these fumes all day. Studies of cleaning workers show elevated rates of asthma and dermatological conditions. The smell of bleach, which signals "clean" to the guest, signals "danger" to the worker.

During the COVID-19 pandemic, this "essential" workforce was pushed to the brink. They were asked to clean rooms that had been occupied by infected guests, often without adequate PPE. The industry marketed "enhanced cleaning protocols" to reassure travelers, but the labor required to sanitize every surface fell on the same overworked staff. They were hailed as heroes in commercials, but in the breakrooms, they were denied sick pay.

The economic logic of the hospitality industry relies on the assumption that service is cheap. We expect a clean room for $89 a night. We expect a meal for $15. These prices are only possible because the labor component has been artificially suppressed. The undocumented worker in the back of the house is the subsidy that allows the American middle class to enjoy the trappings of luxury.

This system relies on the physical and legal erasure of the worker. The hotel is designed with "back of house" corridors so that the guest never has to see a dirty sheet or a mop bucket. This architectural segregation mirrors the legal segregation. We do not want to see the labor; we only want to see the result.

When a housekeeper knocks on a door and says "Housekeeping," she is announcing her function, not her identity. To the industry, she is not a person; she is a set of hands that resets the stage for the next paying customer. She is the ghost in the machine of leisure.

The theft in this industry is not just of wages; it is of dignity. It is the theft of the right to be safe in one's body, the right to breathe clean air, and the right to be paid for every minute of labor. The hospitality underbelly is a place where the "service" economy reveals itself to be a "servitude" economy, maintained by the silence of those who cannot afford to speak.

Every time we check into a hotel or sit down at a restaurant, we participate in this economy. The crisp sheets and the clean plate are the end products of a supply chain that begins with a worker waking up in the dark, hoping that today they will not be hurt, that today they will be paid, and that today they will remain invisible enough to survive.

Chapter 22: Domestic Servitude

The American suburbs are designed to be fortresses of privacy. The cul-de-sac, the fence, the security system, and the hedge are all architectural mechanisms intended to separate the nuclear family from the public gaze. Within these private sanctuaries, the homeowner is sovereign. The laws that regulate the street, the market, and the factory floor seem to fade at the threshold of the front door. It is precisely this sanctity of the private home that makes it the perfect container for the most invisible and intimate form of modern slavery: domestic servitude.

In the tomato fields of Florida or the construction sites of Texas, exploitation has witnesses. There are coworkers, passersby, and the occasional inspector. The violence is public. But in the realm of domestic work, the workforce is atomized. There is no breakroom where workers can compare wages. There is no shop steward. There is often only one worker, alone, trapped behind the double-locked doors of an affluent residence in Bethesda, Beverly Hills, or Scarsdale.

This isolation creates a unique pathology of control. The domestic servant is not just an employee; they are a possession of the household. The boundary between "labor" and "life" is erased completely. For the nanny or the housekeeper living in the home of her employer, there is no "off the clock." The work begins when the baby cries at 4:00 AM and ends only when the last dish is dried and the owners have gone to bed.

The recruitment for this sector often relies on a particularly cruel manipulation of kinship networks. Unlike the industrial recruitment of strangers for agriculture, domestic trafficking frequently involves distant relatives or family acquaintances. A wealthy aunt in the United States offers to bring a niece from a rural village in the Philippines or Nigeria to "help out" and "get an education."

The parents agree, believing they are securing a future for their daughter. But upon arrival, the education never materializes. The "help" turns into eighteen-hour days of cooking, cleaning, and child-rearing. The niece becomes a Cinderella figure, stripped of her passport, forbidden from leaving the house, and told that her unpaid labor is reimbursement for the plane ticket and the food she eats. The "family member" fiction is used to bypass labor laws—"She isn't an employee; she's my cousin"—while the reality is chattel slavery.

The National Human Trafficking Hotline data indicates that domestic work is consistently one of the top venues for labor trafficking reports in the United States. Yet, these cases are notoriously difficult to identify because the victim is hidden in plain sight. They are the woman pushing the stroller in the park who never speaks to the other nannies. They are the shadow moving in the kitchen during the dinner party, whom the guests are trained to ignore.

The legal framework of the United States actively facilitates this exploitation. Historically, domestic workers were explicitly excluded from the protections of the National Labor Relations Act and the Fair Labor Standards Act—a legacy of the Jim Crow era, when Southern legislators refused to grant rights to a workforce that was overwhelmingly Black. While some protections have been extended in recent decades, the cultural and legal presumption remains that household labor is not "real work" worthy of federal oversight.

This deregulation reaches its apex in the visa programs designed for the global elite. The A-3 and G-5 visas allow diplomats and employees of international organizations to bring domestic staff to the United States. In theory, these programs have strict requirements. In practice, they create zones of diplomatic immunity where slavery can flourish without consequence.

The Government Accountability Office (GAO) has documented dozens of cases where diplomats have abused their domestic staff—beating them, starving them, and forcing them to work without pay. When these crimes are discovered, the employer often invokes diplomatic immunity. They cannot be prosecuted. They cannot be sued. The victim is left broken and penniless, while the abuser is simply reassigned to another country to repeat the cycle. It is a state-sanctioned impunity that turns the embassies of Washington D.C. and the penthouses of New York into pockets of foreign territory where the Thirteenth Amendment does not apply.

But the problem extends far beyond the diplomatic corps. The J-1 Au Pair program, marketed as a "cultural exchange," has evolved into a source of cheap, vulnerable childcare for upper-middle-class American families.

Agencies recruit young women from Europe, South America, and South Africa with promises of travel and education. The host families, however, often view the program purely as an economic hack—a way to get full-time childcare for a fraction of the market rate.

Investigations by outlets like *Politico* and labor lawsuits have revealed a pattern where au pairs are treated not as cultural ambassadors but as indentured servants. They are forced to work far beyond the legal hour limits, tasked with heavy housekeeping, and threatened with deportation if they complain. Because their housing is tied to their employment, a fired au pair is instantly homeless in a foreign country. This dependency forces young women to endure harassment, wage theft, and degrading treatment because the alternative is being cast out onto the street.

The psychological control in domestic servitude is distinct from other sectors because it weaponizes intimacy. The trafficker is not a distant foreman; they are the "mother" or "father" of the house. They use a technique known as "fictive kinship" to blur the lines of exploitation. "You are part of the family," they say, usually right before demanding unpaid overtime. "We treat you like a daughter."

This gaslighting makes it incredibly difficult for the victim to conceptualize their abuse. If they are "family," then asking for wages feels like a betrayal. If they are "daughters," then obedience is a duty, not a job requirement.

Furthermore, the trafficker often weaponizes the children. Nannies form deep emotional bonds with their charges. Traffickers exploit this love. "If you leave," they warn, "who will take care of the baby? He loves you. You would be abandoning him." The worker stays not because they fear the employer, but because they cannot bear to leave the child unprotected. It is an emotional hostage situation.

The isolation of the domestic sphere also means there are no witnesses to physical abuse. In a restaurant kitchen, a slap might be seen. In a private home, violence happens behind closed doors. Traffickers withhold food as punishment. They deny access to medical care. They lock workers in basements or closets at night.

The economics of this crime are driven by the "care deficit" in the United States. As the cost of childcare and eldercare has skyrocketed and the two-income household has become the norm, American families are desperate for help. But rather than demanding a public solution to this crisis, the market has privatized it. The "solution" to the high cost of care is to find a worker who can be paid below the cost of living.

The wealthy family that employs a live-in maid for $400 a week—expecting 80 hours of work—is engaging in simple arithmetic. They are saving tens of thousands of dollars a year by stepping outside the legal labor market. The "savings" on their household ledger are directly extracted from the life of the woman in the guest room (or the basement). They are purchasing her time, her energy, and her freedom at a discount rate subsidized by her vulnerability.

When a domestic worker does manage to escape, the challenges are immense. They often have no money, having been paid in "room and board" or infrequent cash allowances. They have no references. And they carry the deep shame of having been abused in a "home."

The prosecution of these cases is notoriously difficult. Defense attorneys paint the victim as an ungrateful relative or a manipulative guest. "We took her in," the wealthy couple testifies. "We gave her a beautiful home. She ate at our table." The jury, often composed of people who aspire to that same lifestyle, finds it hard to believe that the nice doctor or the successful lawyer could be a slaver. The banality of the setting masks the brutality of the crime.

We must recognize that the home is a workplace. It is the site of production for the most essential goods of society: clean clothes, fed children, cared-for elders. When we allow this workplace to operate as a lawless zone, we corrupt the very foundation of the family. We build our domestic comfort on the destruction of another's family.

The domestic servant living in the shadows is the ultimate symbol of the "private" nature of American exploitation. She is the ghost in the machine of the upper class. She makes the career of the female executive possible. She allows the diplomat to attend the gala. She raises the children of the meritocracy. And in exchange, she is erased.

Until we pierce the veil of privacy that protects the household from scrutiny—until domestic workers are granted the full, enforceable rights of every other worker, including the right to organize, the right to overtime, and the right to inspect their workplace—the American home will remain, for thousands of women, a prison disguised as a sanctuary. The "help" are not helping; they are serving time.

Chapter 23: The Intersection of Sex Trafficking

In the geography of American commerce, there exists a specific type of storefront that has become so ubiquitous it renders itself invisible. It is found in the strip malls of suburban boulevards, wedged between a dry cleaner and a takeout restaurant. It occupies the second floor of office buildings in bustling downtowns. It operates out of converted residential homes on the outskirts of rural towns. The signage is often generic—"Asian Bodywork," "Reflexology," or simply "Spa." The windows are obscured by heavy curtains or neon signs that burn late into the night.

To the passerby, these establishments are merely part of the background noise of the service economy. To the labor inspector or the victim advocate, they represent the "health & beauty services" sector—a category the Department of Labor explicitly identifies as a common venue for human trafficking. But within the grim taxonomy of exploitation, these venues occupy a unique and terrifying position: they are the point where labor trafficking and sex trafficking collide, blurring the lines between the extraction of work and the violation of the body.

The public imagination tends to categorize these crimes separately. We visualize labor trafficking as men in dusty fields or women in sweatshops, and sex trafficking as young women on street corners controlled by violent pimps. This binary is a dangerous oversimplification. The reality of the illicit massage business (IMB) and the "cantina" culture reveals a hybrid model of enslavement where the victim is often recruited for "legitimate" work, trapped by the familiar mechanisms of debt and document theft, and then coerced into commercial sex through economic necessity rather than physical abduction.

This intersection is not a marginal phenomenon; it is the financial engine of the modern slave trade. The International Labour Organization (ILO) reports that of the estimated $236 billion in annual illegal profits generated by forced labor, a staggering two-thirds comes from forced sexual exploitation. This disparity reveals a dark economic truth: while the body of a tomato picker or a construction worker generates value through its output, the body of a sex trafficking victim generates value through its access. The commodification is total.

The pathway into this intersection almost always begins with a lie about labor. The "Bait and Switch" is the standard recruitment methodology. A woman in Fujian province or rural Honduras answers an ad for a job in the United States. The ad does not mention sex. It promises work as a masseuse, a waitress, or a hostess. It offers high wages, housing, and the chance to send remittances home—the standard lure of the "American Dream" packaged for the desperate.

Digital platforms facilitate this deception with ruthless efficiency. As documented by the Polaris Project, traffickers utilize apps like WeChat, WhatsApp, and even Tinder to recruit victims, moving the conversation from public forums to encrypted channels where the trap is laid. The victim agrees to the journey, incurring the massive smuggling debts discussed in Chapter 3.

Upon arrival, the reality shifts. The "massage therapy" job requires no license, no training, and involves no therapy. The woman is informed that she owes a debt ranging from $20,000 to $60,000. She is told that to pay off this debt—and to pay for the "rent" of the massage table and the "lodging" in the back room—she must perform "extra services" for male clients.

Here, the coercion is not necessarily a gun to the head; it is the ledger. The trafficker explains the mathematics of survival: providing a standard massage pays $10, which goes to the house. Providing sexual services pays significantly more, allowing the worker to chip away at the mountain of debt. The victim is not forced physically; she is forced economically. She is placed in a situation where the only way to eat, the only way to sleep, and the only way to eventually be free is to submit to the violation of her body.

This is labor trafficking. The victim is working—often 12 to 16 hours a day, cooking and cleaning for the business in addition to serving clients—under conditions of force, fraud, or coercion. But because the *nature* of the work involves sex, society and the legal system often recategorize the victim. She ceases to be a worker in need of OSHA protection and becomes a "prostitute" in the eyes of the law.

This legal stigma is the trafficker's greatest shield. In the tomato fields, a worker fears deportation. In the illicit massage parlor, the worker fears deportation *and* arrest for prostitution. The trafficker weaponizes this double bind. "If you call the police," they warn, "you are the one who will go to jail. You are the criminal here."

The "Cantina" and "Bar" scene in immigrant communities presents a parallel structure of hybrid exploitation. These establishments, often located in Hispanic neighborhoods, operate as social hubs where men drink and pay for the company of women. The women are recruited as "ficheras" or waitresses. Their job, ostensibly, is to flirt with customers to encourage the purchase of overpriced alcohol.

But the economic pressure to "upsell" is relentless. The women are paid a commission on the drinks they sell. To survive and pay their debts to the bar owner—who often acts as the smuggler and landlord—they must keep the customers spending. This creates a slippery slope of coercion. The owner pressures the women to allow touching, then to leave with customers for "dates," and finally to engage in commercial sex acts.

The "debt bondage" mechanism here is identical to that of the sharecropper or the bonded bricklayer. The women are charged for their uniforms, their housing, and even the "protection" provided by the bar. They exist in a state of peonage where their labor is the servicing of men, and their compensation is the reduction of a debt that never vanishes.

The physical environment of these venues reinforces the control. In many illicit massage businesses, the women live on-site. They sleep on the massage tables or in cramped dormitory rooms behind the reception desk. The windows are often covered to prevent the public from looking in, but also to prevent the workers from looking out. This isolation mirrors the "company town" model, where the employer controls every aspect of existence—food, sleep, work, and movement.

The health consequences of this intersectional trafficking are profound and largely untreated. Victims are exposed to sexually transmitted infections, physical violence from customers, and the psychological trauma of repeated rape. Yet, they are rigorously excluded from the healthcare system. A woman who cannot show her face at a bank for fear of deportation certainly cannot walk into a clinic to request an STI test without terrifying repercussions. The "company doctor"—if one exists at all—is often an unlicensed associate of the trafficker who provides antibiotics without diagnosis, aiming only to keep the "asset" in working order.

The profitability of this sector drives its resilience. The ILO's finding that sexual exploitation accounts for $236 billion in profits reveals why this crime is so pervasive. The margins are astronomical. A tomato can be sold only once. The body of a woman in a massage parlor can be sold ten times a day, every day, for years. The trafficker's return on investment is immediate and perpetual.

Law enforcement's approach to this intersection often exacerbates the harm. "Raids" on massage parlors frequently result in the arrest of the women for prostitution or practicing massage without a license. The women are handcuffed, paraded before cameras, and entered into the criminal justice system. The owners and traffickers often evade capture or face minor fines for zoning violations.

This "victim-criminal" paradox is the ultimate victory for the trafficker. The state effectively punishes the slave for the condition of their slavery. By criminalizing the commercial sex act without investigating the coercion behind it, law enforcement becomes an unwitting partner in the cycle of exploitation. The arrest record becomes one more chain binding the victim to the trafficker, one more reason she can never seek legitimate employment.

The intersection of sex and labor trafficking challenges us to broaden our definition of "work" and "workers." If we view these women solely through the lens of morality or vice, we miss the economic reality of their situation. They are laborers trapped in a coercive market. They are victims of contract fraud, debt bondage, and wage theft.

The mechanisms used to hold them—the confiscated passport , the threat of harm to families back home , the manufactured debt —are the exact same tools used to bind the roofer and the farmworker. The only difference is the nature of the service demanded.

We must recognize that the neon "Open" sign on the blacked-out window of the strip mall spa is not just advertising a service. It is marking the location of a prison. Inside, the distinction between labor and body, between work and violation, has been erased by the economics of exploitation. These women are the ultimate casualties of a system that views human beings as extractable resources. They are working in the most dangerous "health & beauty" service in the world, and until we treat their exploitation as a labor crime and a human rights violation rather than a vice crime, the lights will stay on, and the doors will remain locked.

Part IV: The Control Mechanisms (Psychological Warfare)

Why they stay.

Chapter 24: The Threat of Separation

In the calculus of human vulnerability, there is one variable that outweighs all others. It is not hunger. It is not pain. It is not even the fear of death. It is the biological imperative to protect one's offspring. This instinct is the most powerful force in the human experience, capable of driving individuals to acts of supreme heroism.

But in the hands of the modern trafficker or the exploitative employer, this instinct is a weapon.

The ultimate mechanism of control in the undocumented labor market is not the threat of deportation for the worker; it is the threat of separation from their child. This is the nuclear option of labor discipline. It is the leverage that forces a mother to work with toxic chemicals while pregnant. It is the fear that keeps a father on a roof in a lightning storm. It is the silence that allows abuse to fester in the darkness of the American workplace.

To understand the potency of this threat, we must look at the specific demographic reality of the undocumented workforce. As I noted in my analysis of the "Inherited Curse," nearly ten percent of American families with children contain a "mixed-status" fault line—usually an undocumented parent and a U.S. citizen child. These 5.9 million children are the anchor of the parent's life, the very reason they endured the journey and the debt. They are the hope for the future.

They are also the hostages.

The threat is rarely delivered in a formal meeting. It is whispered on the production line or mentioned casually during a pay dispute. "If ICE picks you up," the supervisor might say, "who will take care of Maria? You know the state takes the kids when the parents go to jail."

This statement invokes a bureaucratic nightmare that is terrifyingly real. When an undocumented parent is detained during a workplace raid or a traffic stop, they disappear into the federal detention system. Their children, often at school or daycare, are left stranded. If no relative with legal status can step in immediately, the children are taken into the custody of Child Protective Services (AND) or the foster care system.

Once a child enters the foster system, the timeline for reunification battles the timeline for deportation. If a parent is deported while their child is in state custody, the legal hurdles to regaining custody from a foreign country are nearly insurmountable. The parent faces the permanent loss of their child—not to death, but to the bureaucracy of the state.

Traffickers and unscrupulous employers understand this legal labyrinth better than the workers do. They map the geography of this fear with the precision of a cartographer. They know that for a mother, the prospect of her child growing up in the foster system, perhaps losing their language and culture, perhaps never knowing why their mother "abandoned" them, is a fate worse than any physical torture.

The U.S. Department of State identifies this manipulation as a primary indicator of trafficking, noting that traffickers use threats against family members to maintain control. But in the domestic context, the threat does not require a cartel hitman. It requires only a phone call to the authorities.

The weaponization of Child Protective Services (CPS) is a particularly insidious tactic. In many immigrant communities, CPS is viewed with the same dread as ICE. Predators play on this fear. A domestic worker who complains about working 18-hour days might be told, "You leave your children alone in that apartment all day while you work here. That is neglect. If you quit, I will call CPS and tell them you are an unfit mother."

The worker is trapped in a paradox constructed by the exploiter. She must work excessive hours to feed her children, but working those hours leaves her open to the accusation of neglect. She stays in the abusive job to prevent the call that would take her children away, enduring the very exploitation that makes her vulnerable.

This dynamic is prevalent in the agricultural sector. In the fields, parents often have no access to childcare. They face a brutal choice: leave the children at home unsupervised, or bring them to the fields. If they bring them, they risk exposing them to pesticides and heavy machinery. If they leave them, they risk the "neglect" accusation.

Crew leaders exploit this dilemma. They might allow a mother to bring her child to the edge of the field, effectively charging her for the "favor" by demanding unpaid labor or sexual favors. The child becomes a visible tether, keeping the parent bound to the specific geography of the employer's control.

The psychological toll of this threat creates a specific form of "toxic stress" that permeates the entire family unit. As I documented in Chapter 9, children in these families live in a state of hyper-vigilance. They absorb their parents' terror. They learn that their own existence is the leverage used against their protectors.

This stress is not merely an emotional state; it is a physiological one. The constant flood of cortisol damages the developing brain, leading to the long-term health and educational deficits that cost the U.S. economy over a trillion dollars annually. The employer who uses this threat is not just extracting labor; he is actively damaging the future citizenry of the nation to save a few dollars on payroll.

The threat of separation also serves to silence reports of sexual violence. A woman who is raped by her supervisor in a packing plant or a hotel faces a terrifying calculus. If she reports the crime, she initiates an investigation. Investigations bring scrutiny. Scrutiny can lead to background checks. "If you go to the police," the rapist warns, "they will ask for your papers. You will be deported, and your children will be left here alone."

Faced with the choice between justice for herself and security for her children, the mother chooses the children. She swallows the trauma. She returns to the shift. She endures. The predator relies on her maternal instinct to protect his impunity.

We see this dynamic play out in the aftermath of massive workplace raids. When ICE raided meatpacking plants in Mississippi in 2019, hundreds of children came home from school to find their parents gone. Videos of weeping children begging for their parents went viral. To the public, it was a humanitarian tragedy. To the exploitative employer watching the news, it was a reinforcement of the threat. The raid served as a massive, state-sponsored advertisement for the power of the employer: *Look what happens when the government comes. Stay quiet, keep working, and maybe you will be safe.*

The "Sanctuary" movement in various cities attempts to break this lever of control by separating local law enforcement from federal immigration duties. But the threat remains potent because it does not rely solely on the police. It relies on the administrative state—the social worker, the school administrator, the hospital intake nurse—anyone who has the power to intervene in a family's life.

Traffickers cultivate a myth of omniscience regarding these institutions. They tell workers, "I have a friend in CPS," or "I know the judge." Whether true or not, the worker cannot take the risk. The information asymmetry—the worker's lack of knowledge about their actual rights versus the employer's projected confidence—seals the trap.

The tragedy is that the law *does* provide protections. U visa programs exist for victims of crime. T visas exist for trafficking victims. Policies exist to prevent the separation of families. But these protections are abstract, complex, and slow. The threat of separation is concrete, simple, and immediate.

The parent who accepts degradation and danger that no human should endure rather than face the possibility of being torn from their American-born children is acting rationally. They are making the supreme sacrifice of the parent. The employer is monetizing that sacrifice.

This is the darkest alchemy of the exploitation economy. It transforms love into chains. It turns the most noble human impulse—the desire to provide for and protect one's family—into the mechanism of enslavement. Until we build a firewall that absolutely protects the sanctity of the family from the consequences of labor disputes, until we guarantee that a wage claim will never trigger a foster care case, the threat of separation will remain the ultimate silencer.

We cannot claim to be a "pro-family" society while permitting an economic system that uses the destruction of the family as a management tool. The child waiting at the school bus stop should be a symbol of promise, not a pawn in a game of labor extraction. When we allow this threat to persist, we are not just failing the worker; we are failing the child, and in doing so, we are failing the future.

Chapter 25: Digital Surveillance

In the history of human bondage, the shackle has always been a heavy object. It was made of iron or steel, designed to restrict the movement of the limbs through sheer physical weight. To chain a human being required a blacksmith, a key, and a constant proximity between the master and the slave. The restraint was visible, clumsy, and strictly local. If a captive managed to break the chain and run into the woods, the metal was left behind. The connection was severed.

The modern shackle is weightless. It is made of silicon and radio waves. It does not restrict the movement of the limbs; it tracks the movement of the body. And unlike the iron chain, it does not need to be physically attached to the victim to work. The victim carries it willingly in their pocket, charges it every night, and panics if they lose it.

The smartphone, heralded as the ultimate tool of individual liberation and connection, has been weaponized by the trafficking industry into the ultimate tool of surveillance and control. For the undocumented worker, the device that connects them to their family back home is simultaneously the device that reports their location to their exploiter. It is a digital leash that never goes slack, creating a "digital panopticon" where the worker must assume they are being watched at all times, even—and especially—when they are alone.

To understand how this surveillance operates, we must abandon the Hollywood image of the kidnapped victim locked in a basement without technology. While physical isolation occurs, modern traffickers increasingly prefer "digital containment." It is a far more efficient method of control. Allowing a worker to keep their phone creates the illusion of autonomy while providing the mechanism for total monitoring.

The control begins with the apps. When a labor broker picks up a crew at the border or an airport, a common condition of employment is the installation of location-sharing software. This is often framed as a safety measure or a logistical necessity. "We need to know where you are so the van can pick you up," the contractor explains. Or, "This area is dangerous; download Life360 so we can make sure you don't get lost."

The worker, unfamiliar with the geography and conditioned to trust the "patron," complies. They enable GPS tracking. In that moment, the contractor acquires a god's-eye view of his workforce. He can see if a worker leaves the housing compound at night. He can see if they visit a location he has deemed off-limits, such as a legal aid clinic or a union hall. He creates geofences—virtual perimeters—that trigger alerts on his own phone if a worker crosses them.

This technology resurrects the "pass system" of the antebellum South but strips it of its human fallibility. In 1850, a slave could sneak off the plantation at night if the overseer was asleep or drunk. The digital overseer never sleeps. It does not get drunk. It logs every coordinate, creating a permanent record of movement that can be reviewed and punished retroactively. The worker learns that escape is impossible because their location is broadcast before they even reach the highway.

But the surveillance extends far deeper than geography. It penetrates the private thoughts and communications of the victim. As the Polaris Project has documented in their analysis of trafficking tactics, predators actively monitor and control their victims' social media accounts. This is not merely voyeurism; it is a strategic takeover of the victim's digital identity.

In many cases of labor trafficking, particularly in domestic servitude and the hospitality sector, the employer demands the passwords to the worker's Facebook, WhatsApp, and Instagram accounts. The justification is often framed as "security" or "branding." "We don't want you posting anything that makes the company look bad," the employer claims.

Once the employer has access, they practice a form of digital ventriloquism. They read the messages the worker sends to their mother in Guatemala. They read the complaints vented to a friend. This creates a terrifying chilling effect. The worker cannot tell their family the truth about their abuse because they know the abuser is reading the chat log. "I am fine, the job is good," they type, while the employer looks over their digital shoulder.

Polaris notes that traffickers often impersonate the victim online, posting photographs suggesting all is well. This is a psychological warfare tactic designed to preempt rescue. If a family member becomes worried because they haven't heard from their daughter in weeks, they might check her Facebook page. There, they see a photo of her smiling at a park, or a status update about how busy she is with work. They are reassured. They do not call the authorities.

The photo, of course, was taken months ago, or under duress. The status update was written by the trafficker. The digital façade masks the reality of the dungeon. By maintaining the victim's "virtual alibi," the trafficker neutralizes the only people who might intervene. The victim is screaming for help in reality, but their avatar is projecting contentment.

This surveillance creates a prison of the mind. The worker begins to self-censor not just their speech, but their search history. In a free society, information is power. A worker who feels cheated can Google "minimum wage laws Texas" or "how to report wage theft." But for the trafficker's victim, the search bar is a trap.

Employers often monitor the Wi-Fi networks in company housing. They can see the traffic logs. If they see a device accessing the Department of Labor's website or searching for immigration lawyers, retaliation is swift. The worker learns that curiosity is dangerous. They stop looking for answers. They accept the lies the employer tells them—that they have no rights, that the police will deport them—because they are cut off from the sources of truth.

The architecture of the labor camp itself has been upgraded for the digital age. In the agricultural compounds of Florida and the dairy farms of Vermont, the physical isolation is reinforced by electronic eyes. Cheap, high-definition security cameras are now ubiquitous. They are mounted on the eaves of the trailers, in the hallways of the bunkhouses, and overlooking the fields.

These cameras are rarely installed to protect the workers from outside threats. They are pointed inward. They monitor the assembly of workers in common areas. If a group of workers gathers in the kitchen late at night to discuss a strike or a demand for water, the camera records it. The "ringleader" is identified and fired the next morning. The ability to organize—the fundamental right protected by the National Labor Relations Act—is dismantled by the lens.

In domestic servitude, the "nanny cam" serves a similar function. Marketed to suburban parents as a way to ensure their children are safe, these devices are weaponized against live-in staff. The domestic worker knows she is being watched in the kitchen, in the living room, and sometimes, illegally, in her private quarters. There is no "offstage." She must perform the role of the happy, tireless servant every second of the day, knowing that a moment of rest or a frown could be reviewed by her employer on a smartphone app during a dinner party.

This total lack of privacy degrades the human spirit in a way that physical labor alone cannot. Privacy is the space where the self is reconstituted. It is where we shed the public mask, where we complain, where we dream. To deprive a human being of privacy is to deny them the space to be a person. It reduces them to an object that exists solely for the utility of the owner.

The psychological impact of this "panopticon"—the concept of a prison where the inmates can be watched at any moment and therefore must act as if they are always watched—is profound. It creates a state of hyper-vigilance. The worker creates an internal policeman who monitors their own behavior. They do not need to be told to work faster; they assume the camera demands it. They do not need to be told to smile; they assume the microphone is listening.

This internalization of control is the ultimate goal of the trafficker. It is cheaper than guards. It is more effective than fences. A fence can be climbed; a camera in the mind cannot be evaded.

The digital leash also extends across borders, linking the worker's behavior in the U.S. to the safety of their family abroad. Traffickers often use video calls to demonstrate their reach. They might force a worker to FaceTime with their children back home, ostensibly to say hello. But the subtext is clear: *I know exactly who they are. I know what they look like. I know you love them.* The technology that shrinks the distance between loved ones also shrinks the distance for the threat.

We must also confront the role of data harvesting in the recruitment phase, which feeds the surveillance state of the trafficker. As discussed in Chapter 1, traffickers use social media to "hunt" for victims. But once the victim is ensnared, that data profile becomes a dossier of leverage. The trafficker knows the victim's secrets, their embarrassments, their hidden vulnerabilities. They can threaten "revenge porn" or the release of compromising information to the victim's conservative community back home. The digital footprint becomes a blackmail file.

The defenders of the gig economy and the digital revolution often speak of "transparency" and "connectivity" as unalloyed goods. They do not see how these tools are inverted in the hands of exploiters. They do not see that for the undocumented worker, "connectivity" means "reachability," and "transparency" means "exposure."

When a worker manages to escape—perhaps by leaving the phone behind, severing the digital tether—they often face a new terror: the digital footprint they left behind. Traffickers have been known to use "Find My iPhone" to hunt down runaway workers. They use social media networks to put out "bolos" (be on the lookout) for the escaped victim, framing them as a thief or a criminal to the immigrant community. The digital surveillance follows them even into freedom.

We are building an economy where the lowest-paid workers are the most watched people in America. We track the delivery driver's speed, the warehouse picker's steps, and the tomato harvester's location. We have accepted the premise that if you are paid a wage, you surrender your privacy. But for the trafficked worker, this surrender is not a clause in an employment contract; it is a condition of captivity.

The smartphone in the pocket of the undocumented worker is a paradox. It contains the potential for liberation—the ability to record abuse, to call for help, to find a lawyer. But until the fear of deportation is removed, that potential remains locked. Instead, the device serves its darker purpose. It is the ankle monitor that the prisoner buys for himself. It is the overseer that fits in the palm of the hand. It is the proof that in the modern age, you do not need walls to build a prison; you only need a signal.

Chapter 26: The Company Store Model

In the folklore of American labor, few images are as haunting as the coal miner of Appalachia. We remember him through the lyrics of Tennessee Ernie Ford, the man who loads sixteen tons of number nine coal only to find himself "another day older and deeper in debt." He is the archetype of the worker trapped not by chains, but by a closed economic loop. He lived in a house owned by the mine, bought his food with "scrip" valid only at the company store, and bought his pickaxe and blasting powder from the very company that employed him. He was not just an employee; he was a captive consumer.

We tend to view this arrangement as a relic of the robber baron era, a cruel antiquity abolished by the labor movements of the twentieth century. We assume that the "company store" died when the United States outlawed the payment of wages in scrip.

But the company store did not die; it evolved. It shed its physical walls and its brass tokens, migrating from the coal hollows of West Virginia to the tomato fields of Florida, the cleaning vans of the Midwest, and the migrant camps of California. Today, the mechanism of extracting profit from the worker's own survival needs is more sophisticated, more pervasive, and more profitable than it was in 1920.

The modern iteration of the company store does not rely on monopoly currency. It relies on monopoly access. It exploits the geographical and legal isolation of the undocumented worker to create a captive market where the price of existence is set by the employer.

To understand how this functions, one must examine the paystub of a typical agricultural guest worker or an undocumented laborer. On the left side is the "Gross Pay"—a number that often looks promising, perhaps even meeting the legal minimum wage. On the right side is the "Deductions" column. This is where the modern company store lives.

The first and most lucrative deduction is for housing. In the agricultural sector, labor contractors often house workers in dilapidated trailers, repurposed motels, or barracks. As I noted in my analysis of modern control mechanisms, a rusted trailer that might rent for two hundred dollars a month on the open market is transformed into a gold mine. By cramming ten workers inside and charging each of them fifty or sixty dollars a week, the contractor generates two thousand dollars a month from a liability.

The worker pays premium rates for squalor. Yet, they cannot move. They have no car, no driver's license, and no credit history to rent an apartment in town. They are legally or practically tethered to the employer's land. The landlord and the boss are the same person. Eviction is termination; termination is eviction.

The second pillar of this closed economy is the "raite"—the ride. In the vast, sprawling geography of American agriculture and construction, the workplace is often miles from the housing. The workers cannot walk. Public transit does not run to the onion fields. The only way to get to work is in the contractor's van or converted school bus.

This ride is rarely free. The contractor charges a "transportation fee," often deducted daily or weekly. Five dollars a day, or fifty dollars a week, is skimmed off the top. The worker is paying for the privilege of being transported to the site of their exploitation. In a cruel twist of logic, the expense of the commute—a cost of doing business that legitimate employers absorb or subsidize—is shifted entirely to the worker. If the van breaks down, the workers pay for the repairs. If gas prices rise, the fee goes up.

Then come the tools of the trade. In the coal camps, miners had to buy their own blasting powder. Today, in the fields and construction sites, workers are often required to purchase their gloves, shears, buckets, and safety vests from the employer. The markups are extortionate. A pair of gloves that costs two dollars at a hardware store is sold to the worker for ten.

Why does the worker pay? Because the hardware store is ten miles away, and they are not allowed to leave the camp. Or because the contractor insists that only "approved" equipment can be used. The worker is buying their right to work, one pair of gloves at a time.

Even the most basic biological necessity—water—has been monetized. In the scorching heat of the harvest, hydration is life. Yet, investigations have revealed that some contractors prohibit workers from bringing their own water to the fields, forcing them to purchase sodas or water bottles from the "cantine" truck owned by the crew leader. The price of a bottle of water rises with the temperature. Thirst becomes a profit center.

This constellation of charges creates a specific economic outcome: subsistence. The deductions are calculated with actuarial precision to ensure that the worker's "Net Pay"—the cash they actually receive—hovers just above the level of starvation. If a worker works harder and earns more piece-rate pay, the "rent" might mysteriously increase, or a new "administrative fee" might appear.

Historical precedent for this model is found not just in Appalachia but in the *tiendas de raya* of Mexico. During the Porfiriato period of the late 19th and early 20th centuries, these "line stores" became the symbols of peasant exploitation on the haciendas. Workers were paid in vouchers valid only at the *tienda*, where prices were inflated. The resulting debt was hereditary, passing from father to son.

Today's undocumented workers, many of whom come from the very regions of Mexico where the *tienda de raya* was once hated, find themselves trapped in its American resurrection. The currency is U.S. dollars, but the trap is identical. The worker is not building wealth; they are servicing the costs of their own presence.

Perhaps the most perfect distillation of the modern company store model is found in "traveling sales crews." These groups, often selling magazines or cleaning supplies door-to-door, are notorious for recruiting young, vulnerable people with promises of travel and adventure.

Once inside the van, the reality shifts. As documented by labor trafficking investigations, the crew leader controls every aspect of the worker's economic life. The workers sleep four to a motel room, for which they are charged a "lodging fee." They are driven from neighborhood to neighborhood, incurring a "transportation fee." They are given a daily "food allowance" that is added to their debt.

Most insidiously, they are often required to purchase the product they are selling upfront. The worker goes into debt to buy the spray bottles or the magazine subscriptions from the crew leader, hoping to sell them at a profit to pay back the loan. If they have a bad day and sell nothing, their debt grows. They owe for the room, the ride, the food, and the unsold product.

The van becomes a mobile prison. The workers are often hundreds of miles from home, with no money and no idea where they are. If they try to leave, the crew leader reminds them of their debt and threatens to leave them stranded on the side of the highway. They stay because the van is the only economy they have.

Respect International, in their analysis of business models of modern slavery, categorizes this as "revenue generation." It is a critical distinction. The traditional view of slavery focuses on "cost reduction"—paying people nothing. But the modern trafficker has realized that he can make money coming and going. He saves money by stealing wages (cost reduction), and he *makes* money by overcharging for survival (revenue generation).

This dual strategy transforms the worker into a perpetual motion machine of profit. They generate value when they work, and they generate value when they eat, sleep, or drink. The employer captures the entire economic output of the human being.

The psychological impact of this model is profound. It creates a sense of futility. The worker sees the numbers on the paystub and realizes that no matter how hard they work, the "deductions" will always eat the surplus. It kills the hope of advancement. It teaches the worker that they are working not for their future, but for their maintenance.

This is the definition of a subsistence trap. In a free market, a worker exchanges labor for capital that can be saved, invested, or spent elsewhere. In the company store model, the labor is exchanged for the right to exist in the space controlled by the employer. The capital never leaves the loop.

The legal system has been slow to recognize these deductions as a form of theft. Employers argue that they are providing "services" for the convenience of the worker. "We provide housing because there are no apartments nearby," they claim. "We provide rides because they don't have cars."

But the coercive nature of these "services" strips them of their benevolence. A service you cannot refuse is not a service; it is a tax. A rent that is double the market rate is not housing; it is extortion.

The constitutional implications connect directly to the concept of involuntary servitude. When a person is compelled to work to pay off debts for the very tools and shelter they need to work, they are in a cycle of peonage. The debt is artificial, manufactured by the employer to ensure the worker cannot leave.

In the digital age, this model is adapting yet again. We see it in the "gig economy" arrangements where platform workers must rent their vehicles or equipment from the platform itself, or from partners, creating a cycle where the work pays for the tool, and the tool is required for the work.

But nowhere is it as brutal, as visceral, as in the shadow economy of the undocumented. There, the company store is not a metaphor. It is the trailer where you sleep, the van you ride in, and the water you drink. It is a total institution that monetizes the biological existence of the worker.

We must recognize that when we buy cheap produce or cheap construction, we are often buying from a supply chain where the worker has been forced to subsidize the cost of production. The "efficiency" of the market is an illusion created by the inefficiency of the company store—a system that keeps the worker running in place, loading sixteen tons, and getting another day older and deeper in debt.

Chapter 27: Toxic Stress and Brain Chemistry

The most effective prison is not one built of bars or tracked by GPS; it is one built inside the human nervous system. While debt contracts and confiscated documents create external boundaries, the modern system of labor exploitation relies equally on an internal mechanism of control that is biological, involuntary, and devastatingly effective. It is the weaponization of the human stress response.

To understand why an undocumented worker might endure years of abuse without rebelling, or why a community might remain silent in the face of rampant exploitation, we must look beyond sociology and into physiology. We must examine the medical reality of living in a state of perpetual terror.

The human body is designed to handle threats. When our ancestors encountered a predator, the amygdala—the brain's alarm system—would send a distress signal to the hypothalamus. This command center would activate the sympathetic nervous system, flooding the body with adrenaline and cortisol. The heart rate spikes. Blood pressure rises. Energy is diverted from non-essential functions like digestion and immune response to the muscles. This is the "fight or flight" response. It is a brilliant evolutionary adaptation designed to save our lives in a moment of acute crisis.

But this system was designed for sprints, not marathons. It is meant to activate, resolve the threat, and then switch off, allowing the body to return to homeostasis.

For the undocumented worker in the United States, the tiger never leaves the room.

The threat of deportation is not an event; it is an environment. As I noted in my analysis of the "climate of fear," millions of people live in a state of legal terror where the most mundane activities—driving to work, buying groceries, walking a child to school—carry the risk of family destruction . For these individuals, the alarm bell in the brain is jammed in the "on" position.

The medical profession has a term for this unrelenting activation of the stress response: toxic stress. While often studied in the context of childhood development, its effects on the adult body are equally corrosive. When cortisol floods the system day after day, year after year, it ceases to be a survival aid and becomes a systemic poison.

Research from institutions like the Harvard Center on the Developing Child has established the biological toll of this state. Prolonged exposure to high levels of stress hormones disrupts the brain's architecture and compromises the immune system. It is not merely a feeling of anxiety; it is a physiological dismantling of the self.

Consider the daily existence of a worker in a "mixed-status" family. Every time a police siren wails in the distance, their pulse quickens. Every time a supervisor frowns, the adrenaline spikes. Every time a strange car pulls into the driveway, the cortisol surges. The body is constantly preparing for a catastrophe that could happen at any second.

This state of hyper-vigilance exacts a heavy metabolic price. This is known as "allostatic load"—the wear and tear on the body that accumulates as an individual is exposed to repeated or chronic stress. The consequences are measurable and severe. The constant high blood pressure eventually damages the arteries, leading to hypertension and heart disease. The suppression of the immune system leaves the worker vulnerable to infections and hampers recovery from the physical injuries sustained in the fields or factories. The disruption of metabolic processes contributes to diabetes and obesity.

In the context of labor exploitation, this biological degradation serves a dark utilitarian purpose for the employer. A brain under the influence of toxic stress functions differently than a brain at rest. The prefrontal cortex—the area responsible for executive function, long-term planning, and complex decision-making—is inhibited by high levels of catecholamines (stress chemicals). The brain shifts control to the primitive, reactive centers.

In practical terms, this means a person in a state of toxic stress is biologically primed for survival, not strategy. They are focused on getting through the next hour, the next shift, the next day. They are less likely to engage in the complex, abstract planning required to organize a union, file a lawsuit, or navigate a bureaucratic grievance process. The "fight or flight" response, paradoxically, often results in a "freeze" response when the threat is an overpowering authority figure.

This is the biology of compliance. The employer does not need to drug the workforce to keep them docile; the environment of illegality does it for them. The worker is exhausted not just by the physical labor, but by the metabolic cost of fear.

This medical reality also explains the paradox of why workers often stay in abusive situations even when "exit" seems possible. Chronic stress reshapes the neural pathways related to fear and reward. It creates a psychology of scarcity where the known danger (the abusive boss) feels safer than the unknown danger (the world outside the gates).

Furthermore, the physical manifestations of this stress—the chronic headaches, the digestive issues, the insomnia—are often weaponized against the worker. An employer might notice a worker slowing down due to fatigue or pain. Instead of offering medical care, they threaten termination. "You look sick," the foreman says. "If you can't do the work, I'll find someone who can." The worker, terrified of losing their livelihood, forces their body to push through the warning signs, deepening the damage.

As the American Immigration Council has documented, the psychological trauma of this existence extends to the entire family unit. Children absorb the tension of their parents, leading to the same toxic stress responses in the next generation. But for the adult worker, the tragedy is compounded by the fact that they are excluded from the very systems designed to treat these conditions.

The undocumented worker suffering from stress-induced hypertension cannot walk into a clinic for beta-blockers without fear. They cannot see a therapist to process the trauma of the journey or the anxiety of the workplace. They are locked out of the healthcare system by the same lack of status that causes their illness.

The "company doctor" discussed in previous chapters—the one who glues cuts shut to avoid OSHA reports—is certainly not equipped or inclined to treat complex stress disorders. The remedy for the worker's condition is not pharmaceutical; it is legal. The cure for deportation anxiety is status. Without it, the body continues to erode.

We must also recognize the gendered dimension of this biological warfare. For female workers, who often face the dual threat of labor exploitation and sexual harassment, the stress load is compounded. The constant vigilance required to avoid a predator in the fields or the hotel hallway adds another layer of cortisol to an already toxic mix. The trauma of sexual violence, or the fear of it, creates a deep, persistent psychological wound that the body carries as chronic pain or dissociation.

This biological perspective reframes the debate about "unskilled" labor. There is no such thing as unskilled labor when the job requires the physical endurance to work while one's own nervous system is attacking itself. The resilience required to wake up every morning, suppress the screaming instinct to hide, and go to work in a hostile environment represents a profound expenditure of human energy.

When we look at the mortality rates of immigrant communities—the early onset of strokes, the prevalence of kidney failure, the "weathering" effect where bodies age faster than their chronological years—we are seeing the scorecard of this warfare. We are seeing the receipt for the cheap labor.

The modern slaveholder does not need to use a whip to break a worker's spirit. He relies on the slow, invisible drip of chemistry. He relies on the fact that a human being can only live in the red zone for so long before something snaps. And when it does—when the worker collapses in the field or can no longer get out of bed—the system simply discards the broken part and replaces it with another body, one whose adrenal glands are still fresh, ready to be consumed by the fear.

Chapter 28: Stockholm Syndrome in the Fields

When federal agents or labor inspectors finally descend on a site of exploitation—whether it is a tomato field in Florida or a garment factory in Los Angeles—they often encounter a reaction that baffles them. They arrive expecting to be greeted as liberators. They expect the workers to point accusing fingers at the foreman, to cheer the arrival of the law, and to pour out their grievances.

Instead, they are often met with silence, hostility, or active defense of the exploiter.

"He is a good man," a worker might say of the boss who has stolen wages for years. "He gave me a job when no one else would." "He lets me live in the trailer." "He protects us from *La Migra*."

This phenomenon is the most confounding barrier to prosecution in human trafficking cases. It is the moment when the chains of the mind prove stronger than the chains of debt. To the outsider, it looks like madness or stupidity. Why would a person defend the architect of their own misery?

The answer lies in a psychological adaptation known popularly as Stockholm Syndrome, but known clinically as "trauma bonding." It is a survival strategy forged in the crucible of total dependency. In the context of the undocumented labor market, it is not a pathology of the individual; it is a rational response to an environment where the employer holds the power of life and death.

To understand this bond, we must first dismantle the cartoon image of the "evil slaveholder." If the exploiter were purely sadistic, 100 percent of the time, rebellion would be inevitable. Pure cruelty breeds pure hatred. But the successful trafficker is rarely a caricature. He is a complex figure who mixes abuse with kindness, extraction with provision, and terror with protection.

He is the *Patron*.

In many Latin American cultures, the *Patron* is a figure of immense cultural weight. He is the godfather, the provider, the authority figure who demands loyalty but offers security in return. Traffickers exploit this cultural archetype ruthlessly. They position themselves not as mere employers, but as patriarchs.

The mechanism of control relies on "intermittent reinforcement." This is a well-documented psychological principle: a reward that is given unpredictably is far more addictive than a reward given consistently. The employer who screams, threatens, and steals wages on Monday might, on Tuesday, buy pizza for the crew or offer a small loan for a sick child.

These small acts of "kindness" take on immense psychological weight against the backdrop of total deprivation. In a world where the worker has nothing, the man who gives a bottle of cold water is a savior, even if he is the same man who prohibited water breaks an hour earlier. The worker's brain seizes on the kindness as evidence of the boss's humanity, while minimizing the abuse as "necessary discipline" or "just a bad day."

Furthermore, the employer constructs a reality where he is the *only* barrier between the worker and destruction. This is the core lie of the trauma bond. "The police want to deport you," the trafficker whispers. "The neighbors hate you. The government wants to put you in a cage. *I* am the only one willing to hide you. *I* am the only one who gives you work."

By framing the outside world as a landscape of absolute terror—a framing that is reinforced by the reality of immigration raids and anti-immigrant rhetoric—the trafficker positions himself as the protector. The exploitation is reframed as the price of protection. The stolen wages are the "tax" for safety. The worker defends the exploiter because, in their truncated reality, the exploiter is the only thing keeping the wolves at bay.

This dynamic is reinforced by "comparative suffering." The worker compares their current situation not to the American standard of labor rights—which they may not know exists—but to the desperate poverty they left behind.

"At least I am eating," the worker tells the inspector. "Back home, we starved."

The trafficker weaponizes this gratitude. "Look at what I have done for you," he says. "I brought you to America. I gave you a roof." He creates a debt of gratitude that operates alongside the financial debt. To speak out against him feels like a betrayal of the person who "saved" them from poverty. The victim feels guilt for their own victimization.

This bond is deepened by the isolation I documented in previous chapters. When a domestic worker or a farmworker is cut off from the outside world, their reality is defined entirely by the abuser. The abuser becomes the source of all information, all validation, and all social interaction. The victim begins to see the world through the abuser's eyes. They adopt the abuser's justifications. "He yells because the business is under pressure," the worker rationalizes. "He doesn't pay us because the market is bad." They become the apologists for their own enslavement.

We must also confront the role of the "straw boss" or *capataz* in cementing this dynamic. Often, the direct supervisor is not the white owner but a member of the worker's own community. This person has risen from the ranks. They speak the language; they know the hometown. They represent the possibility of success.

The straw boss is often the most brutal enforcer, but they also serve as a "trauma blocker." The worker directs their anger at the immediate supervisor while maintaining a reverence for the distant owner, the "Big Boss" who occasionally waves from his truck. Or, conversely, the straw boss plays the "good cop," mediating between the workers and the owner, convincing the crew that he is doing his best to protect them from the owner's wrath, if only they work a little harder.

Breaking a trauma bond is excruciatingly difficult. It is not as simple as opening a gate. When a victim is removed from the control of the trafficker, they often experience a psychological collapse. They feel exposed, guilty, and terrified. They have lost their protector.

This is why victims often return to their exploiters, or why they refuse to testify. The prosecutor sees a crime scene; the victim sees a broken family. The prosecutor offers "justice," an abstract concept that puts no food on the table; the trafficker offers the familiarity of the known hell.

The legal system is ill-equipped to handle this ambiguity. Courts demand clear victims and clear villains. They struggle with a victim who says, "He didn't mean to hurt me," or "I agreed to do it." Juries look at a worker who had a cell phone and a chance to run but didn't, and they conclude there was no coercion. They fail to see the invisible wires of dependency that paralyzed the will.

We must understand that Stockholm Syndrome in the fields is not a sign of weakness. It is a testament to the human capacity to adapt to intolerable conditions. It is the mind's way of surviving a situation where resistance seems futile and dangerous.

To dismantle this bond, we cannot simply arrest the bad guy. We must provide an alternative structure of safety that is more robust than the one the trafficker provided. We must prove to the worker that the state can offer genuine protection, not just deportation. We must replace the false benevolence of the *Patron* with the true dignity of rights that do not depend on anyone's kindness.

Until we do, we will continue to see the tragic spectacle of the slave shielding the master, fighting to preserve the only security they have ever known.

Part V: The Economics of Theft (Follow the Money)

The financial incentives.

Chapter 29: The Mechanics of Wage Theft

If a man walks into a convenience store, points a gun at the clerk, and empties the register of two hundred dollars, we have a clear vocabulary for his actions. He is a criminal. The police are called, a report is filed, and if he is caught, he faces a felony charge and potential prison time. Society recognizes the violation of property rights as a breach of the social contract that demands an aggressive state response.

But if a construction foreman stands at the edge of a job site on a Friday afternoon and tells a crew of ten workers that he doesn't have their paychecks—that the "general contractor hasn't paid him yet," or that there was a "glitch in the payroll system"—and effectively steals two thousand dollars from them, the vocabulary shifts. This is not called a crime; it is called a "civil dispute." The police will not come. The district attorney will not file charges. The state will not intervene.

This disparity in language and enforcement creates a zone of impunity where the single largest category of property crime in the United States flourishes. Wage theft—the systematic non-payment of wages owed—dwarfs all other forms of theft combined. As the Economic Policy Institute has documented, the total value of wages stolen from workers annually exceeds the combined value of all bank robberies, convenience store holdups, street muggings, and car thefts in the nation. It is a multi-billion-dollar transfer of wealth from the poor to the profiting class, executed not with weapons, but with spreadsheets, silence, and the specific vulnerabilities of the undocumented workforce.

To understand how billions of dollars are siphoned from the pockets of the working poor, we must move beyond the abstract concept of "exploitation" and examine the specific mechanics of the theft. It is rarely a dramatic refusal to pay a month's salary. It is a game of inches, played $50 at a time, using techniques that have been refined into an industrial art form.

The most common instrument of this theft is the "ghost hour." In industries defined by fluid schedules—hospitality, agriculture, and construction—time is a malleable concept. The mechanism is simple: rounding. If a dishwasher clocks out at 10:47 PM, the payroll software—often deliberately configured by management—rounds the time back to 10:45 PM or even 10:30 PM.

Two minutes here, fifteen minutes there. It seems trivial. But aggregated across a workforce of fifty people over a year, these shaved minutes accumulate into thousands of unpaid hours. For the undocumented worker, who keeps track of their time in a notebook or by memory, proving this discrepancy is nearly impossible. They lack the digital audit trail held by the employer. The theft is invisible because it occurs in the gap between the time worked and the time recorded.

Then there is the "automatic break" deduction. Labor laws generally require unpaid meal breaks for shifts over a certain length. Employers frequently program their payroll systems to automatically deduct thirty minutes for lunch every day, regardless of whether the worker actually took the break. In the high-pressure environment of a poultry plant or a harvest crew, workers are often pressured to work through lunch to meet quotas. They work the time, but the computer steals it. When a worker notices the discrepancy, the explanation is bureaucratic: "The system does it automatically. You should have taken your break." The burden of proof shifts to the victim to prove a negative.

But for the undocumented worker paid in cash, the theft is even more direct. The "envelope game" is a standard practice on non-union construction sites. At the end of the week, the worker receives a cash envelope. On the outside, a number is scribbled: $600. Inside, there is $550.

When the worker confronts the foreman, the response is a shrug or a threat. "I deducted for the ride," the foreman might say, inventing a fee on the spot. Or, "I had to pay a tax." Or simply, "Take it or leave it. There are ten guys who want your spot on Monday." The worker, standing on a street corner with no contract and no recourse, takes the $550. The $50 difference is the price of their silence. Multiply that $50 by ten workers, fifty-two weeks a year, and the foreman has pocketed $26,000—a tax-free bonus extracted directly from the subsistence of his crew.

A more sophisticated variation involves the "bounced check" loop. In this scenario, the labor broker pays the workers with checks issued from a bank account that he knows is empty, or he issues them late on a Friday afternoon. The workers, unbanked and unable to use traditional financial services, must take these checks to predatory check-cashing storefronts that charge high fees.

When the check bounces, the check casher comes after the worker, not the employer. Or, the worker returns to the employer on Monday, check in hand, only to be told, "Hold onto it until Wednesday, cash flow is tight." Wednesday becomes Friday. Friday becomes next week. The worker is strung along, continuing to work in the hope of eventually getting paid for the past. They are trapped by the "sunk cost" of their own labor. If they quit, they know they will never see the money. If they stay, they might. The employer leverages this hope to extract weeks of free labor before the worker finally breaks.

The "vanishing subcontractor" is perhaps the most devastating mechanic in the construction and disaster recovery sectors. As discussed in previous chapters regarding the liability shield, large projects rely on layers of subcontracting. The theft occurs at the very bottom of this chain. A labor broker, often an LLC created just for a specific project, hires a crew of undocumented framers or roofers. They work for two weeks, completing a critical phase of the job.

On payday, the broker is gone. His phone is disconnected. The job site trailer is locked. He has collected the draw from the general contractor and disappeared. The workers turn to the general contractor, who throws up his hands. "I paid him," the big boss says. "It's not my fault he didn't pay you."

This is not always an accident; it is often a feature of the business model. The "burn and churn" strategy relies on hiring a crew, working them to exhaustion, stealing their final paycheck, and then replacing them with a new crew. By stealing the final week's wages from every worker, a contractor can lower his labor costs by 20 percent over the life of a project. In a low-bid environment, that 20 percent is the profit margin.

The theft also operates through the manipulation of the "prevailing wage." On government-funded projects, contractors are legally required to pay a set wage, often significantly higher than the minimum wage, to prevent government spending from driving down labor standards. Unscrupulous contractors win these bids by claiming they will pay the prevailing wage, but then engaging in a kickback scheme.

They issue a check for the full legal amount—say, $40 an hour—to create a paper trail for government auditors. But they force the undocumented worker to cash the check and return the difference between the prevailing wage and their "real" wage (perhaps $15 an hour) in cash to the boss. "If you don't bring me the cash," the boss says, "you don't get the next job." The worker is forced to become an accomplice in their own robbery, laundering the money that was stolen from them.

In the agricultural sector, the piece-rate system provides its own unique opportunities for larceny. Workers are paid by the bucket or the pound. But who counts the buckets? The "token system" relies on a field walker handing a plastic chip to the worker for every bucket dumped. It is remarkably easy for a supervisor to "run out of tokens" or to simply undercount.

"You picked 40 buckets," the worker argues. "My count says 32," the supervisor replies. In a field where the worker has no status and the supervisor controls the water and the ride home, the supervisor's count is law. The eight stolen buckets are pure profit for the grower or the crew leader.

Furthermore, the "waiting time" theft is endemic in agriculture. Workers are told to arrive at 5:00 AM to be transported to the fields. They arrive, but the dew is still on the crops, so they cannot pick until 8:00 AM. They sit on the bus for three hours, unpaid. The Fair Labor Standards Act is complex regarding waiting time, but in many cases, if the worker is required to be there, they must be paid. In the shadow economy, this time is stolen. The worker donates three hours of their life every morning to the employer's logistics.

The digital age has introduced new vectors for wage theft through the "payroll card." Instead of checks or direct deposit, unbanked workers are issued debit cards loaded with their wages. These cards are often laden with fees—a fee to check the balance, a fee to withdraw cash, a fee for inactivity. The bank and the employer effectively tax the worker's wages after they are earned. A worker earning $300 a week might lose $15 or $20 just to access their own money. It is a friction tax applied to the poor.

Why does this system persist? Why is the theft of billions of dollars treated with a shrug by the legal system?

The answer lies in the legal classification of the act. As I noted in the analysis of the legal black hole, the theft of wages is generally treated as a breach of contract, not a crime against property. It is a civil matter. The remedy is restitution, not incarceration.

This classification creates a risk-reward ratio that encourages theft. If a contractor steals $50,000 in wages and is caught, the worst-case scenario in most states is that he has to pay the $50,000 back. There is no punitive multiplier. There is no jail time. He has essentially received an interest-free loan from his workers. If he is *not* caught—and given the decimated state of labor enforcement, he likely won't be—he keeps the money.

For the undocumented worker, the mechanism of theft is reinforced by the mechanism of deportation. The moment a worker asserts their right to be paid, they cease to be a "worker" in the eyes of the employer and become a "problem." The employer plays the ultimate trump card: "You want your money? Come to the office. I have ICE waiting for you."

We must recognize that wage theft is not an aberration; it is a structural component of the business models in agriculture, construction, and hospitality. It is the margin. It is the buffer that allows the subcontractor to bid low and still buy a new truck. It is the subsidy that keeps the price of the salad and the hotel room artificially low.

Every dollar stolen from a worker is a dollar that does not buy food for a child, does not pay rent, and does not circulate in the local economy. It is wealth concentrated in the hands of the lawbreaker. The mechanics of this theft are banal—a rounded number, a missing check, a cash kickback—but the cumulative effect is a grand larceny that hollows out the working class $50 at a time. The ledger of the American economy is balanced on the back of the worker who looks at his pay envelope, sees that it is light, and knows that he cannot say a word.

Chapter 30: The Tax Gap

In the American civic imagination, the Internal Revenue Service is an omniscient, all-seeing eye. We are raised to believe that death and taxes are the only two certainties in life, and that the federal government possesses the power to track every dime, audit every deduction, and punish every evader. We assume that if we miss a payment, a letter will arrive. We assume the system works.

But there is a parallel economy where the IRS is blind. It is a cash-based ecosystem where billions of dollars in wages change hands every Friday without a single W-2 form being issued, without a single Social Security contribution being made, and without a cent of Medicare tax being collected. This is the underground economy, and it is not a small leak in the ship of state; it is a hull breach.

The "Tax Gap"—the official term for the difference between what the federal government is owed and what it actually collects—has exploded in recent years. Recent estimates suggest this gap now approaches $700 billion annually. While this figure includes all forms of non-compliance, a massive and growing portion is attributable to the underreporting of business income and employment taxes in sectors dominated by undocumented labor.

To understand the mechanics of this theft, one must look at the pay stub—or rather, the absence of one.

In a legitimate employment relationship, the employer acts as a tax collector for the government. For every dollar paid to a worker, the employer must withhold federal income tax. More importantly, they must deal with FICA—the Federal Insurance Contributions Act. This tax funds Social Security and Medicare. It is a flat 15.3 percent tax on wages, split evenly between the employer and the employee.

When a construction contractor or a farm labor broker pays a worker in cash "under the table," they are not just simplifying paperwork; they are pocketing that 15.3 percent.

Consider the math of a medium-sized framing crew with an annual payroll of $1 million. If the contractor pays legally, he owes $76,500 in FICA taxes on top of the wages. If he pays in cash, he keeps that $76,500. This is pure profit, extracted directly from the Social Security Trust Fund.

But the theft is actually double that amount. Because he is not withholding the worker's share of the tax, and because the worker is undocumented and likely not filing a return, the other 7.65 percent is also lost to the system. The total loss to the public treasury is over $150,000 for just one crew, in one year.

Multiply this by the thousands of crews operating in the shadows of the American housing market, the thousands of kitchens paying dishwashers in cash, and the vast agricultural networks operating off the books. The aggregate loss is staggering. We are witnessing the systematic defunding of the American safety net by the very industries that claim to be essential to the economy.

The defenders of the status quo often argue that undocumented immigrants are a drain on the tax system. This narrative is a convenient inversion of reality. The truth is that undocumented workers are often desperate to pay taxes. They know that a tax return is the primary evidence of "good moral character" and continuous residence—proof that might one day help them legalize their status. Millions of undocumented workers file taxes using Individual Taxpayer Identification Numbers (ITINs), contributing billions to a Social Security system they will never access.

The real drain is the employer. The employer has no incentive to create a paper trail. In fact, the employer has a criminal incentive to hide the existence of the workforce entirely.

The mechanism for hiding this payroll has become increasingly sophisticated. It is rarely as simple as a boss handing out bills from his wallet. It involves a financial shell game designed to fool auditors and insurance adjusters.

A common tactic in the construction industry involves "check-cashing" schemes. A general contractor writes a large check to a shell company—let's call it "XYZ Construction"—ostensibly for "materials" or "consulting." This creates a legitimate-looking expense on the general contractor's books, reducing his taxable income.

The operator of XYZ Construction takes the check to a check-cashing store, pays a fee, and walks out with a bag of cash. He then distributes this cash to the workers. The money has been "laundered." On paper, it was a business expense. In reality, it was a payroll run. The taxes that should have been generated by those wages have vanished.

Stanford University researchers have identified "pass-through" business entities—partnerships and S-corporations often used in these schemes—as responsible for a disproportionate share of the tax gap. These structures are opaque, fluid, and difficult to audit. They can be formed online in minutes and dissolved just as quickly. They are the getaway cars of tax evasion.

The impact of this evasion extends beyond the federal deficit. It creates a competitive distortion that destroys honest businesses. The contractor who complies with the law—paying his 7.65 percent share, withholding income tax, paying unemployment insurance premiums—starts every bid at a massive disadvantage. He is effectively subsidizing his competitor's criminality.

When we hear politicians lament the insolvency of Social Security or the rising cost of Medicare, they rarely point to the construction site down the street. They talk about demographics and the aging population. They do not talk about the billions of dollars in covered wages that are being paid every year without a single contribution to the fund.

This is a form of embezzlement. The employer is utilizing the public infrastructure—the roads that bring workers to the site, the schools that educate their children, the emergency rooms that treat their injuries—but refusing to pay the "membership dues" that maintain that infrastructure. They are free-riders on the American social contract.

Furthermore, this tax gap represents a massive, regressive transfer of wealth. When the tax base erodes, the government must either cut services or raise taxes on those who *do* pay. The nurse, the teacher, and the factory worker who have their taxes automatically deducted from their paychecks are forced to carry the burden for the millionaire developer who pays his framing crew in cash.

The solution to this problem is not a mystery. It requires bringing the shadow workforce into the legal light. If the eleven million undocumented people in this country were legalized, the "cash economy" would shrink overnight. Workers would demand W-2s. Employers would be forced to withhold taxes. The tax base would expand by billions of dollars, shoring up the safety net for decades to come.

But until that happens, we must recognize the "cheap" labor of the undocumented workforce for what it is: a subsidized commodity. The discount on the price of a new home or a restaurant meal is not the result of market efficiency. It is the result of tax fraud. We are paying for it not at the cash register, but on April 15th, and in the crumbling infrastructure of a nation that is being robbed by those who claim to be building it.

Chapter 31: The Healthcare Subsidy

In the accounting of American capitalism, every asset has a depreciation schedule. A factory machine, a delivery truck, or a computer server is understood to have a lifespan. The owner calculates the wear and tear, invests in maintenance to prolong utility, and sets aside capital to replace the asset when it inevitably fails. This is basic stewardship; to run a machine until it breaks without maintenance is considered bad business.

But in the shadow economy of undocumented labor, the human body is the only machine that does not require a depreciation schedule. It is the only asset that can be run at maximum capacity without maintenance, broken without consequence, and discarded without cost.

When a construction worker falls from a roof in Texas, or a poultry worker's tendon finally snaps in Arkansas, the employer does not face a crisis of capital. He faces a logistical inconvenience. He does not pay for the repair. He does not pay for the replacement. Instead, he shifts the entire financial burden of that broken body onto a third party that never agreed to the contract: the American public healthcare system.

This transfer of liability—from the private profit of the employer to the public ledger of the emergency room—is one of the most massive and least discussed subsidies in the modern economy. It is a hidden tax levied on every citizen who pays an insurance premium or a hospital bill, a financial mechanism that allows industries to extract the vitality of a workforce while outsourcing its mortality.

To understand how this subsidy functions, we must examine the legal architecture of the American emergency room. In 1986, Congress passed the Emergency Medical Treatment and Labor Act, known by the acronym EMTALA. The law was born of a humanitarian imperative: to prevent "patient dumping," the practice of private hospitals refusing to treat indigent patients and transferring them to public hospitals, often with fatal results. EMTALA mandates that any hospital accepting Medicare payments—which is virtually all of them—must stabilize anyone who comes to the emergency department, regardless of their ability to pay or their citizenship status.

It is a noble law. It asserts that in the United States, we do not let people bleed to death on the sidewalk because they lack a credit card.

But for the exploitative employer, EMTALA is not a humanitarian safeguard; it is a business plan. It effectively creates a free catastrophic insurance policy for their workforce. The employer knows that he does not need to provide health insurance. He does not need to pay into workers' compensation funds. He does not need to keep a nurse on site. He knows that if the worst happens—if the chemical burns become unbearable, or the heat stroke induces a seizure—the local hospital *must* take the worker in.

The emergency room becomes the primary care physician for the undocumented workforce. But it is the most expensive, least efficient form of care imaginable. A condition that could be treated with a $50 course of antibiotics in a clinic becomes a $50,000 sepsis treatment in the ER because the worker, terrified of the cost and the questions, waited until they were dying to seek help.

Consider the economics of a typical workplace injury in the residential construction sector. A framer cuts his hand on a table saw. In a legitimate workplace, this triggers a workers' compensation claim. The insurance pays for the stitches, the follow-up visits, and the physical therapy to restore function. The cost is borne by the employer's premiums, which rise to reflect the risk of the job. This creates a financial incentive for the employer to improve safety.

On the shadow job site, the calculus is inverted. The foreman wraps the hand in a rag and tells the worker to go to the hospital. "Don't tell them you work for me," he warns. "Tell them you did it at home."

The worker walks into the ER. He has no insurance. He has no money. Under EMTALA, the hospital treats the wound. They stitch the hand. They generate a bill for $3,000. The worker cannot pay it. The hospital writes it off as "uncompensated care" or "charity care."

But in economics, there is no such thing as a write-off. The cost does not vanish; it is redistributed. The hospital recovers that $3,000 by raising the prices on every aspirin, every bandage, and every MRI charged to patients *with* insurance. The cost of the injury is baked into the premiums paid by teachers, police officers, and office workers. The construction company that profited from the framer's labor pays zero. They have successfully privatized the profit of the house they built while socializing the cost of the blood spilled to build it.

The scale of this cost-shifting is staggering. As noted in the fiscal analysis of immigration, spending on Emergency Medicaid for non-citizens—which covers the specific costs of emergency treatment for those who would otherwise be eligible for Medicaid—totals billions of dollars annually. But this figure captures only the government's direct reimbursement. It does not capture the billions more in "bad debt" absorbed by hospital systems, costs that ultimately drive up the price of healthcare for the entire nation.

The brutality of this system is most visible in what happens *after* the emergency room. EMTALA requires only that the patient be "stabilized." It does not require a cure. It does not require rehabilitation. It effectively mandates that the hospital save the life, but it permits the destruction of the livelihood.

If an undocumented worker shatters a leg falling from a ladder, the ER will set the bone and stop the bleeding. But they will not provide the six months of physical therapy required to walk again. They will not provide the follow-up surgeries needed to restore full function. The worker is discharged with a pair of crutches and a bottle of painkillers into a void.

Without workers' compensation to provide wage replacement during recovery, the worker is instantly destitute. They cannot work, so they cannot pay rent. They become a burden on their family, their church, or the local community. The "human capital" they represented—the years of skill and strength—is liquidated. The employer simply returns to the day-labor corner and rents a new body.

This creates a disposable workforce in the most literal sense. The industry consumes the healthy years of a worker's life and discards them the moment they falter. We see this in the meatpacking towns of the Midwest, where a generation of workers who arrived in the 1990s are now aging into disability. Their bodies are wrecked by the repetitive motion of the line— shoulders frozen, backs fused, nerves deadened. Because they are undocumented, they are ineligible for Social Security Disability Insurance or Medicare. They are the "industrial refuse" of the food system, left to navigate old age with broken bodies and no safety net.

There is a specific, gruesome sub-genre of this crisis involving end-stage renal disease. In the agricultural fields of California and Florida, chronic dehydration and heat stress are destroying the kidneys of young men at epidemic rates. When their kidneys fail, they need dialysis to live—a treatment that costs tens of thousands of dollars a year.

Because they are ineligible for standard Medicaid or the Affordable Care Act marketplaces, these workers occupy a grisly legal niche. In many states, "Emergency Medicaid" interprets the law to mean that dialysis is only covered when the patient is in immediate danger of death.

This leads to the practice of "emergency-only dialysis." Instead of receiving scheduled treatment three times a week, which keeps the patient healthy and able to function, the worker must wait until their blood toxicity reaches a lethal level. They must wait until they are seizing, vomiting, or struggling to breathe. Only then, when they are at death's door, does the "emergency" threshold trigger coverage. They are dialyzed, stabilized, and sent home to wait for their body to poison itself again.

This practice is not only torturous; it is fiscally insane. Emergency dialysis costs significantly more than scheduled dialysis. It requires ambulance rides, ICU stays, and emergency interventions. We spend millions of dollars to torture these workers and keep them on the brink of death, rather than spending a fraction of that amount to keep them alive and functional. It is a policy dictated not by medical logic or fiscal prudence, but by a punitive desire to deny "benefits" to the undocumented, even if that denial costs the taxpayer more.

The healthcare subsidy also masks the true danger of these industries. By hiding injuries from the official record, employers avoid the scrutiny of OSHA and the insurance markets. If a company's workers' compensation premiums rose every time a worker was hurt, the market would force the company to improve safety. But when the injuries are off the books—treated in the ER as "domestic accidents" or "falls at home"—the feedback loop is broken. The company maintains a pristine safety record while the hospital fills up with its casualties.

The "company doctor" or on-site nurse plays a critical role in this deception. In the poultry and meatpacking industries, on-site medical staff are often instructed to treat injuries with "first aid" measures—ice, aspirin, bandages—precisely to avoid creating a medical record that would trigger a reportable incident. Workers with repetitive strain injuries are told they are "just sore" and sent back to the line. By the time the injury requires surgery, the worker has often quit or been fired, severing the link to the workplace.

This system creates a public health risk that extends beyond the workers themselves. An undocumented workforce that is terrified of the medical system is a workforce that does not seek care for communicable diseases. During the COVID-19 pandemic, this vulnerability became a vector. Workers in meatpacking plants, terrified of losing a paycheck and afraid to go to the doctor, went to work while sick. They had no paid sick leave, no health insurance, and no trust in the system. The result was mass outbreaks that spread from the plants to the surrounding communities. The virus did not respect immigration status. The health of the public proved to be inextricably linked to the health of the most vulnerable worker.

We must recognize that the "cheap goods" we consume are subsidized by this deferred maintenance of the human body. The low cost of a new roof is possible because the contractor does not pay for the broken ankles. The low cost of a chicken breast is possible because the processor does not pay for the carpal tunnel surgery. We are not paying the true cost of production at the register; we are paying it in our insurance premiums and our tax bills.

The solution is not to close the emergency room doors; that would be a moral abomination. The solution is to force the beneficiaries of this labor to pay for its maintenance. If an industry relies on human labor, it must bear the cost of keeping those humans alive and whole.

This requires bringing the workforce out of the shadows. A legalized worker demands health insurance. A legalized worker files for workers' compensation. A legalized worker sues when a machine cuts off their arm. Legalization forces the externalized cost of injury back onto the balance sheet of the employer.

Until that happens, the American healthcare system will continue to serve as the reluctant, unpaid maintenance department for the exploitation economy. We will continue to run a system where profits are private, but pain is public. And we will continue to treat the worker not as a patient to be healed, but as a component to be used until failure, and then dumped at the door of the emergency room for the taxpayer to salvage.

Chapter 32: The "Cheap Goods" Lie

There is a persistent, whispering fear that haunts the American consumer. It is the fear that if we were to pay the people who harvest our food and build our homes a legal, living wage, our way of life would collapse under the weight of hyperinflation. We are told, implicitly and explicitly, that the $2.99 pint of strawberries and the affordable starter home are fragile gifts made possible only by the suffering of the undocumented. To end the exploitation, the argument goes, would be to usher in the era of the $10 tomato.

This is the "Cheap Goods" Lie. It is the economic shield that protects the moral rot of the labor market. It posits a zero-sum game between the dignity of the worker and the wallet of the consumer. It suggests that you, the shopper, are the primary beneficiary of modern slavery.

But when we take a forensic look at the price tag of a tomato or a house, this argument disintegrates. The math simply does not support the mythology.

Let us begin in the produce aisle. When you buy a pound of tomatoes for $2.00, how much of that money actually reaches the hand of the person who picked it? The answer is measured in pennies. According to agricultural economic analysis, farm labor costs typically account for less than 10 percent of the retail price of fresh produce. The vast majority of that $2.00 goes to the retailer, the wholesaler, the transportation company, and the marketing budget.

The Fair Food Program, discussed in Chapter 47 as a model for reform, provides a real-world test case for the cost of dignity. To transform the Florida tomato fields from "ground zero for modern-day slavery" into a workplace with decent wages and enforceable rights, the major buyers—Walmart, McDonald's, Whole Foods—agreed to pay a premium. That premium was exactly one penny per pound.

One penny.

That single cent, passed directly to the worker, was enough to nearly double the wages of the pickers, lifting them out of extreme poverty. For the consumer, the impact was invisible. If a tomato costs $2.00, raising the price to $2.01 is statistically irrelevant. It is less than the fluctuation caused by a minor shift in diesel prices. It is lost in the rounding error at the register. Yet, we are told that enforcing such standards nationwide would bankrupt families.

The reality is that the "efficiency" of exploited labor is not passed on to the consumer; it is captured by the supply chain. When a grower squeezes his workforce to save five cents a bucket, that nickel does not lower the price of your salsa. It pads the margin of the retailer or the processor. The consumer is not saving money; they are unwittingly subsidizing the profits of the corporate middleman with the misery of the picker.

The housing market reveals a similar deception. As I documented in the analysis of the construction industry, the use of misclassified, undocumented labor allows contractors to slash their labor costs by approximately 30 percent by avoiding taxes and insurance.

But does a home built by exploited labor cost 30 percent less than a home built by union carpenters?

It does not. The price of a home is determined by interest rates, land values, zoning laws, and the maximum amount the market will bear. In a hot housing market, a developer charges what the buyer can borrow. If the developer saves $20,000 on framing labor by hiring a crew of undocumented workers and paying them in cash, he does not lower the listing price of the house by $20,000. He keeps the difference.

The "affordability" of American housing is not driven by cheap labor; it is threatened by the high cost of land and materials. Labor is a shrinking fraction of the total cost. By devastating the wages of construction workers, we have not made homes cheaper; we have simply made the business of building them more profitable for those at the top of the food chain, while destroying the middle-class livelihood that construction work once provided.

This lie also ignores the dynamic nature of markets. When Henry Ford doubled the wages of his assembly line workers to $5 a day—a shocking sum at the time—critics predicted he would go bankrupt. Instead, he created a workforce that could afford to buy the cars they were building. He understood that workers are also consumers.

Today, the millions of undocumented workers in the United States are consumers in a state of suspended animation. They buy the bare minimum because they earn the bare minimum. If their wages were to rise to legal levels, the cost of goods might tick upward fractionally, but the aggregate demand in the economy would explode. They would buy more clothes, more cars, more electronics. The "velocity of money"—the speed at which a dollar circulates through the economy—would increase, generating growth that would dwarf the minor increase in prices.

Furthermore, we must account for the "hidden tax" discussed in Chapter 31. The "cheap" goods we buy are subsidized by the public purse. The low cost of the chicken breast is artificial because the taxpayer is picking up the tab for the emergency room visits of the injured workers . The low cost of the roof is a mirage because the community is paying for the indigent care of the roofer who fell.

If we were to force employers to internalize these costs—to pay living wages and provide health insurance—the sticker price of goods would reflect their true cost. A hamburger might cost fifty cents more. A house might cost one percent more. But our tax bills for uncompensated care and social services would go down. We are currently paying the bill; we are just paying it on April 15th instead of at the checkout counter.

The "Cheap Goods" Lie is a mechanism of social control. It recruits the American consumer as an accomplice to exploitation. It encourages us to view the worker not as a fellow citizen or a human being, but as an input cost that must be minimized to preserve our standard of living. It tells us that our comfort depends on their suffering.

But the data proves this is a false choice. We can afford justice. The margins exist. The wealth is there. The penny per pound is there. The only thing lacking is the honesty to admit that the "bargain" we think we are getting is the most expensive purchase we will ever make.

Chapter 33: The Impact on Native Workers

In the heated public square where immigration policy is debated, two loud and contradictory narratives often drown out reality. One side screams that immigrants are "stealing jobs," painting a picture of a zero-sum game where every new arrival subtracts an opportunity from a native-born citizen. The other side insists, with equal fervor, that immigrants are merely doing "jobs Americans won't do," suggesting a neat division of labor where foreign workers take the tasks that have become culturally or physically beneath the dignity of the native workforce.

Both narratives are dangerously incomplete. They miss the specific, devastating mechanism that is actually reshaping the American labor market. It is not a simple case of theft, nor is it a benign case of filling a vacuum. It is a rigged competition where the rules of the game have been altered to favor the player who has the least power.

Economists call it the "substitution effect." In a healthy market, labor competes on a relatively level playing field. A carpenter competes with another carpenter based on skill, speed, and reliability. But when a large segment of the workforce is undocumented, a fourth variable is introduced: exploitability.

The American worker—whether white, Black, or a legal immigrant who has been here for decades—carries a "regulatory backpack." Inside this backpack are the costs of their legal status: the requirement for minimum wage, the expectation of overtime pay, the necessity of workers' compensation insurance, and the employer's mandate to pay payroll taxes. These are not luxuries; they are the baseline costs of hiring a person who exists within the protection of the law.

The undocumented worker arrives without this backpack. Or rather, the unscrupulous employer strips it off them at the door. Because this worker can be paid in cash, denied benefits, and fired without consequence, they effectively offer a 30 to 40 percent discount on labor costs compared to their legal counterpart.

This creates a market distortion that is often invisible to the consumer but fatal to the American worker. The native-born worker is not losing their job because they are lazy, or because they lack skill, or because they demand too much. They are losing their job because they are competing against a violation of the law. They are competing against a price point that is chemically impossible to match while remaining legal.

We see this dynamic most vividly in the construction industry. Fifty years ago, residential construction was a path to the middle class. A young man with a strong back and a willingness to learn could start as a laborer, learn a trade, join a union (or just a reputable crew), and eventually buy the house he was building. Today, in many parts of the country, that ladder has been kicked away.

As I noted in the analysis of the "crossfire" in which American workers are caught, the native worker competes not against the immigrant himself, but against the illegality itself. When a general contractor takes bids for a framing job, he looks at the bottom line. Contractor A, who hires legal workers and pays taxes, bids $50,000. Contractor B, who hires undocumented workers as "independent contractors" and pays cash, bids $35,000. Contractor B wins.

Contractor A has two choices: go out of business, or fire his legal crew and adopt the model of Contractor B. The "market" has spoken, but the market was rigged. The American carpenter finds himself priced out not by superior efficiency, but by tax evasion and wage theft.

This reality exposes the lie of "jobs Americans won't do." There is virtually no job an American won't do if the price is right and the conditions are safe. Americans work on oil rigs in the Gulf of Mexico, one of the most dangerous jobs on earth. They work in sanitation, hauling garbage in the summer heat. They work in coal mines. Why? Because these jobs pay a premium for the danger and the dirt.

In the agricultural and hospitality sectors, however, the wage mechanism is broken. The influx of exploitable labor freezes wages at the subsistence level. If the pay for picking tomatoes is $50 a day, it is true that few Americans will do it. But if the pay were $25 an hour with overtime and benefits—the rate that might prevail if the labor supply weren't artificially inflated by exploitable workers—Americans would line up. The phrase "jobs Americans won't do" is incomplete; it should end with "...at the wages exploiters want to pay."

The victims of this substitution effect are not the wealthy. The lawyer, the doctor, and the software engineer are largely insulated from this competition; in fact, they benefit from it through cheaper services. The impact falls squarely on the most vulnerable segments of the native-born population: high school dropouts, workers in rural areas, and, disproportionately, Black and Latino men.

Historically, low-skilled entry-level jobs served as the on-ramp to the economy for these groups. But today, a young Black man in Chicago or a Latino citizen in Los Angeles looking for entry-level work in construction or logistics finds himself competing with men who are terrified to complain about safety or pay. The employer prefers the undocumented worker not because they work "harder" in some abstract cultural sense, but because they are "pliant." They don't file workers' comp claims. They don't take breaks.

This pushes the low-skilled native worker out of the labor force entirely. It contributes to the crisis of prime-age male non-employment that plagues the Rust Belt and the inner cities. When work no longer pays a living wage because the wage floor has been destroyed by the shadow economy, the rational choice for some is to stop looking, or to turn to the illicit economy.

The historical parallels to the post-Civil War South are striking. After Emancipation, the sharecropping system was designed to re-subjugate Black labor. But as historians have documented, it also devastated poor white farmers . The white yeoman farmer could not compete with the plantation that relied on debt-peonage labor. The presence of a captive workforce dragged down the wages and land values for everyone who tried to work the land freely. The poor white farmer and the Black sharecropper were pitted against each other by a system that exploited both, but the white farmer was told his enemy was the Black worker, rather than the planter class that rigged the market.

Today, we see a similar misdirection. The anger of the displaced American worker is often directed at the immigrant standing on the corner. This is a mistake. The immigrant is the ammunition, not the shooter. The shooter is the employer who exploits the system, and the politicians who maintain the loophole.

The native worker and the undocumented worker are, in a tragic sense, on the same side. They are both victims of a system that devalues labor. The undocumented worker is exploited directly through theft and abuse; the native worker is exploited indirectly through displacement and wage suppression.

Defenders of the current system often point to macroeconomic studies showing that immigration has a net positive or neutral effect on wages. These studies often suffer from the "forest and trees" problem. They look at the economy as a whole, averaging the gains of the CEO with the losses of the janitor. They obscure the specific, concentrated damage done to the bottom quartile of the workforce.

For the construction worker in Dallas who hasn't seen a real raise in twenty years despite a building boom, the "net positive" GDP growth is irrelevant. He knows what he sees on the job site: crews arriving in vans, paid in cash, working without harnesses, for wages he cannot accept if he wants to feed his family legally.

The "substitution effect" ultimately erodes the social contract. It breaks the link between productivity and pay. It teaches the American worker that following the rules is a sucker's game. It validates the cynicism that says the economy is rigged against the little guy.

And perhaps most dangerously, it fuels a nativist resentment that misidentifies the problem. By allowing the exploitation of undocumented workers to fester, we have created the conditions for a culture war. We have turned the working class against itself, while the benefits of the cheap labor flow upward to the owners of capital.

To protect the American worker, we do not need to close the border to all migration; we need to close the border to *exploitation*. If every immigrant who entered this country did so with full legal rights—the right to the minimum wage, the right to organize, the right to switch jobs—the "discount" would vanish. The substitution effect would disappear. The immigrant would no longer be a weapon against the native worker, but a colleague and a competitor on a level playing field.

Until we achieve that, the American worker remains caught in the crossfire, their standard of living collateral damage in the war for the lowest possible bid.

Chapter 34: The Competitive Disadvantage

In the quiet office of a small construction firm in suburban Chicago, or at the kitchen table of a landscaping business in Denver, a specific tragedy plays out every week. It is a tragedy of arithmetic. An owner sits with a calculator, a set of blueprints, and a bottle of antacids, preparing a bid for a commercial project. He calculates the cost of materials, which is fixed. He calculates the cost of fuel and equipment. And then he calculates the cost of labor.

He puts in the numbers required by law. He adds the hourly wage—let's say $25 for a skilled carpenter. He adds the 7.65 percent for the employer's share of Social Security and Medicare. He adds the unemployment insurance premium. He adds the workers' compensation insurance, which in construction can run as high as 15 or 20 percent of payroll because the work is dangerous. He adds the cost of safety harnesses, hard hats, and training time.

He submits the bid. A week later, he gets the call. He lost. And he didn't just lose; he was blown out of the water. The winning bid came in 30 percent lower than his cost for materials and labor combined.

He knows, with the certainty of a mathematician, that the winning number is impossible. It is physically impossible to buy the lumber, run the trucks, and pay human beings a legal wage for that price. The only variable that could have moved that much is the labor cost. The winner is cheating.

This is the "Competitive Disadvantage." It is the existential crisis facing every American business owner who attempts to follow the law in an industry permeated by undocumented labor. We often speak of the "free market" as a mechanism that rewards efficiency and innovation. But in the shadow economy, the market has been corrupted. It no longer rewards the company that builds the best wall or grows the tastiest tomato. It rewards the company that is most willing to break the law.

The dynamic creates a "Gresham's Law" of labor: bad ethics drive out good. The honest contractor acts as a proxy for the rule of law. When he pays his taxes and insures his workers, he is upholding the social contract. He is ensuring that if a worker falls, the medical system is paid. He is ensuring that when a worker retires, Social Security is funded.

But the market punishes him for this virtue. As I noted in the analysis of the "race to the bottom," the honest contractor faces not a disadvantage but a death sentence. In a competitive bidding situation, he simply cannot match the price of a competitor who treats payroll taxes as optional and safety gear as an unnecessary expense.

The margin of theft is the margin of victory. Consider the specific economics. A law-abiding business pays roughly 30 to 40 percent on top of the hourly wage for mandatory taxes and insurance. A shadow operator pays zero. That 40 percent gap is insurmountable. No amount of "efficiency" or "better management" can close it. You cannot out-innovate tax evasion. You cannot manage your way around the cost of a severed limb.

This reality forces the honest business owner into a brutal decision tree.

Branch one: He can hold the line. He can continue to bid honestly, lose contract after contract, and slowly bleed his reserves until he goes bankrupt. This is the path of the martyr.

Branch two: He can exit the market. He can sell his trucks, fire his crew, and find a new line of work. This is the path of capitulation. When this happens, the community loses a pillar of stability. A legitimate business that paid taxes and supported middle-class families is replaced by a fly-by-night operator who contributes nothing to the public weal.

Branch three: He can join them. This is the most insidious outcome. The owner, desperate to save his business and feed his own family, begins to compromise. Maybe he pays overtime in cash. Maybe he stops asking for papers. Maybe he misclassifies half his crew as independent contractors.

This is how the corruption spreads. It is not always driven by greed; often, it is driven by survival. The "race to the bottom" transforms otherwise decent people into exploiters because the system leaves them no other viable option. The law, by failing to enforce itself against the cheaters, effectively mandates cheating for the survivors.

The general contractors and large developers at the top of the food chain are often complicit in this destruction. They know the math as well as anyone. When they see a bid that is 30 percent below market rate, they know it relies on illegality. But the structure of the "Subcontracting Shield" allows them to accept the low bid while feigning ignorance . They pocket the savings and leave the honest subcontractor to die on the vine.

We see this most vividly in the construction industry, where unionized contractors—who are contractually obligated to follow the rules—have been decimated in the residential sector. The economic exploitation of undocumented workers became a cornerstone of the non-union industry's strategy, effectively pricing union labor out of the market. The result is not just a loss for unions; it is a loss for the entire economy, as skilled trades that once supported a middle-class life are degraded into poverty-wage gigs.

The defenders of the current system often argue that these low bids are good for the consumer. "It keeps housing affordable," they say. But this is the "Cheap Goods Lie" revisited. The savings from the honest contractor's demise are rarely passed on to the homebuyer; they are absorbed as profit by the developers and the shadow operators. And even if prices were slightly lower, the cost is borne by the honest business owner who pays for the "subsidy" with his livelihood.

Furthermore, the honest business owner suffers a double injury. Not only does he lose the work, but he is forced to subsidize his competition. Through his tax payments, he funds the emergency rooms that treat the injured workers of the shadow contractor. He pays the unemployment insurance premiums that cover the system his competitor evades. He is forced to pay for his own destruction.

This dynamic destroys innovation. In a healthy market, businesses compete by investing in better technology or training. A framing contractor might buy a robotic layout station to work faster. But why invest $50,000 in a machine when your competitor can just hire five more undocumented workers for $10 an hour and discard them when the job is done? The availability of cheap, exploitable labor acts as a drag on technological progress. It encourages industries to remain labor-intensive and primitive rather than capital-intensive and modern.

The story of the Texas contractor interviewed by *Newsweek* offers a glimpse of the alternative. When immigration raids scared away the undocumented workforce, he admitted, "We are forced to hire inexperienced laborers at higher rates to replace our employees". He framed this as a disaster. But from the perspective of a functioning market, it was a correction. The "higher rates" were simply the true market price of labor when the distortion of illegality was removed. If every competitor faced that same reality, the honest contractor would finally have a fighting chance.

The competitive disadvantage is the mechanism by which the shadow economy cannibalizes the legitimate economy. It rewards the rule-breaker and penalizes the rule-follower. It turns the American ethos of fair play into a suicide pact. Until we level the playing field—by enforcing the laws against those who cheat, or by bringing the workforce into the legal system so they cannot be undercut—we are telling every honest business owner in America that they are a fool for following the rules.

Part VI: The Historical Mirror (The Argument)

Direct comparison to 1850s slavery.

Chapter 35: Calhoun's Ghost

On February 6, 1837, John C. Calhoun stood on the floor of the United States Senate and delivered a speech that would define the moral architecture of the South for a generation. The senator from South Carolina was not interested in apology. For decades, many Southerners had treated slavery as a "necessary evil"—a burden inherited from the British, a dangerous but unavoidable economic crutch. Calhoun rejected this defensive crouch. He declared, with the cold certainty of an aristocrat, that slavery was not an evil at all. It was, in his famous formulation, "a positive good."

Calhoun's argument was sophisticated, seductive, and terrifying. He contended that the institution benefited the enslaved as much as the enslaver. It "civilized" the African, he argued, lifting him from barbarism and providing a level of care and security that the free laborer in the North could never hope to attain. He posited that there has never existed a wealthy and civilized society in which one portion of the community did not, in point of fact, live on the labor of the other.

Fast forward nearly two centuries. The setting has shifted from the Senate floor to the cable news studio, the agricultural lobbyist's office, and the construction site trailer. The vocabulary has been sanitized; we no longer speak of "masters" and "savages." But if you listen closely to the arguments used to defend the permanent presence of an undocumented underclass, you will hear a spectral voice. It is the ghost of John C. Calhoun, speaking through the mouths of modern Americans.

The modern iteration of the "positive good" theory is the mantra that undocumented immigrants are doing "jobs Americans won't do."

This phrase is repeated with such frequency that it has achieved the status of folk wisdom. It suggests that there is a category of labor—harvesting crops, scrubbing toilets, slaughtering livestock—that is so inherently degrading that no citizen, no matter how poor, would deign to perform it. Therefore, the argument goes, we *need* a caste of workers who are desperate enough to accept it.

Just as Calhoun argued that the enslaved person was "better off" on the plantation than in the wilds of Africa, modern defenders of exploitation argue that the undocumented worker is "better off" in a U.S. meatpacking plant than in a rural village in Guatemala. "We are giving them an opportunity," the employer says. "They earn ten times here what they could earn at home."

This is the Calhounian alchemy: it transforms the extraction of value into an act of benevolence. It reframes the payment of sub-minimum wages not as theft, but as charity. By focusing on the relative improvement in the worker's condition (compared to absolute destitution), it distracts from the absolute exploitation of their labor (compared to legal standards). The logic is identical: because the worker's alternative is starvation, the employer is a savior, and the exploitation is a kindness.

The intellectual continuity extends to the arguments of George Fitzhugh, the antebellum theorist who took Calhoun's ideas to their logical extreme. Fitzhugh argued that the enslaved person was "but a grown up child" who needed the economic and social protections that only bondage could provide. He contrasted the security of the plantation, where the master had a financial interest in the slave's survival, with the "war of the rich with the poor" that defined Northern capitalism. In Fitzhugh's view, the free market was too brutal for the "inferior" races; they needed the paternalistic shield of slavery to survive.

Today's paternalism is subtler but no less insidious. We hear it in the arguments that undocumented workers cannot handle the complexities of the legal system, or that they prefer the "flexibility" of cash payments. We hear it when employers claim to "protect" their workers from the police, while simultaneously using the threat of the police to enforce discipline. The employer casts himself as the benevolent *Patron*, the only barrier between the "child-like" worker and the harsh machinery of the state.

Most strikingly, the economic threats issued by today's industries mirror the warnings of the Cotton Kingdom. In the 1850s, the defenders of slavery insisted that the entire American economy—and indeed, the global economy—rested on the back of the slave. "Cotton is King," they declared. To abolish slavery would be to destroy the textile mills of Massachusetts and the banks of New York. It would bring civilization to a halt.

Today, the agricultural lobby warns that without undocumented labor, "food prices would soar." The construction industry claims that "housing would become unaffordable." The hospitality sector insists that "hotels would close." The argument is structural: our way of life depends on the existence of a rightless class. We cannot afford justice.

This argument naturalizes exploitation. It presents the $2.00 pint of strawberries not as the product of a specific set of policy choices, but as a fragile miracle that can only be preserved by human suffering. It suggests that the economy is a delicate machine that will explode if we pay the person picking the fruit a legal wage.

But we know how the story of King Cotton ended. The South did not vanish into the sea after Emancipation. The economy adjusted. The price of cotton fluctuated, but the mills kept spinning. The "economic necessity" of slavery was a lie—a profitable lie for the planter, but a lie nonetheless.

Similarly, the claim that Americans will not do physical labor is demonstrably false. Americans drill for oil in the Gulf of Mexico. They mine coal in West Virginia. They frame houses in unions where the pay is fair. The variable is not the work; it is the wage and the conditions.

Calhoun's ghost persists because it serves a vital psychological function for the beneficiary of exploitation. It allows the employer to look in the mirror and see a philanthropist rather than a predator. It allows the consumer to eat the cheap salad without tasting the bitterness of the labor. It provides a moral framework for immorality.

When we accept the premise that certain people are "better off" being exploited because of where they were born, we are channeling the spirit of 1837. We are accepting the "positive good" of modern bondage. And until we exorcise this ghost—until we reject the idea that any human being is made for servitude—we remain trapped in the moral logic of the plantation.

Chapter 36: The Fugitive Slave Act vs. Modern Deportation

In the autumn of 1850, the United States Congress passed a piece of legislation that would ultimately tear the nation apart. It was called the Fugitive Slave Act, but among the abolitionists and the terrified Black populations of the North, it was known simply as the "Bloodhound Law."

This statute did not merely reaffirm the right of a slaveholder to recover his "property." It radicalized the federal government's role in that recovery. It stripped alleged fugitives of the right to a jury trial. It denied them the right to testify in their own defense. It compelled ordinary citizens to assist federal marshals in the capture of runaways, under pain of imprisonment. And, most infamously, it created a rigged financial incentive: the federal commissioners who heard these cases were paid ten dollars if they ruled in favor of the slaveholder, but only five dollars if they ruled in favor of the captive's freedom.

The law was designed to extend the power of the plantation into the free states. It meant that a person living in Boston or Ohio, perhaps having lived there for years, raising a family and working a trade, could be snatched off the street and sent in chains to a cotton field in Mississippi based on nothing more than a sworn affidavit from a white man. It erased the border between freedom and bondage.

Today, we look back on this law as a grotesque aberration of justice. Yet, if we examine the machinery of modern deportation—the expedited removal orders, the detention quotas, the workplace raids, and the suspension of due process in immigration courts—we find that the Bloodhound Law has been resurrected. It has been updated with biometric technology and bureaucratic euphemisms, but its essential function remains the same: to use the overwhelming power of the federal state to hunt down human beings and forcibly transport them to a place where they have no desire to be.

The parallels between the 1850 Act and the modern immigration enforcement apparatus are precise and disturbing. Both systems rely on the suspension of standard legal protections to achieve efficiency. In 1850, the goal was the swift return of labor to the owner. Today, the goal is the swift removal of labor from the interior. In both cases, the government decided that "due process"—the slow, deliberative search for truth—was an obstacle to the logistical imperative of moving bodies.

Consider the modern immigration court. It is a civil, not criminal, tribunal. This distinction allows the government to bypass the protections of the Sixth Amendment. An undocumented worker facing deportation has no right to a government-appointed attorney. Toddlers have been forced to appear before immigration judges without counsel. The burden of proof is often reversed or lowered. And in the case of "expedited removal," the judge is removed entirely; an immigration officer acts as prosecutor, judge, and jury, signing the deportation order on the spot.

This is the modern version of the 1850 commissioner. It is a system designed for "throughput," not justice.

The financial incentives, too, have found a modern echo. The ten-dollar fee of 1850 has been replaced by the multi-billion-dollar private prison industry. Corporations like GEO Group and CoreCivic run the vast majority of immigration detention centers. Their contracts often include "guaranteed minimums"—quotas that require the government to pay for a certain number of beds, regardless of whether they are filled.

This creates a market demand for prisoners. Just as the 19th-century commissioner had a financial reason to find against the fugitive, the modern detention complex has a financial reason to lobby for aggressive enforcement. A free immigrant generates no revenue for a private prison; a detained one generates a daily per diem paid by the taxpayer. The commodification of the captive body remains central to the system.

The "deputization" of local authorities is another shared feature. The Fugitive Slave Act compelled local marshals and citizens to aid the slave catchers. Today, programs like 287(g) and Secure Communities effectively deputize local police to serve as force multipliers for ICE. When a sheriff in a rural county holds a traffic violator for ICE, he is fulfilling the same function as the antebellum marshal who detained a suspected runaway for the slave catcher. He is prioritizing the federal mandate of control over the local mandate of public safety.

The psychological terror inflicted by these laws is identical. In the 1850s, the "kidnapping crews" roamed Northern cities, creating a climate of fear where no Black person felt safe. Parents told their children not to talk to strangers. People slept with one eye open.

Today, the ICE raid serves the same function. When armed agents surround a poultry plant in Mississippi or a factory in Tennessee, sealing the exits and hunting workers through the aisles, they are enacting a ritual of state terror. The goal is not just to apprehend specific individuals; it is to send a shockwave through the entire community. It is to remind every undocumented worker that they are hunted.

This terror serves a crucial economic purpose. As I documented in Chapter 4, the "climate of fear" is the ultimate tool of labor discipline . A worker who is terrified of being snatched by the state is a worker who will not complain about unpaid wages. The deportation machine does not need to remove everyone to be effective; it only needs to be visible enough to terrify the rest.

The conflict between federal enforcement and local resistance also mirrors the antebellum struggle. In the 1850s, Northern states passed "Personal Liberty Laws" to try to hinder the enforcement of the Fugitive Slave Act, forbidding the use of local jails for holding captives. Today, "Sanctuary Cities" pass ordinances forbidding the use of local resources for federal immigration enforcement.

The federal response then, as now, was fury. Antebellum Southern politicians, usually champions of "states' rights," suddenly became fierce advocates of federal supremacy when it came to recovering their property. Modern politicians who decry federal overreach in every other sphere demand that the federal government punish sanctuary cities by withholding funds. The pattern holds: the enforcement of the labor hierarchy trumps all other political principles.

There is, however, one critical difference between the two eras. The Fugitive Slave Act was designed to return the worker to the specific master who owned them. Modern deportation removes the worker from the economy entirely.

Or does it?

In reality, the threat of deportation functions to *keep* the worker in the specific master's employ. As discussed in the chapters on guest worker programs and debt bondage, the employer uses the threat of the "snatch squad" to bind the worker to the job. "If you leave," the message goes, "you are out in the open, and they will get you." The deportation apparatus acts as the electric fence around the labor camp. It defines the perimeter of the shadow economy.

When we watch the footage of families being separated at the border, or of workers being led away in zip-ties, we are witnessing the modern enforcement of an old idea: that certain people are movable objects, subject to the will of the state and the needs of the market, with no inherent right to remain where they have built their lives. The Fugitive Slave Act treated human beings as property to be repatriated. Our current immigration laws treat them as contraband to be seized. The legal terminology has changed, but the dehumanization remains absolute.

Chapter 37: The Slave Codes vs. Immigration Law

In the legal archives of the American South, nestled among property deeds and wills, one can find the "Slave Codes." These were not federal laws but a patchwork of state and local ordinances designed with a single, comprehensive purpose: to construct a legal cage so tight that escape, rebellion, or even independent thought became impossible. They criminalized literacy. They forbade assembly. They restricted movement. They defined the enslaved person not as a subject of rights, but as an object of regulation.

When we examine the sprawling, complex, and punitive body of modern immigration law—from the Immigration and Nationality Act to the thousands of pages of administrative rules governing visas and deportation—we find a disturbing structural echo. The language has shifted from "chattel" to "alien," but the function remains the containment and control of a labor force that is present but rightless.

The most famous prohibition of the Slave Codes was the ban on literacy. Laws in states like South Carolina and Virginia made it a crime to teach an enslaved person to read or write. The logic was clear: knowledge is power. A slave who could read could understand the abolitionist pamphlets circulating from the North. They could forge a pass. They could communicate with others. Ignorance was a necessary condition of bondage.

Today, we do not ban literacy, but we enforce linguistic isolation. The immigration system is a labyrinth designed to be navigated only by those with expensive legal counsel. Forms are complex, proceedings are conducted in English legal-speak, and errors are fatal. For the indigenous Guatemalan worker who speaks Mam or K'iche', or even for the Spanish speaker with limited education, the legal system is a locked book.

Furthermore, we deny access to the "literacy" of rights. As noted in the discussion of OSHA, undocumented workers are often not trained in safety protocols. They are not informed of their right to workers' compensation. This enforced ignorance serves the same function as the antebellum ban on reading: it keeps the worker from knowing the tools of their own liberation.

The restriction on movement is another direct parallel. Slave Codes required written passes for any travel off the plantation. Modern immigration law creates a de facto pass system through the driver's license. In many states, undocumented immigrants are barred from obtaining a license. This transforms every commute into a criminal act. It means the worker cannot drive to a better job in the next county. It tethers them to the employer who provides the ride or the housing, recreating the geographic confinement of the plantation.

The prohibition on assembly is perhaps the most politically potent echo. Slave Codes forbade gatherings of enslaved people without a white overseer present, fearing that any collective meeting was a prelude to revolt. Today, the law does not explicitly ban assembly, but it weaponizes it. When undocumented workers gather to protest or organize a union, the employer calls ICE. The threat of a raid breaks the assembly.

Moreover, the exclusion of agricultural and domestic workers from the National Labor Relations Act—a legacy of the 1930s compromise with Southern segregationists—is a statutory ban on the most effective form of assembly: collective bargaining. The law says, in effect, "You may gather, but your gathering has no legal force." It strips the collective of its power, reducing the workforce to a collection of vulnerable individuals.

The Slave Codes also deputized the entire white population as enforcers. Any white person could stop a Black person and demand their pass. Today, we have "E-Verify" and "No-Match Letters." We have laws in states like Texas and Florida that require hospitals to ask for immigration status, or that compel landlords to check papers. The state recruits the HR manager, the landlord, and the nurse to serve as the modern patrol.

We must also look at the criminalization of aid. In the 1850s, helping a runaway slave was a federal crime. Today, leaving water in the desert for migrants is prosecuted. Providing sanctuary in a church is legally fraught. The law seeks to isolate the undocumented person by criminalizing the act of human solidarity.

The Slave Codes defined the status of the child through the mother: *partus sequitur ventrem*. The child followed the condition of the womb. In modern immigration law, we see a complex inversion of this. The U.S.-born child is a citizen, but the mixed-status family is punished for that citizenship. The parent is "illegal," and therefore the family unit is unstable. The law punishes the biological bond, using the parent's status to impoverish the citizen child.

Finally, the Slave Codes created a separate judicial system. Enslaved people were often tried in special "slave courts" without juries or due process. Today, we have the immigration court system—Article I courts under the executive branch, not the independent judiciary. Here, as noted in Chapter 36, the normal protections of the Constitution are suspended. There is no right to counsel. Hearsay is admissible. The goal is administrative efficiency, not justice.

The Slave Codes were not static; they evolved in response to fears of rebellion. After the Nat Turner revolt, they became harsher. Similarly, modern immigration laws tighten in cycles of political panic. The Illegal Immigration Reform and Immigrant Responsibility Act of 1996 (IIRIRA) was the modern tightening of the screws, expanding the grounds for deportation and stripping judges of discretion.

We are living under a new set of codes designed to manage a new caste. They are codes of containment. They are designed to ensure that the labor is available but the laborer is disposable. They construct a legal reality where a human being can be essential to the economy but illegal to the state. Until we dismantle this architecture—until we align our laws with the reality of our economy and the principles of our Constitution—we are merely updating the statute book of slavery for the digital age.

Chapter 38: The Overseer vs. The Foreman

In the visual hierarchy of the American plantation, the most terrifying figure was often not the master. The master was a distant authority, a man who lived in the Big House, concerned with ledgers, cotton prices, and politics. The figure who inhabited the nightmares of the enslaved was the overseer, or more intimately, the "driver." He was the man on the horse, the man with the whip, the immediate, breathing presence of control. He was the interface between the capital of the owner and the body of the worker.

Today, on the tomato farms of Florida, the construction sites of Nevada, and the slaughterhouses of Iowa, that figure has returned. He does not ride a horse; he drives a white Ford F-150. He does not carry a whip; he carries a clipboard or an iPad. He is called the foreman, the crew leader, the *capataz*, or the *mayordomo*. But his function remains perfectly preserved from the nineteenth century: he is the mechanism by which the impossible demands of the market are translated into the physical exhaustion of the worker.

To understand the durability of this role, we must look at the specific architecture of control used in antebellum slavery. As PBS documents in its analysis of plantation conditions, discipline was enforced through a chain of command involving "drivers, overseers, and masters." The driver was often an enslaved man himself, promoted to a position of authority over his peers. He was given minor privileges—better food, a cabin of his own, perhaps a slightly larger ration of whiskey—in exchange for a terrible duty: he was responsible for maintaining the pace of the work and administering punishment.

This system served a dual purpose. First, it maximized production. The driver knew the capacity of his fellow slaves better than any white overseer could. He knew who was faking illness, who was strong, and who was hiding. He could extract the last ounce of effort because he knew exactly where it was hidden.

Second, and more insidiously, it fractured the solidarity of the workforce. By elevating one member of the oppressed group and giving them power over the others, the master created a class of collaborators. The anger of the field hands was often directed at the driver—the traitor in their midst—rather than at the distant master who orchestrated the entire system.

The modern exploitation economy has replicated this structure with devastating fidelity. In industries dominated by undocumented labor, the direct supervisor is almost never a white English-speaker. He is a man from the same country, often the same region, and sometimes the same village as the workers he commands. He speaks their dialect. He understands their cultural codes. He knows the names of their children back home.

This shared identity is not a source of solidarity; it is a tool of extraction. The modern "driver" uses his cultural fluency to manipulate, coerce, and silence his crew in ways a white manager never could.

Consider the dynamic on a residential framing crew. The developer—the "master" in this analogy—sets a price and a schedule that are objectively unreasonable. He demands a house be framed in three days for a fixed sum. He does not scream at the workers to run faster; he simply tells the crew leader, "Get it done, or you don't get the next contract."

The pressure travels downward. The crew leader, whose own livelihood depends on meeting this impossible metric, turns on his men. He uses the specific leverage of their shared background. "Come on, *paisanos*," he might say, invoking national solidarity. "Don't be lazy. Show them how we work." When that fails, he shifts to threats that are specifically calibrated to their vulnerabilities. "If you slow down, I know where you live. I know your family in Michoacán."

Because the foreman often doubles as the recruiter—the "coyote" or smuggler discussed in earlier chapters—he holds the debt. He is not just the boss; he is the creditor. The worker cannot defy the foreman because the foreman controls the remittances that keep the worker's children alive. The authority is total because the dependency is total.

This structure allows the corporate entities at the top of the supply chain to maintain a "moral distance" from the brutality on the ground. This is the modern version of the planter sitting on his veranda while the driver whips a slave in the distant field. The CEO of a major poultry producer or a national homebuilder can honestly say, "We have a strict code of conduct. We do not tolerate abuse." And in their corporate offices, they don't.

But they hire the middleman—the labor contractor or the staffing agency—specifically to do the dirty work. They outsource the enforcement of discipline. When a foreman screams at a female worker, denies a bathroom break, or shaves hours off a timecard, he is doing exactly what the system requires him to do to meet the price point set by the CEO. He is the shock absorber for the cruelty of the market.

In the legal realm, the foreman serves as the "fall guy." When the Department of Labor investigates a case of wage theft or child labor, the trail often stops at the crew leader. The large corporation claims, "We paid the contractor in full. We didn't know he wasn't paying his people." The contractor is fined, perhaps even prosecuted. He dissolves his LLC, declares bankruptcy, and disappears. The corporation hires a new contractor the next day. The structure remains intact because the foreman is disposable.

The "straw boss" dynamic is particularly prevalent in the agricultural sector. Here, the power of the *mayordomo* is absolute because the isolation is absolute. In a rural labor camp, the foreman controls access to food, medicine, and transportation. He decides who gets the "good rows" (where the crops are plentiful and money can be made on the piece rate) and who gets the "bad rows" (where the picking is slow and the wages are starvation-level).

This power to allocate opportunity creates a patronage system. Workers must curry favor with the foreman to survive. This often leads to a culture of bribery and sexual exploitation. Female farmworkers frequently report that they must engage in sexual acts with crew leaders to keep their jobs or get assigned to decent fields. This is the *droit du seigneur* of the tomato patch, a feudal right exercised by the petty tyrant of the labor camp.

The psychological toll on the foreman himself is a complex element of this tragedy. In many cases, he was once a picker or a laborer. He rose through the ranks by being faster, tougher, or more compliant than his peers. He views his position as a hard-won achievement, a precarious foothold in the middle class.

But his position is fragile. He knows that he is only useful to the "Big Boss" as long as he delivers the numbers. If the harvest is slow, he is blamed. If the workers organize, he is fired. He punches down because he is being crushed from above. He is the classic middle-management functionary of a totalitarian system, enforcing rules he did not write to protect a position he can lose in an instant.

This precariousness makes him vicious. A foreman who feels secure might be lenient. A foreman who is terrified of losing his truck and his contract will drive his crew to the breaking point. The anxiety of the undocumented status—even if the foreman himself has achieved some form of residency, his crew likely hasn't—creates a pressure cooker where violence becomes the default management tool.

The use of ethnic affinity as a weapon is perhaps the most cynical aspect of this arrangement. Employers specifically hire foremen from indigenous communities to manage indigenous workers, or Haitians to manage Haitians, utilizing the specific social hierarchies of the home country to enforce discipline in the U.S. In the fields of California, Mixteco-speaking foremen are used to manage Mixteco pickers, exploiting internal caste systems that predate the Spanish conquest. The American plantation absorbs and repurposes every form of inequality it touches.

We must also confront the role of the foreman in the "company store" model. Often, the foreman runs the side hustles that extract wealth from the workers. He sells the beer, the cigarettes, and the phone cards. He operates the van that charges for rides to the laundromat. He acts as the predatory lender, advancing cash at usurious interest rates. He is the gatekeeper of the local economy, taxing the very wages he hands out.

This creates a closed loop of exploitation. The worker earns money from the foreman and spends it back to the foreman. The capital never leaves the ecosystem of control. This mirrors the post-Reconstruction peonage of the South, where the sharecropper was perpetually indebted to the planter's merchant. Today, the merchant is the guy driving the van.

In the construction industry, the foreman is the linchpin of the "independent contractor" fraud. He is the one who hands out the 1099 forms. He is the one who tells the workers, "No taxes taken out today, lucky you." He frames the loss of rights as a benefit, using his influence to sell the deception. He coaches the workers on what to say if an inspector shows up: "Tell them you own your own business." He is the instructor in the curriculum of silence.

The historical continuity is undeniable. The antebellum "driver" was a tragic figure, a victim turned victimizer, trapped in a system where his only path to relative safety was the betrayal of his own people. The modern foreman occupies the same moral gray zone. He is the hands of the exploitation machine.

But we must not mistake the hands for the head. The foreman does not set the line speed at the poultry plant. He does not determine the market price of a bushel of apples. He does not write the contracts that indemnify the developer. He is merely the instrument of those decisions.

To focus solely on the cruelty of the crew leader is to miss the systemic nature of the crime. We arrest the foreman for trafficking, but we leave the supply chain that demanded the trafficking intact. We punish the middleman for delivering exactly what the market ordered: cheap, compliant, disposable labor.

The foreman is the visible face of abuse, but the invisible face—the corporate board, the private equity firm, the consumer demanding the lowest price—is the true architect of the plantation. The foreman is just the one holding the whip; the order to strike comes from much higher up. Until we hold the "masters" accountable for the actions of their "drivers," the hierarchy of the plantation will remain the operating system of the American shadow economy.

Chapter 39: Physical Chains vs. Paper Chains

The popular iconography of American slavery is dominated by metallurgy. When we visualize the loss of freedom, we see iron collars, ball-and-chain restraints, wrist shackles, and the intricate, terrifying architecture of the barracoon. We associate bondage with the weight of metal against skin. This imagery is accurate to the historical reality of the nineteenth century, but it has become a liability in the twenty-first. It has trained us to look for the wrong evidence. We scan the wrists and ankles of the workers in our fields and factories, and finding no iron, we declare them free.

We fail to see that the technology of enslavement has undergone a revolution. The modern slaveholder has discovered a fundamental inefficiency in the use of physical restraints: iron is heavy, expensive, and visible. It requires blacksmiths to forge and guards to monitor. It leaves marks that can be photographed and used as evidence in court. Most critically, it provokes a visceral moral outrage in the observer. A man in chains is undeniably a victim; a man in a uniform is presumed to be an employee.

To solve this inefficiency, the exploitation economy has transitioned from physical chains to paper chains.

This evolution represents a technological leap comparable to the shift from steam power to digital networks. Paper chains—in the form of debt ledgers, confiscated passports, tied visas, and the lack of legal status—are lighter, cheaper, and stronger than iron. They do not restrict the movement of the limbs; they restrict the movement of the life. They bind the worker not to a specific post, but to a specific vulnerability. And unlike iron, which must be forced upon the victim, paper chains are often forged with the victim's signature.

The economic logic of this transition is ruthless. In 1860, a prime field hand cost approximately $1,800—the equivalent of roughly $60,000 to $80,000 in today's currency. This high capital cost dictated the terms of physical bondage. The slave was a valuable asset, a piece of capital equipment that the master had to protect. If a slave ran away, the master lost a significant investment. This necessitated walls, dogs, and patrols—the infrastructure of physical containment.

Today, the cost of acquiring an undocumented worker is effectively zero for the employer. The worker pays for their own transport. The worker pays the smuggler. The worker arrives at the factory gate carrying a debt that functions as a self-enforcing shackle. If this worker runs away or is broken by the work, the employer loses nothing. He simply hires the next person in line.

This shift from "capital investment" to "disposable input" required a new mechanism of control. Physical chains are designed to keep valuable property from escaping. Paper chains are designed to keep disposable people from complaining.

The strongest link in this new chain is the debt contract. As I analyzed in Chapter 4, the debt incurred to cross the border or secure a job functions as a "negative dowry" that the worker brings to the employment relationship . A worker who owes $15,000 to a smuggler is not free to leave a job that pays sub-minimum wage, because leaving means defaulting, and defaulting means violence against their family back home.

This financial restraint is far more effective than a physical wall. A wall can be climbed. A debt cannot be outrun. It travels with the worker, a psychological weight that presses down on every decision. The employer does not need to hire guards to keep the worker in the field; the debt does the guarding for him. The worker wakes up every morning and puts on the yoke voluntarily, driven by the terror of the ledger.

The second link is the document. The passport, the visa, or the lack thereof, defines the radius of the worker's existence. In the antebellum South, the "pass system" controlled movement; a slave caught off the plantation without a written pass was subject to capture. Today, the lack of a driver's license or a valid visa serves the exact same function.

When a labor broker confiscates a worker's passport "for safekeeping," he has effectively locked the worker in a cell the size of the United States. The worker cannot board a plane. They cannot enter a government building. They cannot legally rent an apartment or open a bank account. They are physically free to walk down the street, but legally paralyzed. The confiscation of the document is the theft of the legal self. As the State Department has noted, this tactic is the primary means of coercion in modern trafficking because it is bloodless and silent.

For the millions of undocumented workers who never had a visa to begin with, the "paper chain" is the absence of paper. The lack of legal status creates a "prison without walls." The perimeter of this prison is defined by the reach of the surveillance state. The worker knows that driving past a police car, entering a hospital, or applying for a better job could trigger the digital tripwire of deportation.

This fear performs the work of the overseer. In the 19th century, the overseer rode a horse and carried a whip to ensure the pace of work. Today, the employer simply mentions "La Migra." The threat of the state replaces the violence of the individual. The employer outsources the cost of enforcement to the taxpayer-funded deportation apparatus. He does not need to whip the worker; he only needs to remind them that the government will destroy their life if they step out of line.

This reliance on state terror as a labor discipline tool is the ultimate efficiency of the paper chain. The taxpayer funds the ICE raids, the detention centers, and the border patrols that keep the workforce terrified and compliant. The employer captures the profit of the cheap labor while the public bears the cost of the coercion.

The "tying" provision of the H-2A and H-2B visa programs represents the paper chain in its most bureaucratic form. Here, the government explicitly writes the bondage into the law. The worker's legal right to exist in the country is contractually tied to a single employer. If they quit, they become illegal. This is indentured servitude codified by statute. The visa is a leash, and the employer holds the handle. A worker on an H-2A visa who faces sexual harassment or wage theft cannot simply walk away and find a new job; they must choose between endurance and deportation.

Comparing the psychological impact of these two systems reveals a disturbing paradox: paper chains can be more damaging to the psyche than iron ones. Physical enslavement is an external condition; the slave knows they are being held by force. Paper slavery often masquerades as choice. The worker "chose" to sign the debt contract. They "chose" to cross the border. They "chose" to accept the visa conditions.

This illusion of choice creates a sense of personal failure and shame that physical slavery did not. The trafficker gaslights the victim: "You agreed to this. You owe me." The victim internalizes the oppression, believing they are honor-bound to pay a fraudulent debt. This is why we see the phenomenon of "Stockholm Syndrome in the fields," where workers defend their exploiters. The paper chain entangles the worker's sense of honor and obligation, turning their own morality against them.

Furthermore, the paper chain allows the exploiter to maintain a self-image of benevolence. The antebellum master could not deny the violence of his position; he owned people. The modern CEO of a construction firm or a sprawling agribusiness can claim, "I don't own anyone. These are independent contractors. They can leave anytime they want."

This "plausible deniability" is the distinct advantage of the modern system. The paper chain is constructed of shell companies, subcontractors, and staffing agencies that act as legal buffers. The iron chain connected the master directly to the slave. The paper chain is long, winding, and designed to break if anyone pulls on it too hard, leaving the worker holding the liability while the profits flow upward.

We must also consider the durability of the paper chain. An iron chain can be cut. A physical escape, once successful, is often final. But how do you escape a digital record? How do you outrun a biometric database? The modern worker who flees an abusive employer leaves a digital trail. If they are undocumented, their biometrics are often in a federal database. If they are H-2A, their "absconding" is reported to the government, barring them from future legal work.

The paper chain follows the worker even after they have left the field. It creates a permanent record of vulnerability. The "blacklist" used by agricultural recruiters ensures that a worker who strikes or complains in North Carolina will be denied a job in Mexico the following season. The control extends across borders and through time, enforced by the flow of data rather than the reach of the patrol.

The transition from physical to paper chains also explains why modern slavery is so difficult to prosecute. A jury can see the bruises from a beating. They can see the padlock on the door. It is much harder to show a jury the coercion inherent in a complex web of debt, visa regulations, and cultural obligation. The prosecutor must prove the "invisible force" that kept the worker in the field. They must explain why a person who was physically free to walk to the road was psychologically unable to do so.

This is why the "Modern Slavery" terminology, while accurate, is often resisted. We are trained to look for the whip. When we see a worker with a smartphone, we assume they are free. We do not see that the phone is being monitored by the trafficker. We do not see the text messages threatening their children. We do not see the spreadsheet that shows their debt increasing every week.

The paper chain is the perfect technology for a neoliberal age. It turns human beings into contractual obligations. It financializes the soul. It allows the economy to consume the labor of millions without ever having to acknowledge their humanity.

As we close this examination of the historical mirror, the conclusion is stark: we have not abolished slavery; we have merely modernized it. We have engineered a system that delivers all the economic benefits of the plantation—cheap, reliable, compliant labor—without the capital investment or the moral stigma of ownership.

We have traded the overseer on the horse for the foreman with the spreadsheet. We have traded the bloodhound for the deportation officer. We have traded the iron collar for the tied visa. The mechanism has changed, but the result is the same: a class of people who are forced to work for the profit of others, held in place not by the laws of nature, but by the laws of men.

The paper chain is the ultimate accomplishment of the exploitation economy. It is invisible to those who benefit from it, yet unbreakable to those who wear it. To shatter it requires more than a bolt cutter; it requires a fundamental rewriting of the social contract that declares, once and for all, that no piece of paper can ever justify the ownership of a human being.

Part VII: The Collateral Damage
The societal cost.

Chapter 40: The Citizen Child

In a kindergarten classroom in El Paso, or a middle school in Nashville, or a high school in rural Iowa, the day begins with a ritual of assimilation. The bell rings. The students stand. They place their hands over their hearts and recite the Pledge of Allegiance. They promise loyalty to the flag and to the republic for which it stands, concluding with the assurance of "liberty and justice for all."

For most of the students, this is a rote exercise, a monotonous prelude to the morning announcements. But for a specific subset of the American student body, this ritual is a daily exercise in cognitive dissonance. They are pledging allegiance to a flag that represents the entity they fear most in the world. They are citizens of a republic that is actively hunting their parents.

There are approximately 5.9 million children in the United States who occupy this precarious dual reality. They are U.S. citizens by birth, holders of the same blue passports as the President or the Chief Justice. They are constitutionally entitled to every right and privilege of American membership. Yet they go to sleep every night knowing that the federal government possesses the power to orphan them by morning.

These are the "citizen children" of the undocumented workforce. They represent nearly 10 percent of all families with children in the United States. They are not a niche demographic; they are a generation. And we are systematically dismantling their future to punish their parents.

To understand the collateral damage of our immigration policy, we must look away from the border and into the developing brain of a six-year-old. Childhood development relies on a foundation of "felt safety." A child needs to know that their caregivers are secure in order to explore the world, learn new concepts, and form healthy relationships. When that foundation is cracked, the architecture of the mind shifts from growth to survival.

The medical profession has a specific term for the environment in which these children live: "toxic stress." As research from the Harvard Center on the Developing Child has established, this is not merely a mood; it is a physiological state. When a child lives in constant fear that their mother will not return from her shift at the poultry plant, or that their father will be pulled out of his construction van by police, their body is flooded with stress hormones like cortisol and adrenaline.

In short bursts, these chemicals are adaptive; they help us survive danger. But when the system is activated 24 hours a day, 365 days a year, the chemicals become corrosive. They attack the body from the inside. They disrupt the formation of neural connections in the prefrontal cortex, the area of the brain responsible for impulse control, planning, and complex learning
.

We are effectively chemically lobotomizing a generation of American citizens. We are creating a cohort of children whose brains are wired for threat detection rather than algebra or literature. The American Immigration Council notes that these children exhibit rates of anxiety, depression, and Post-Traumatic Stress Disorder (PTSD) that mirror those seen in children from war zones. They suffer from sleep disturbances, aggression, and withdrawal. They are fighting a war on American soil, but the battlefield is their own living room.

The impact of this trauma is not limited to childhood. The longitudinal health data paints a grim picture of the future we are manufacturing. High levels of adverse childhood experiences (ACEs) are causally linked to chronic diseases in adulthood. The terrified ten-year-old becomes the forty-year-old with heart disease, diabetes, and a shortened life expectancy. By terrorizing these children now, we are creating a massive public health liability for the future—a bill that will be paid by the Medicare and Medicaid systems decades from now.

But the damage is not just biological; it is educational. The schoolhouse, which should be a sanctuary of opportunity, becomes another zone of anxiety. When immigration enforcement ramps up in a community—when rumors of a raid circulate on WhatsApp, or when ICE vehicles are spotted near a bus stop—attendance plummets.

Educators report that following enforcement actions, classrooms empty out. Parents keep their children home, fearing that the drive to school is too dangerous or that the school itself might be targeted. Even when the children attend, their minds are elsewhere. A child who is worried about whether their parents are safe cannot conjugate verbs or memorize the periodic table. The "achievement gap" that plagues Latino students in many districts is, in significant part, a "fear gap." It is the measurable difference between a student who can focus on the blackboard and a student who is watching the door.

This educational sabotage is compounded by economic devastation. The citizen child is the primary victim of the wage theft and exploitation documented throughout this book. When a parent is paid sub-minimum wage, the child goes hungry. When a parent is injured and denied workers' compensation, the family loses its housing.

The American Immigration Council has quantified the economic cliff that these families face. If an undocumented breadwinner is deported, the household income drops by an average of 70 percent within six months. This is a catastrophic collapse. It transforms a working-poor family into a destitute one overnight. The research estimates that nearly one million households with U.S. citizen children would fall below the poverty line if their undocumented earners were removed.

This poverty is not a result of parental negligence; it is a result of state action. We are actively manufacturing poverty among American citizens. We are taking families that are self-sufficient, however precariously, and pushing them into the social safety net. The child who was eating food bought with their father's wages is forced to rely on SNAP benefits. The family that was paying rent is forced into a shelter.

The cruelty reaches its apex in the legal anomaly of "de facto deportation." When a single parent is deported, they face an impossible choice: take their U.S. citizen child with them to a country the child has never known, often a place of violence and poverty, or leave the child behind in the U.S. foster care system.

Thousands of American children have effectively been exiled by this policy. They grow up in rural Guatemala or Mexico, stripped of the advantages of their birthright, unable to access the American education or healthcare to which they are entitled. They are citizens in exile, punished for the status of their parents.

Alternatively, those who stay behind enter the foster care system, a state apparatus ill-equipped to deal with the trauma of separation. As discussed in Chapter 24, the threat of this separation is used to discipline labor. But for the child, the *reality* of separation is a death of the self. To be torn from a loving parent and placed with strangers because the government declared the parent "illegal" creates a wound that never heals. It teaches the child a devastating lesson about their own country: that the law is an enemy of love.

This dynamic creates a profound crisis of identity and allegiance. How do we expect these children to grow up into patriotic, engaged citizens when their formative experience of the state is one of terror? We are raising a generation of Americans who view the police, the courts, and the government not as protectors, but as predators. We are eroding the social contract for millions of future voters, workers, and leaders.

The defenders of the current system often argue that this suffering is the fault of the parents—that by bringing their children here or having them here illegally, they "chose" this risk. This argument relies on a concept of "corruption of blood" that the U.S. Constitution explicitly rejects. We do not punish children for the crimes of their fathers. We do not deny rights to a citizen because of their lineage.

To punish a six-year-old for the immigration violations of their mother is a moral abomination. To construct an entire economy that relies on the labor of the mother while systematically traumatizing the child is a societal suicide pact.

The economic loss alone is staggering. As economists Mark Rank and Michael McLaughlin found, child poverty costs the U.S. economy over $1 trillion annually in lost productivity, increased crime, and health expenditures. By maintaining policies that keep the children of immigrants poor and traumatized, we are burning human capital. We are ensuring that these children will earn less, pay fewer taxes, and require more social services than they would if their parents were legalized.

We look at these children and see "anchor babies" or "liabilities." We should see future doctors, engineers, and teachers. We should see the demographic salvation of an aging nation. But potential is fragile. It requires stability to grow. By denying that stability to the citizen child, we are robbing ourselves.

The classroom bell rings. The pledge ends. The child sits down and opens their book, trying to learn the history of a nation that wishes they did not exist, trying to solve math problems while calculating the odds of their own survival. They are the collateral damage of our addiction to cheap labor, the human cost we have decided is acceptable to pay for a lower overhead. They are Americans, and we are failing them.

Chapter 41: Educational Trauma

The schoolhouse is the cornerstone of the American promise. It is the one institution where, theoretically, the accident of birth is neutralized by the opportunity of merit. In the classroom, the son of a billionaire and the daughter of a janitor open the same textbook, take the same test, and are graded on the same scale. We tell ourselves that education is the great equalizer, the ladder by which the poor climb into the middle class.

But for the children of the undocumented workforce, the ladder is missing rungs. The school is not a sanctuary; it is a surveillance zone. It is a place where the trauma of the home follows the student into the hallway, where the fear of deportation colonizes the mind, and where the "achievement gap" is revealed to be a scar of systemic terror.

To understand educational trauma, we must first understand the cognitive load of fear. Learning requires a brain that is calm, focused, and secure. It requires the ability to ignore the immediate environment and engage with abstract concepts. A child who is worried about whether their mother will be home when the bus drops them off cannot perform this mental leap. Their brain is stuck in the limbic system, scanning for threats.

Educators in immigrant communities report a specific, heartbreaking phenomenon: the "empty chair." When rumors of an ICE raid circulate—often amplified by social media or local news—classrooms empty out. Parents keep their children home, fearing that the drive to school is too dangerous, or that agents might target the school itself. Even though ICE has a policy of avoiding "sensitive locations" like schools, the trust is gone. The parents know that policies can change, and agents can go rogue.

This absenteeism is not truancy; it is a survival strategy. But its educational cost is catastrophic. A child who misses three days of school every time a raid rumor surfaces falls behind. They miss the introduction of fractions. They miss the chapter on the Civil War. They return to a class that has moved on without them. Over the course of a year, these gaps accumulate. The student is present in body but absent in curriculum.

Even when the child is physically present, they are often psychologically absent. Teachers describe students who are withdrawn, hyper-vigilant, or prone to sudden outbursts of aggression. These are the classic symptoms of Post-Traumatic Stress Disorder (PTSD). But unlike a soldier returning from war, these children are still on the battlefield. The threat is not a memory; it is a daily probability.

This trauma is compounded by the economic exploitation of the parents. As documented in previous chapters, undocumented workers are often paid sub-minimum wages and denied overtime. This poverty translates directly into educational disadvantage. The child goes to school hungry because the pantry is empty. They do not have a quiet place to do homework because three families are sharing a two-bedroom apartment to afford rent. They do not have internet access to complete online assignments because the parent cannot get a contract without a social security number.

Furthermore, the "mobility" of the migrant workforce disrupts educational continuity. When a parent follows the harvest from Florida to Michigan, or moves from a construction site in Texas to one in Colorado, the child moves too. They are pulled out of one school and dropped into another, often mid-semester. Curricula do not align. Credits do not transfer. The child is perpetually the "new kid," struggling to catch up, socially isolated, and academically adrift.

The language barrier adds another layer of difficulty. Many children of recent arrivals are English Language Learners (ELL). To succeed, they need specialized instruction. But schools in high-poverty districts—precisely where these families live—are often underfunded and understaffed. The child sits in a mainstream classroom, unable to understand the lesson, silent and ashamed.

The "school-to-deportation" pipeline is a specific, terrifying mechanism that links disciplinary issues to immigration enforcement. In some jurisdictions, School Resource Officers (SROs)—sworn police officers stationed in schools—share information with local law enforcement, who in turn share it with ICE. A fight in the cafeteria, a truancy violation, or a minor act of vandalism can trigger a chain reaction.

If a student is arrested, their immigration status (or that of their parents) can be exposed. The school, intended to be a site of correction and growth, becomes a funnel into the detention system. Parents know this. They warn their children: "Do not draw attention to yourself. Do not get in trouble. Do not speak up."

This enforced passivity destroys the educational experience. We want students to raise their hands, to debate, to challenge ideas. But the undocumented child is taught that visibility is dangerous. They learn to be small, quiet, and unnoticed. They do not join the debate team. They do not run for student council. They self-censor their own potential to protect their family.

The trauma extends to higher education. For the "Dreamers"— undocumented students brought to the U.S. as children—high school graduation is often a collision with a brick wall. They see their peers applying for college, filling out the FAFSA for federal financial aid, and planning their futures. But the undocumented student is ineligible for federal aid. In many states, they are ineligible for in-state tuition.

They realize, often in their senior year, that the meritocracy was a lie. Their grades do not matter. their hard work does not matter. The door is locked. This realization can lead to profound depression and disengagement. Why study for the SATs if you cannot go to college? Why strive for excellence if your destiny is the same tomato field or dish pit where your parents labor?

This despair is a loss not just for the student, but for the nation. We have invested thirteen years of public education in these children. We have paid for their teachers, their books, and their lunches. To then deny them the opportunity to use that education is a spectacular waste of human capital. We are training engineers and then forcing them to be busboys. We are educating nurses and then forcing them to be housekeepers.

The Deferred Action for Childhood Arrivals (DACA) program offered a temporary reprieve, proving the economic case for inclusion. DACA recipients went to college, started businesses, and entered professions. They showed what is possible when the fear is lifted. But DACA is a fragile, temporary fix, subject to the whims of the courts and the executive branch. It is a band-aid on a hemorrhage.

We must also confront the bullying that occurs in the shadow of political rhetoric. When national leaders demonize immigrants, that language filters down to the playground. Children are told by their peers to "go back to Mexico" or that "ICE is coming for you." This harassment creates a hostile learning environment where the child feels unsafe and unwanted. The school becomes a site of rejection rather than belonging.

The educational system itself is often complicit. School administrators, facing budget cuts and overcrowding, may subtly discourage the enrollment of immigrant children. They may demand documents they are not legally allowed to ask for, or fail to provide translation services for parents. They view these students as burdens rather than assets.

But the data tells a different story. Immigrant children are often highly motivated. They possess "immigrant optimism"—a drive to succeed to justify their parents' sacrifice. When given the chance, they outperform their native-born peers. They are the demographic engine that can revitalize aging communities and fill the skills gap in the economy.

By traumatizing them, we are sabotaging this engine. We are taking the most ambitious, resilient population in our schools and crushing their spirit. We are creating a self-fulfilling prophecy of an underclass.

The cost of this educational trauma will be paid for decades. A student who drops out of high school earns significantly less over their lifetime, pays fewer taxes, and is more likely to rely on social services or enter the criminal justice system. By failing to educate these children, we are creating a future liability for the state.

More importantly, we are failing the moral test of our society. A child is not responsible for their immigration status. They are not responsible for the labor market. They are responsible only for learning. When we make that impossible—when we fill their backpacks with fear instead of books—we are betraying the fundamental covenant of the schoolhouse. We are teaching them that in America, some children are the future, and others are just debris.

Chapter 42: The Public Health Risk

In the epidemiology of a pandemic, or even a seasonal flu, the virus operates as a biological detective. It seeks out the cracks in a society's infrastructure. It finds the overcrowded room, the unventilated factory floor, and the individual who cannot afford to stay home. It exploits weakness. And in the United States, there is no greater weakness in our public health armor than the existence of eleven million people who are terrified to see a doctor.

We tend to view healthcare as a private good—a commodity we purchase for ourselves and our families to ensure our own well-being. But communicable disease operates on a different logic. It is a public event. My health depends entirely on the health of the person standing next to me in the grocery line, the person cooking my food in the restaurant, and the person cleaning the hospital room where I recover.

By maintaining a massive, undocumented workforce that is systematically excluded from the healthcare system, we have created a biological time bomb. We have engineered a population that is incentivized to work while sick, forced to live in conditions that breed contagion, and terrified to seek treatment until they are at death's door. We have compromised the "herd immunity" of the nation to preserve the low cost of labor.

To understand the mechanics of this risk, we must look at the concept of "presenteeism." In the corporate world, this refers to the annoying colleague who comes to the office with a cold. In the undocumented labor market, it is a survival imperative.

As documented in the chapters on agriculture and meatpacking, these workers rarely have paid sick leave. If they do not work, they do not eat. But the coercion goes deeper. In many industries, the "point system" for attendance means that calling in sick is a strike against employment. Three strikes, and you are fired. Losing a job means losing company housing, which means homelessness and potential deportation.

Therefore, the undocumented worker does not call in sick. They take Tylenol to lower their fever so they can pass the thermal scanner at the plant entrance. They suppress their cough. They wrap their infected wounds in duct tape. They enter the workplace carrying the virus or the bacteria, not out of malice, but out of a desperate need to survive.

The workplace itself then acts as an incubator. In a poultry plant, where workers stand shoulder-to-shoulder in cold, damp air, a respiratory virus moves with terrifying speed. During the COVID-19 pandemic, this dynamic was laid bare. Meatpacking plants became the epicenters of community spread in the Midwest and South. The virus did not magically appear in these facilities; it was carried in by workers who had no other choice, and it was spread by an industrial architecture designed for density and speed.

The industry's response was often to put up plastic dividers and hand out masks, but they refused to slow the line or offer paid leave that would allow sick workers to stay home. The result was mass infection that spilled over into the surrounding towns. The rural hospitals of Nebraska and Georgia were overwhelmed not just by workers, but by the teachers, nurses, and shopkeepers they interacted with. The health of the undocumented worker proved to be inextricably linked to the health of the citizen.

The risk is compounded by the housing conditions I described in Chapter 7. When wages are low and rents are high, workers crowd into high-density living arrangements. It is common to find three families sharing a two-bedroom apartment, or a dozen single men in a trailer. In some migrant communities, "hot bedding" is practiced—workers on the night shift sleep in the beds vacated by workers on the day shift. The sheets never cool down.

From an epidemiological perspective, this is a catastrophe. If one person in that household contracts tuberculosis, meningitis, or influenza, everyone contracts it. There is no "quarantine room" in a trailer sleeping ten people. The disease rips through the household and then radiates out to the multiple workplaces where the occupants labor.

The specific threat of tuberculosis (TB) deserves careful attention. TB is a disease of poverty and overcrowding. It has been largely eradicated in the U.S. general population, but it persists in the shadows. Treating TB requires a strict regimen of antibiotics taken over six to nine months. If the treatment is interrupted, the bacteria can mutate into Multi-Drug Resistant TB (MDR-TB), a strain that is incredibly difficult and expensive to treat and highly lethal.

The current immigration enforcement regime makes effective TB treatment nearly impossible for the undocumented. A patient must visit a clinic regularly for months. But if that patient fears that the clinic is a trap, or if they are forced to move to follow the harvest, or if they are deported mid-treatment, the regimen breaks.

When we deport a person with active, partially treated TB, we are not solving a health problem; we are exporting a biological hazard and potentially creating a superbug. That person may return to the U.S. (as many do), carrying a resistant strain that does not respond to our standard medicines. By prioritizing deportation over public health continuity, we are actively sabotaging disease control.

The "chilling effect" of anti-immigrant rhetoric has created a shadow healthcare system that operates outside of regulation. In neighborhoods like Jackson Heights in Queens or East Los Angeles, you can walk into a *botanica* or a backroom of a grocery store and buy antibiotics brought in from abroad. These medicines are sold without prescription, without dosage instructions, and often without quality control.

Workers self-medicate because the legitimate system is walled off. They take antibiotics for viral infections, contributing to the global crisis of antibiotic resistance. They receive injections from unlicensed practitioners. This is not because they prefer "folk medicine"; it is because the front door of American medicine is locked to them.

Even the public health infrastructure that is supposed to be accessible—county health departments, vaccination drives—is viewed with deep suspicion. When the Trump administration expanded the "Public Charge" rule, suggesting that using public benefits could disqualify an immigrant from a green card, it sent a shockwave through the community. Even though the rule has been legally contested and modified, the fear remains.

Mothers stopped bringing their U.S. citizen children to clinics for standard vaccinations—measles, mumps, rubella—fearing that their name on a government list would trigger a raid. We are now seeing the resurgence of preventable diseases in these communities. A measles outbreak does not check papers. It jumps from the unvaccinated child of an undocumented worker to the child of a citizen in the same kindergarten class. The "herd immunity" we rely on is fractured by the fear we have instilled.

The food safety implications of this excluded workforce are equally disturbing. We entrust our food supply—the vegetables we eat raw, the meat we serve our families—to the hands of the very people we deny healthcare to.

In the fields, as noted in Chapter 15, hygiene facilities are often inadequate. In the processing plants, workers are denied bathroom breaks. Combine this with the pressure to work while sick with gastrointestinal illnesses like Norovirus or Hepatitis A, and you have a recipe for foodborne outbreaks. When we hear of an E. coli outbreak linked to romaine lettuce, we focus on the bacteria. We rarely focus on the labor conditions that made hygiene impossible for the picker.

We cannot have a safe food supply if the people handling the food are sick, terrified, and denied access to toilets. Food safety is labor safety.

The defenders of the status quo argue that providing healthcare to undocumented immigrants would be a burden on the taxpayer. This is the "fiscal drain" argument. But as we saw in the chapter on the Healthcare Subsidy, we are *already* paying for their healthcare—we are just paying for it in the most expensive way possible, in the emergency room, after the disease has advanced or spread.

Proactive public health—vaccinations, prenatal care, early treatment of chronic conditions—is infinitely cheaper than reactive emergency care. Treating high blood pressure costs pennies a day. Treating a stroke costs tens of thousands. By denying the former, we guarantee the latter.

Furthermore, the "burden" argument ignores the cost of contagion. What is the cost to the economy of a flu season that is extended by weeks because a segment of the workforce cannot isolate? What is the cost of a localized TB outbreak? These costs are borne by businesses in lost productivity and by the public in medical expenses.

The solution requires a "firewall" between public health and immigration enforcement. A doctor's office must be a sanctuary. A vaccination record cannot be a deportation lead. But more than that, it requires bringing this population into the insurance pool.

If undocumented workers were legalized, they would be eligible for employer-sponsored insurance or could purchase plans on the exchange. They would have a primary care doctor. They would get flu shots. They would manage their chronic conditions. They would stop being vectors of untreated illness and start being partners in public health.

The lesson of the pandemic was unambiguous: biology connects us. The air in the meatpacking plant is the same air that circulates in the town. The health of the "essential" worker dictates the health of the community. We cannot build a wall against a virus.

By maintaining a caste of workers who are legally excluded from the right to be healthy, we are engaging in a grotesque experiment. We are testing whether a nation can remain robust while keeping ten million of its residents in a state of medical apartheid. The results are in, written in the excess deaths of the working poor and the vulnerability of the entire population. We are only as healthy as the sickest person we refuse to treat.

Chapter 43: Erosion of the Rule of Law

The phrase "Rule of Law" is perhaps the most revered incantation in American civic life. It is the bedrock principle upon which the Republic stands: the idea that no person is above the law, no person is below it, and that the statutes written by the legislature apply equally to the billionaire and the beggar. We are taught that this principle is the firewall against tyranny and chaos. It is the invisible force that allows us to trust the contract, the court, and the cop on the beat.

But in the American labor market, the firewall has collapsed.

We have allowed a system to metastasize where the violation of federal law is not an aberration, but a standard operating procedure. We have created a sector of the economy where the "Rule of Law" has been replaced by the "Rule of Power." When we permit entire industries to build their business models on the systematic commission of felonies—tax evasion, visa fraud, perjury, and grand larceny in the form of wage theft—we are not just exploiting workers. We are poisoning the legal legitimacy of the state itself.

To understand this erosion, we must look beyond the statutes and into the culture they have spawned. We must examine the message that selective enforcement sends to the broader society. The asymmetry is stark: if an undocumented worker uses a fake Social Security number to get a job—a crime of survival—they face felony charges for identity theft, deportation, and a permanent ban from the United States. The law falls on them with its full, crushing weight.

But if an employer knowingly hires that worker to pay them sub-minimum wages, strips them of safety gear, and evades payroll taxes—crimes of profit—the law often responds with a shrug. The employer might face a civil fine, which they negotiate down and pay as a "cost of doing business." They do not lose their business license. They do not go to jail. They do not lose their right to operate in the American economy.

This asymmetry creates a culture of cynicism that radiates outward, infecting the broader society. The corrosion begins with the concept of the "open secret." In almost every American town, there are sites of known illegality: the construction site where no one wears a harness, the restaurant back-of-house where cash is king, the agricultural field where children work.

These are not clandestine operations; they are visible from the street. They operate in the daylight, often within view of the police station or the city hall.

When the state ignores these visible violations, it sends a message of tacit approval. It signals that certain laws—those protecting labor, safety, and tax revenue—are "optional." This is the definition of a "dead letter" law. The statutes remain on the books, promising protection and order, but they have been rendered void by the refusal to enforce them.

This selective enforcement destroys the competitive integrity of the market. In a functioning capitalist system, success should depend on efficiency, innovation, and quality. But as we have seen, our current system rewards criminality. The contractor who follows the law is driven out of business by the contractor who breaks it. We have created an economic environment where integrity is a liability. The honest business owner looks at their competitor—who is cheating on taxes, stealing wages, and winning contracts—and draws the only rational conclusion: *The law is for suckers.*

This realization is the death knell of a law-abiding society. When the "good guys" start cutting corners because they see the "bad guys" winning, the rot becomes systemic. We see this in the proliferation of "independent contractor" misclassification, a fraud that has moved from the fringes to the mainstream of corporate strategy. It is no longer just the shady crew leader; it is the national logistics company and the gig economy giant adopting the tactics of the black market. The logic of the shadow economy infects the legitimate economy, dragging standards down to the lowest common denominator.

The normalization of corporate lawbreaking also degrades the power of the contract. Contract law relies on the assumption that agreements will be enforced. But in the shadow economy, the employment contract is a fiction. The worker agrees to work for a wage, but the employer decides whether to pay it. The "Subcontracting Shield" allows major corporations to sign contracts forbidding exploitation while knowingly forcing price points that make exploitation inevitable. This renders the contract an instrument of deception rather than obligation. It transforms the written word of the law into a tool for "plausible deniability" rather than accountability.

When a society loses faith in the validity of contracts, trust evaporates. Business becomes a game of predation. The handshake deal becomes a risk. The written agreement becomes a trap.

Furthermore, this erosion compromises the integrity of our public officials. The existence of a massive underground economy creates opportunities for corruption at the local level. Inspectors can be bribed to look the other way. Sheriffs can be incentivized to target specific populations for political gain rather than public safety. The "rule of man"—the whim of the official—replaces the rule of law. We see this in small towns where local power brokers protect exploitative industries, creating fiefdoms where federal law is treated as a foreign suggestion.

By treating these systematic thefts as administrative nuisances, we are engaging in a form of "decriminalization for the rich." We have effectively decriminalized the theft of labor while hyper-criminalizing the theft of goods. If a worker steals $50 from the cash register, they leave in handcuffs. If the owner steals $50 from the worker's paycheck, it is a "civil dispute." This disparity reveals that our legal system prioritizes the protection of capital over the protection of people. It tells the worker that their property—their labor—is less valuable than the inventory on the shelf.

The long-term consequence is a loss of social cohesion. A society cannot function when a significant portion of its population believes the game is rigged. The anger of the displaced American worker is fueled by the correct perception that the rules are not being applied equally. They see the law failing to protect their wages while protecting the profits of those who undercut them. They see their communities hollowed out by an economic model that rewards the race to the bottom.

This breeds a dangerous populism that rejects institutions entirely. If the Department of Labor won't protect wages, and OSHA won't protect safety, why should anyone trust the government? If the courts protect the wage thief but punish the trespasser, why respect the judiciary? The erosion of the rule of law in the labor market contributes to a broader crisis of legitimacy for the American state.

We are teaching a generation of Americans—both citizens and immigrants—that laws are merely suggestions for those with power. We are validating the cynical view that justice is a commodity to be bought, not a right to be defended. We are creating a culture where "getting away with it" is seen as smart business, and compliance is seen as weakness.

Restoring the Rule of Law requires more than just "law and order" rhetoric directed at the border. It requires the "Hammer of the Law" to fall equally on the boardroom and the breakroom. It requires treating the white-collar criminal who steals wages with the same severity as the street criminal. It requires acknowledging that a business model built on the violation of federal statutes is not a business; it is a criminal enterprise, and it should be dismantled.

Until we do this, the "Rule of Law" will remain a hollow slogan, mocked by the reality of the daily harvest and the construction bid. We cannot have a law-abiding society built on a foundation of lawless labor. The integrity of our legal system depends on its universality. When we carve out exceptions for exploitation, we crack the foundation of the Republic itself.

Part VIII: The Abolition (Solutions)

How to end it.

Chapter 44: The "Minnesota Model" (Wage Theft as Felony)

For decades, the American legal system has operated on a quiet, unwritten consensus regarding the theft of labor. If a worker reaches into the cash register and takes fifty dollars, it is a crime, handled by police, prosecutors, and the penal code. If an owner reaches into a worker's paycheck and takes fifty dollars, it is a "dispute," handled by administrative clerks, civil fines, and the slow-moving machinery of bureaucracy.

This distinction has long served as a subsidy for the unscrupulous. It signaled that the property rights of the employer were sacrosanct, while the property rights of the worker—their right to the wages they earned—were negotiable. But in 2019, the state of Minnesota shattered this consensus. By passing the Wage Theft Prevention Act, the state declared that the theft of wages is not a misunderstanding or a clerical error; it is a felony, indistinguishable in the eyes of the law from grand larceny or embezzlement.

The "Minnesota Model" represents the most significant shift in labor enforcement in a generation because it attacks the root of the problem: the risk-reward calculation of the exploiter. Under the old civil system, the worst-case scenario for a wage thief was restitution—simply paying back what was stolen, perhaps with a modest penalty. It was an interest-free loan forced upon the worker. Under the Minnesota statute, the calculation changes violently. Intentional wage theft in excess of $1,000—a threshold that represents less than two weeks' pay for many workers—can now trigger imprisonment and a permanent criminal record.

The abstract power of this law became concrete reality in the case of Frederick Newell. In 2025, Newell, the owner of a painting company, became the first employer in the state to be convicted of felony wage theft. His crime was the theft of over $37,000 from five employees. These were men who had labored on his projects, expecting the compensation they were promised, only to be stiffed by the man who profited from their sweat.

In the pre-2019 era, Newell's actions would likely have resulted in a Department of Labor investigation. He might have negotiated a settlement, paid a portion of the wages years later, and continued to bid on contracts without a blemish on his personal record. The theft would have been a line item in his business expenses.

Instead, Newell faced the full weight of the criminal justice system. He stood before a judge not as a businessman involved in a dispute, but as a criminal defendant. His conviction was not a private administrative matter; it was a public branding. As legal experts have noted, criminal charges serve as a deterrent far stronger than civil penalties because they carry the unique stigma of incarceration and "significant reputational harm". A felony conviction is a bell that cannot be unrung. It appears on background checks. It disqualifies contractors from government bids. It makes securing a business loan or a surety bond nearly impossible.

The genius of the Minnesota Model lies in how it leverages the market to enforce the law. When wage theft is a felony, the "reputational harm" acts as a force multiplier. Banks do not want to lend to felons. General contractors do not want to hire subcontractors who might be arrested mid-project. The law effectively deputizes the entire business community to shun the wage thief, not out of morality, but out of risk management.

Critically, the law does not require the creation of a massive new police force. It utilizes the existing infrastructure of the criminal courts. It empowers prosecutors—who are elected and responsive to their communities—to take up the cause of workers who have been historically ignored. It transforms the county attorney into a labor enforcer.

The Minnesota experiment has proven that the "business climate" does not collapse when workers are protected. Honest employers have nothing to fear from a law that punishes theft; in fact, they benefit from the removal of competitors who undercut them by cheating. The only businesses that suffer are those whose models are predicated on fraud.

This shift is spreading. Following Minnesota's lead, states like California, Colorado, and Virginia have enacted their own criminal wage theft statutes, recognizing that civil remedies have failed to stem the tide of exploitation. This is how abolition happens: not always from the top down, but from the laboratories of the states, where innovative policies prove that the status quo is not inevitable.

By treating wage theft as a felony, we do more than punish individual bad actors like Frederick Newell. We restore the moral weight of the law. We assert that the money a roofer earns on a hot shingle is just as much their property as the car in the driveway or the money in the bank. We declare that the "taking" of labor is a violation of the social contract that demands the handcuffs, not just the fine. The Minnesota Model provides the blueprint for a national standard where the phrase "wage theft" is finally legally redundant, because the law simply calls it what it is: theft.

Chapter 45: Funding the Labor Police

In the taxonomy of American law enforcement, there is a clear hierarchy of prestige and power. At the top sit the Federal Bureau of Investigation and the Secret Service, agencies endowed with billion-dollar budgets, cutting-edge technology, and a cultural mythology that equates their work with the preservation of the Republic. Below them are the sprawling apparatuses of Homeland Security—Immigration and Customs Enforcement (ICE) and Customs and Border Protection (CBP)—which command fleets of drones, Blackhawk helicopters, and a combined budget that rivals the GDP of small nations.

At the very bottom of this hierarchy, effectively invisible to the public and starved by Congress, sits the "Labor Police."

They do not carry guns. They do not wear body armor. They are the investigators of the Department of Labor's Wage and Hour Division (WHD) and the Occupational Safety and Health Administration (OSHA). They are armed only with spreadsheets, calculators, and the dusty statutes of the Fair Labor Standards Act. Yet, in the fight against modern slavery, they are the only officers on the beat.

The central thesis of the abolitionist movement I propose is that exploitation thrives in a vacuum of enforcement. We have constructed a legal reality where the probability of being caught stealing wages or endangering workers is statistically indistinguishable from zero. To end this impunity, we must do more than rewrite laws; we must fund the people who enforce them. We must elevate the labor inspector to the same status as the border agent, backing them with the same resources, the same manpower, and the same political mandate to stop crime.

The current disparity is not a matter of penny-pinching; it is a policy of deliberate neglect. As Daniel Costa of the Economic Policy Institute has rigorously documented, the federal government spends nearly twelve times more on immigration enforcement than it does on all labor standards enforcement combined. We spend $25 billion annually to hunt the worker, and barely $2 billion to hunt the exploiter.

This ratio—12 to 1—is the mathematical expression of our national hypocrisy. It declares that the "crime" of crossing a border to work is twelve times more dangerous to the nation than the crime of stealing that worker's life or livelihood.

To dismantle the plantation economy, we must invert this ratio. We must launch a "surge" in labor enforcement that rivals the surges we routinely deploy to the southern border. This is not a call for "big government" in the abstract; it is a call for "effective government" in the specific. It is a proposal to fund the Labor Police at a level where they can actually police.

The blueprint for this transformation begins with staffing. In 1978, the Wage and Hour Division employed more investigators than it does today, despite the U.S. workforce nearly doubling in size. Today, each investigator is theoretically responsible for protecting 175,000 workers . This creates a workload that forces the agency into a purely reactive posture. They sit at their desks waiting for the phone to ring, processing complaints from the brave few who dare to speak, while the silent majority of victims remain untouched.

A properly funded Labor Police would operate on a different model: the "beat cop" model. Imagine a Wage and Hour Division with 5,000 investigators instead of 700. This force would not wait for complaints. They would conduct randomized, unannounced audits of high-risk industries. They would walk onto construction sites in Dallas, into poultry plants in Arkansas, and into restaurant kitchens in New York City with the frequency and unpredictability of a health inspector.

The psychological impact of this presence cannot be overstated. Currently, the rational employer calculates that they will likely never see a federal investigator in their lifetime. If we raise the probability of inspection to even 10 percent annually, the calculus of exploitation collapses. The risk of getting caught becomes a line item on the balance sheet that is too high to ignore. Deterrence works, but only when the threat is credible.

This funding must also modernize the weaponry of the Labor Police. While ICE utilizes biometric tracking, cell-site simulators, and massive data mining operations to locate undocumented immigrants, labor inspectors are often fighting 21st-century wage theft with 20th-century tools.

A funded Labor Police would employ forensic accountants and data scientists capable of piercing the "Subcontracting Shield" discussed in Chapter 11. They would use algorithms to detect patterns of "time shaving" in digital payroll systems. They would have the software to map the complex networks of shell LLCs used by labor brokers to hide assets. We need to arm our labor enforcers with the same level of technological sophistication that we grant to those who hunt money launderers or drug traffickers.

Critically, this proposal is not a drain on the treasury; it is a revenue generator. This is the "ROI of Justice." Every dollar spent on a Wage and Hour investigator generates a multiple in recovered wages. When workers are paid what they are owed, they pay more taxes and consume more goods.

But the return on investment goes deeper. By cracking down on the misclassification of independent contractors—the "sham" described in Chapter 10—a robust Labor Police would recover billions in unpaid Social Security, Medicare, and unemployment insurance taxes. The Treasury Department loses vast sums every year to employers who pay in cash to avoid these obligations. Funding the investigators who stop this fraud is not spending; it is collections. It pays for itself.

The political resistance to this proposal is predictable. Corporate lobbyists will decry "regulatory overreach" and warn of a "war on business." They will paint the labor inspector as a bureaucrat strangling the free market with red tape.

We must reject this framing. The enforcement of property rights—including the worker's property right to their wages—is the foundation of a free market. A market where theft is permitted is not free; it is a kleptocracy. The honest business owner, currently suffering the "Competitive Disadvantage" of bidding against cheaters, is the primary beneficiary of a strong Labor Police.

When the Labor Police shut down a construction firm that relies on wage theft, they act as the protector of the firm that follows the law. They level the playing field. They ensure that efficiency and innovation, rather than criminality, determine who wins the contract. This is a pro-business policy for every business that operates with integrity.

Furthermore, we must reallocate the budget to reflect the reality of harm. The current obsession with border enforcement is justified by the language of "national security" and "public safety." Yet, the data shows that undocumented immigrants have lower crime rates than native-born citizens. Meanwhile, the corporations that poison workers with chemicals, maim them with machinery, and steal their wages are inflicting demonstrable, quantifiable violence on the public.

Why is a fall from a roof due to negligence considered an "accident," while a minor drug offense is a "crime"? Why do we send SWAT teams to arrest drug dealers, but send letters to employers who kill workers?

A funded Labor Police would require a cultural shift in how we view these offenses. It would require the Department of Justice to partner with the Department of Labor to prosecute the worst offenders criminally, not just civilly. As seen in the "Minnesota Model" (Chapter 44), criminal penalties change behavior. But federal prosecutors need the investigative referrals that only a robust labor inspectorate can provide.

The reallocation of funds from DHS to DOL is the logistical mechanism for this moral shift. We do not need to raise taxes to fund the Labor Police; we simply need to stop spending billions on the performative cruelty of the border and start spending it on the interior protection of the workforce. If we took just 10 percent of the budget for ICE and CBP—roughly $2.5 billion—and moved it to the Department of Labor, we would more than double the enforcement capacity of the United States.

We would go from a token force to a formidable one. We would send a message to every corner of the economy: *The era of impunity is over. The state is watching.*

This proposal also includes a mandate for linguistic and cultural competence. The new Labor Police must look like the workforce they protect. They must speak Spanish, Mam, K'iche', and Haitian Creole. They must be embedded in the communities where exploitation happens, building trust rather than fear.

Unlike ICE, whose presence triggers panic and silence, the Labor Police must operate as partners to the community. They must possess the "firewall" authority to assure workers that speaking to an inspector will never, under any circumstances, lead to deportation. Their badge must symbolize protection, not persecution.

The failure to fund labor enforcement is the single greatest subsidy the government provides to the exploitation economy. It is a decision to look the other way. It is a decision to let the market devour the vulnerable. By reversing this decision—by putting our money where our values supposedly are—we can transform the law from a dead letter into a living shield.

We have the money. We have the laws. What we have lacked is the admission that a crime in the workplace is as serious as a crime in the street. Funding the Labor Police is the first step in acknowledging that the theft of a life, whether by inches or by dollars, is a matter for the state to stop.

Chapter 46: Supply Chain Transparency

In the modern global economy, information is the most valuable currency. A multinational corporation can track a shipping container from a port in Shenzhen to a distribution center in Ohio with GPS precision. A supermarket chain knows exactly which field in California produced a specific head of romaine lettuce within minutes of an E. coli outbreak. The data infrastructure of American commerce is a marvel of omniscience. We track temperature, humidity, velocity, and inventory levels in real-time.

Yet, if you ask that same supermarket chain to identify the specific human beings who picked that lettuce, or if you ask the fashion brand to name the women who sewed their t-shirts, the screen goes black. The omniscience evaporates, replaced by a sudden and convenient amnesia. "We buy from a distributor," the executive says. "We don't have visibility past the first tier of our supply chain."

This blindness is not a technical failure; it is a legal strategy. It is the deliberate cultivation of ignorance to preserve immunity. As I documented in Chapter 11, the "Subcontracting Shield" allows corporations to sever the link between their profits and the people who generate them. They have constructed a "fissured workplace" where the brand holds the power while the subcontractor holds the liability.

To dismantle the exploitation economy, we must shatter this shield. We must enact laws that force corporations to map their labor supply chains with the same rigor they apply to their logistics. We must move from an era of "plausible deniability" to an era of "inescapable responsibility." The solution is not to ask companies to be better; it is to make it legally dangerous for them not to know who works for them.

The legislative mechanism for this transformation is known as "chain of commerce" liability.

Currently, the legal firewall protects the lead firm—the brand or the general contractor—from the crimes of its vendors. If a subcontractor steals wages, the brand is insulated. A transparency law would invert this presumption. It would establish that any entity profiting from the sale of a good or service is strictly liable for labor violations committed at any point in its production.

If a roofer falls to his death on a construction site because the labor broker didn't buy harnesses, the lawsuit would not stop at the bankrupt broker; it would travel up the chain to the developer who commissioned the house. If a child is found cleaning a slaughterhouse, the fines would not be levied solely against the sanitation service, but against the meatpacking giant that owns the facility.

This legal shift changes the risk calculus instantly. Today, corporations choose the lowest bidder because they pay no price for the bidder's criminality. Under a regime of chain liability, the lowest bidder becomes a radioactive risk. The General Counsel of the corporation would look at a bid that is 30 percent below market rate and see not a bargain, but a potential lawsuit. They would demand proof of compliance. They would audit not just the paperwork, but the actual conditions. They would become the enforcers of labor standards because their own balance sheet would be on the line.

We have a precedent for this kind of "tracing" liability in the Fair Labor Standards Act (FLSA), specifically the "Hot Goods" provision. This law allows the Department of Labor to stop the shipment of goods produced in violation of minimum wage or child labor laws. It freezes the product in the supply chain, turning the inventory into a liability.

However, the "Hot Goods" provision has been weakened by court rulings and lacks the resources for broad enforcement. A robust Transparency Act would modernize this provision for the twenty-first century. It would require "digital passports" for products—a blockchain-verified record of every hand that touched the item, linking the final product to the specific payroll records of the workers who made it.

Critics will argue that this is technologically impossible, that supply chains are too complex to map. This is the "complexity defense," and it is demonstrably false.

When the FDA demanded traceability for food safety to prevent salmonella outbreaks, the industry complained, then complied. They implemented barcoding systems that can trace a bag of spinach back to the specific row of the specific farm where it was harvested. If we can track a pathogen through the supply chain to protect the consumer's stomach, we can track a paycheck through the supply chain to protect the worker's livelihood. The technology exists; only the will is missing.

The second pillar of this legislative reform is the expansion of the "Joint Employer" standard. Corporate lobbyists have fought a decades-long war to narrow the definition of an employer. They argue that because they do not directly hire, fire, or supervise the subcontractor's workers, they are not employers.

But economic reality tells a different story. When a fast-food corporation dictates the uniform, the menu, the prices, the training protocols, and the computer systems used by a franchisee, they are exercising control. When a construction developer sets a schedule that requires twenty-hour days to meet, they are dictating working conditions.

A Transparency Act would codify the "economic realities" test. It would state that if a company dictates the economic terms of the work—the price, the deadline, the quality standards—they are a joint employer of the workforce, regardless of whose name is on the paycheck. This would pierce the corporate veil that allows brands to dictate everything except the responsibility for the human beings involved.

This transparency must also extend to the consumer. Currently, the "ethically sourced" label is a marketing term, not a legal one. Corporations police themselves with voluntary "Codes of Conduct" that, as noted in Chapter 11, are often exercises in theater.

We need a "Truth in Labor" labeling law, modeled on the nutritional facts label. Imagine scanning a QR code on a pint of strawberries and seeing a "Labor Score": a grade based on the producer's compliance with wage laws, safety regulations, and collective bargaining rights. This data would be drawn not from the company's own marketing department, but from Department of Labor audits and independent verifiers.

This would unleash the power of the market. American consumers have shown repeatedly that they are willing to pay a premium for values—organic, fair trade, cruelty-free. But they cannot make ethical choices if the market is opaque. By forcing transparency, we empower the consumer to punish exploiters and reward ethical businesses. The "Competitive Disadvantage" suffered by honest companies would evaporate; instead, their compliance would become their greatest marketing asset.

We can look to international models for inspiration. Germany's Supply Chain Due Diligence Act creates a legal obligation for large companies to identify and mitigate human rights risks in their supply chains. The United States' own Uyghur Forced Labor Prevention Act creates a "rebuttable presumption" that goods from a specific region are made with forced labor unless the importer can prove otherwise with clear and convincing evidence.

We should apply this "rebuttable presumption" to domestic industries with high rates of violation. We know that the residential roofing industry, the hand-harvested vegetable sector, and the garment industry are rife with exploitation. The law should presume that goods from these sectors are "tainted" unless the seller can provide a transparent, audited chain of custody proving that workers were paid legally. The burden of proof should shift from the underfunded investigator to the profitable corporation.

This shift would also destroy the business model of the "labor broker"— the middleman whose only value add is the ability to source undocumented workers and shield the client from liability. If the client is liable regardless of the broker, the broker becomes a risk. Corporations would move toward direct hiring, bringing workers back onto their own payrolls where they can be monitored, trained, and protected. It would re-integrate the workforce, ending the fragmentation that allows abuse to fester in the gaps.

The defenders of the status quo will scream that this "regulatory burden" will increase costs. They are correct. It will increase the cost of doing business for criminals. It will force the internalization of costs that are currently externalized onto the worker and the taxpayer. It will end the subsidy of theft.

But for the honest business, transparency is a shield. It protects them from being undercut by rivals who cheat. It stabilizes the market. It creates a predictable environment where competition is based on excellence, not exploitation.

Ultimately, Supply Chain Transparency is about ending the era of willful blindness. It is about declaring that in the American economy, you cannot profit from what you refuse to see. You cannot build a brand on a foundation of anonymous suffering. If you have the technology to track a widget across an ocean, you have the ability to know if the person who made it was paid. And if you refuse to look, the law will assume you knew what you would have found.

Chapter 47: The Fair Food Program

In the annals of American labor history, the narrative arc usually bends toward tragedy. We read of strikes crushed by strikebreakers, of safety regulations written in the blood of the Triangle Shirtwaist Factory fire, and of reforms that are whittled down by lobbyists until they are toothless. But in the swampy interior of Florida, a different story has been written—one that provides a concrete, operational blueprint for the abolition of modern slavery.

This transformation occurred in the tomato fields of Immokalee, the very region we visited in Chapter 15. As we saw then, these fields were once a zone of exclusion where the Constitution seemed to hold no sway. It was a landscape defined by extreme heat, toxic chemical exposure, and a piece-rate system that drove workers to the brink of physiological collapse. It was here that federal prosecutors repeatedly found cases of workers chained in box trucks, beaten for moving too slowly, and held in debt bondage—a reality that led U.S. Attorneys to prosecute multiple slavery rings in the 1990s and 2000s.

Today, however, those same fields are described by the *New York Times* as arguably the "best work environment in U.S. agriculture."

This miracle did not occur because the federal government suddenly decided to enforce the law. It did not happen because the Department of Labor received a massive budget increase, nor because the growers underwent a spontaneous moral awakening. It happened because a group of workers, the Coalition of Immokalee Workers (CIW), designed a mechanism to harness the immense power of the market to enforce human rights. They created the Fair Food Program (FFP).

To understand why the FFP succeeds where federal law fails, we must look at its architectural difference. Traditional labor law relies on a "complaint-driven" model: a worker must be brave enough to call the government, which must then have the resources to investigate, which then must litigate against the employer. As we have seen throughout this book, for an undocumented worker facing the threat of deportation, this chain is broken at the very first link. The risk of reporting abuse far outweighs the potential benefit of a slow-moving investigation.

The Fair Food Program replaces the power of the subpoena with the power of the purchase order.

The model is known as Worker-driven Social Responsibility (WSR). It represents a radical departure from the failed "Corporate Social Responsibility" models of the past, where companies monitored themselves. The WSR model begins with a binding legal agreement between the Coalition and the massive corporations that buy tomatoes—giants like Walmart, McDonald's, Burger King, Taco Bell, and Whole Foods. These "Participating Buyers" pledge to purchase Florida tomatoes only from growers who comply with a Code of Conduct designed not by public relations executives, but by the workers themselves.

This Code of Conduct is not a vague corporate mission statement. It is a rigorous, granular set of standards that addresses the specific abuses we documented in Chapter 15. It includes zero tolerance for forced labor and sexual assault. It mandates requirements for shade and water in the fields— a direct response to the heat stress deaths that plagued the industry. It establishes the right to form health and safety committees, giving workers a voice in their own protection.

But a code without enforcement is merely poetry. The genius of the FFP lies in the consequence of violation. If a grower is found to be using forced labor, permitting sexual harassment, or engaging in systematic wage theft, the Participating Buyers stop buying their tomatoes.

Consider the economic leverage this creates. For a large grower, losing the contract to supply Walmart or McDonald's is an existential threat. It is a business death sentence. Under the old system, cheating a worker out of wages might save a grower a few thousand dollars, with a negligible risk of a small government fine. Under the FFP, that same act of theft risks millions of dollars in revenue. The program completely inverts the risk-reward calculation of exploitation. It makes dignity the prerequisite for profitability.

The second pillar of the program addresses the economic desperation that fuels vulnerability. As discussed in Chapter 32 regarding the "Cheap Goods Lie," the Participating Buyers agree to pay a "Fair Food Premium"— a small surcharge, typically one penny per pound of tomatoes—that is passed down through the supply chain directly to the workers.

To the consumer buying a burger or a salad, this penny is invisible. It is a rounding error at the register. But to the worker who picks two tons of tomatoes a day, it is transformative. Since the program's launch, these pennies have aggregated into nearly $40 million in additional payroll for farmworkers. This wage increase lifts workers out of the desperate poverty that makes them vulnerable to debt bondage and predation. It creates a financial buffer that allows a worker to say "no" to dangerous work, or to take a day off when sick. It proves that we can afford to pay workers fairly without bankrupting the economy or the consumer.

But the most revolutionary aspect of the FFP is its monitoring system. In the shadow economy, the worker is silenced by the fear that reporting abuse will lead to retaliation or deportation. The FFP breaks this silence through the Fair Food Standards Council (FFSC), an independent monitoring body funded by the buyers' premiums.

The FFSC conducts rigorous audits—not the scheduled "compliance theater" tours used by other industries where auditors are walked through sanitized facilities by management. FFSC auditors go into the fields. They get on the buses at 5:00 AM. They interview workers confidentially, away from the supervisors. They look at the books with forensic intensity.

Crucially, they operate a 24-hour confidential hotline staffed by bilingual investigators who speak Spanish, Haitian Creole, and indigenous languages. This hotline is not a voicemail box; it is a rapid-response mechanism.

When a worker calls this hotline to report a supervisor demanding bribes or sexual favors, the investigation is swift. Because the growers know that the FFSC holds the keys to the market—that a bad report from the Council means Walmart stops buying—they cooperate. Retaliation is strictly prohibited and swiftly punished. If a foreman fires a worker for calling the hotline, the grower must reinstate the worker or face suspension from the program.

This mechanism effectively deputizes every worker in the field as a monitor. It creates a "safety net of eyes and ears." The foreman, who previously acted as the petty tyrant of the labor camp (as described in Chapter 38), now finds his power checked. He knows he cannot abuse his crew because any one of them can make the call that shuts down the farm's access to its biggest customers. The "culture of fear" is replaced by a culture of accountability.

The results are empirically verifiable. The United Nations has lauded the Fair Food Program as an "international benchmark" in the fight against modern-day slavery. In the fields covered by the program, cases of forced labor and sexual assault—once endemic—have virtually disappeared. When violations do occur, they are identified and resolved, often within days, rather than festering for years.

The elimination of sexual assault in these fields is perhaps the most striking achievement. For decades, the "green motel"—the fields themselves—was a site of rampant sexual violence against female farmworkers. Supervisors used their power to hire and fire to coerce women into sex. Under the FFP, sexual harassment is a "zero tolerance" violation. A grower can be suspended immediately if it is found. This has changed the culture of the fields overnight. Women report feeling safe for the first time in their working lives.

The success of the FFP challenges the cynicism that pervades the immigration debate. Defenders of the status quo argue that agriculture relies on an undocumented workforce that cannot be protected because they are "illegal." Yet, the FFP operates in fields where the workforce remains largely undocumented. It proves that legal status, while crucial, is not the *only* way to protect rights. Even without a visa, a worker protected by the Fair Food Program has more functional power than a non-unionized U.S. citizen working in an unprotected industry.

By linking the worker directly to the brand, the FFP pierces the "Subcontracting Shield" discussed in Chapter 11. Walmart cannot say, "We didn't know." They are contractually obligated to know. The transparency is forced by the contract. The distance between the boardroom and the field is collapsed.

Furthermore, the program offers a pathway for the rehabilitation of the industry. Growers who were once skeptical, who fought the CIW tooth and nail, have come to embrace the program. They found that being a "Fair Food" farm reduced turnover. It improved safety, lowering insurance risks. It attracted a more stable, professional workforce.

It turns out that the "Competitive Disadvantage" of being honest—discussed in Chapter 34—disappears when honesty is the only way to access the market. When every major grower must follow the same rules to sell to the major buyers, the race to the bottom ends. The competition shifts to efficiency and quality, rather than who can steal the most wages.

The scalability of this model is its most promising feature. While it started with Florida tomatoes, it has expanded to other crops and states. The "Milk with Dignity" program in Vermont, modeled directly on the FFP, has secured agreements with Ben & Jerry's to protect dairy workers in the frigid north. The model is being adapted for the construction industry in places like Minneapolis and Austin, creating "Better Builder" programs that link density bonuses for developers to safety standards for workers.

This expansion proves that the principles of WSR are universal. Wherever there is a concentration of corporate buying power and a vulnerable workforce, this lever can be pulled. The construction industry, dominated by massive developers and retailers, is ripe for this intervention. The hospitality industry, controlled by global brands, could implement it tomorrow.

This is the abolitionist blueprint. It does not wait for Congress to pass comprehensive immigration reform. It does not wait for the Department of Labor to double its budget. It seizes the existing levers of power—the capital of the corporation and the consumption of the public—and uses them to enforce the social contract.

The Fair Food Program demonstrates that the "market" is not inherently immoral; it is a machine that does what it is programmed to do. For centuries, it was programmed to value the product and devalue the person. The CIW rewrote the code. They proved that when you make the sale conditional on the soul, the market adjusts.

We have spent decades asking, "How can we stop illegal immigration?" The Fair Food Program asks a better question: "How can we stop exploitation?" By answering the second question, they have rendered the first one less relevant. An undocumented worker in a Fair Food field is no longer a shadow person; they are a recognized participant in a system of rights and responsibilities. They are, in every way that matters to their daily survival, free.

This model serves as a rebuke to every industry that claims abuse is inevitable. It stands as proof that we do not have to choose between abundance and justice. We can have both, but only if we are willing to pay the penny, sign the contract, and listen to the worker. The tomato fields of Florida, once a scene of national shame, are now a beacon. They show us that the plantation is not an eternal condition of American agriculture; it is a choice, and it is a choice we can unmake.

Chapter 48: Visa Portability

In the lexicon of free-market capitalism, the most powerful phrase is not "you're hired." It is "I quit."

The ability to walk away from a job is the fundamental fulcrum upon which the entire theory of labor economics rests. It is the mechanism that forces wages to rise; if an employer pays too little, the worker leaves for a competitor who pays more. It is the mechanism that enforces safety standards; if a workplace is dangerous, the worker exits to protect their life. It is the mechanism that ensures dignity; if a boss is abusive, the worker takes their skills elsewhere. The power to quit is the invisible hand that keeps the employer honest.

But for the hundreds of thousands of guest workers currently laboring in the United States under the H-2A and H-2B visa programs, this right does not exist. As I noted in the analysis of the "H-2A Loophole," these workers are bound by a "tying" provision that links their legal status to a single, specific employer. They cannot shop their labor. They cannot negotiate. If they utter the phrase "I quit," they are not entering the job market; they are effectively deporting themselves.

This restriction creates a profound distortion in the American economy. We have constructed a system where the employer operates in a capitalist market—selling their crops or construction services to the highest bidder—while the worker is trapped in a feudal relationship, unable to sell their labor to anyone but the lord of the manor.

The solution to this structural imbalance is perhaps the single most effective legislative fix available to policymakers. It requires no massive new enforcement agency, no border wall, and no complex biometric surveillance. It requires only a simple administrative change known as "visa portability."

Visa portability is the concept that a worker's visa should belong to the worker, not the boss. Under a portable system, a guest worker would be vetted by the government and authorized to work in a specific sector—agriculture, hospitality, or construction—for a specific period. But within that sector and that timeframe, they would be free to move between certified employers.

The implementation of this simple freedom would trigger an immediate and revolutionary market correction. Consider the dynamic on a farm in

Georgia where the owner abuses his crew, houses them in squalor, and steals their wages. Under the current "tied" system, the crew stays because they have no choice. The bad employer is subsidized by the law; he retains his workforce despite his abuse.

Under a portable system, that crew would simply walk down the road to a neighboring farm that offers better wages and humane conditions. The abusive farmer would face an immediate labor crisis. He would be forced to either improve his standards to attract workers or go out of business.

This is the "market mechanism" at its purest. Portability forces employers to compete for labor. As the Center for American Progress and other reform advocates have argued, when workers can search for positions that value their skills appropriately, the entire character of the employment relationship changes. The employer ceases to be a jailer and becomes a customer who must buy the worker's time with fair compensation.

The economic logic of portability is unassailable. The current system of "bound labor" creates massive inefficiencies. It traps workers in jobs where they may be underutilized or unhappy, while other employers desperate for labor cannot hire them. It freezes the labor market, preventing the fluid movement of human capital to its highest and best use.

Historically, this rigidity was the fatal flaw of indentured servitude and the *Bracero* program. As economic historians have documented, binding workers to specific employers destroys the incentive for those employers to invest in productivity. If a farmer knows his workers cannot leave, why should he buy better equipment to make their work easier? Why should he invest in safety training? He has a captive audience. Portability restores the incentive to innovate. To retain free workers, an employer must make the job attractive, often by investing in technology or processes that boost productivity for everyone.

Critics of portability—primarily the lobbyists for industries that rely on captive labor—argue that the "tying" provision is necessary to protect the employer's investment. They point out that growers pay for the transportation, visas, and recruitment of these workers. "Why should I pay $2,000 to bring a worker from Mexico," they ask, "only to have him leave me for the farm next door?"

This argument treats the human being as a capital asset, a piece of equipment to be amortized. It is the logic of ownership. But even accepting the premise of "investment," the solution is simple contract law, not bondage.

A portable system could easily include a mechanism for "reimbursement." If a worker moves to a new employer, the new employer could be required to pay a pro-rated portion of the recruitment costs to the original sponsor. Or, the industry could establish a shared pool or bonding system to cover recruitment costs, socializing the expense across the sector rather than pinning it to a specific human being.

We solve this "investment" problem in every other sector of the economy without resorting to bondage. When a tech company pays for a software engineer to relocate, and that engineer quits six months later to join a competitor, the company does not have the power to deport him. They might demand the repayment of a signing bonus, but they cannot revoke his right to exist in the country. We recognize that the freedom of the worker outweighs the sunk cost of the corporation. There is no moral or economic reason why a tomato picker should be held to a lower standard of freedom than a programmer.

Furthermore, portability acts as the ultimate whistleblower protection. Currently, as noted in the discussion of enforcement failure, reporting abuse is a high-risk proposition. A worker who reports a safety violation risks being fired and losing their visa. The remedy for the crime punishes the victim.

With portability, the "exit option" becomes a form of enforcement. A worker does not need to wait for a Department of Labor investigation that might take years. They can enforce the law with their feet. By leaving an abusive employer, they deprive that employer of the labor they need to profit. If enough workers leave, the abusive workplace collapses. This "voting with their feet" creates a real-time feedback loop that penalizes bad actors far faster than any bureaucracy can.

The introduction of portability would also shatter the power of the "blacklists" used by recruiters to control the workforce. Currently, workers who complain or organize are marked as "ineligible for rehire" and banned from future seasons. This blacklisting is effective because the worker relies on the recruiter to match them with a specific employer. In a portable system, the worker could bypass the blacklisted employer and find work with others who are desperate for help. The monopoly power of the recruiter would be broken.

We must also consider the impact on the "substitution effect" discussed in Chapter 33. The current system artificially depresses wages for American workers because H-2A workers are trapped in a non-negotiable contract. They cannot bargain for higher wages, which means they anchor the market rate at the legal minimum.

If guest workers were free to bargain—if they could say, "I won't work for less than $18 an hour"—wages in the sector would rise to their natural market level. This would benefit native-born workers who compete in the same labor pool. The "discount" on foreign labor would vanish, leveling the playing field for everyone.

The design of a portable visa system is not a radical experiment; it is a return to the norms of a free society. It would require a central clearinghouse or a digital job registry where certified employers could post vacancies and workers with valid visas could apply. It would require a "grace period" allowing a worker to remain in the country for 60 or 90 days between jobs to find new employment, ensuring that a momentary gap in work does not result in deportation.

These are administrative details, easily solvable with modern technology. The barrier is not logistical; it is political. The industries that rely on H-2A and H-2B labor fight portability ferociously because they know exactly what it would mean: the end of their absolute control. They prefer the certainty of a captive workforce to the competition of a free market.

But we must be clear about what that preference represents. It is a preference for a subsidy extracted from the liberty of the worker. It is a demand that the government act as a private security force to keep workers from quitting.

Implementing visa portability would transform the guest worker program from a system of modernized indenture into a genuine labor mobility program. It would align the law with the economic reality that labor is a service to be sold, not a property to be owned.

The worker who holds a portable visa stands up straighter. They look the foreman in the eye. They negotiate. They join with others. They possess the dignity of agency. By granting this simple right—the right to quit—we do not just free the immigrant; we free the market from the distortion of bondage, and we restore the basic American premise that employment must always be an agreement between free people, not a sentence served by the bound.

Chapter 49: Earned Legalization

In the polarized lexicon of American politics, there is one word that functions as a conversation stopper, a linguistic grenade that detonates any attempt at rational policy discussion: "Amnesty." To the opponents of immigration reform, any proposal to grant legal status to the eleven million undocumented people currently living in the United States is viewed as an unforgivable capitulation. It is framed as a reward for lawbreaking, a suspension of the rule of law, and a betrayal of those who waited in line.

This framing is not just politically convenient; it is economically illiterate. It relies on the pretense that the current status quo—a permanent, shadow underclass of millions—is a form of punishment. It assumes that by keeping these workers illegal, we are upholding the law.

But as I have documented across forty-eight chapters, the current system is not a punishment for the undocumented; it is a subsidy for their exploiters. The status quo *is* an amnesty—a *de facto* amnesty for the sweatshop owner, the shady labor broker, and the tax-evading contractor. By refusing to regularize this workforce, we have granted a permanent pardon to the industries that profit from their vulnerability. We have created a sanctuary jurisdiction for exploitation.

To dismantle the plantation economy, we must move beyond the bumper-sticker slogans and confront the economic reality. We cannot deport eleven million people; the logistical and economic cost would be catastrophic, shrinking the GDP by trillions and destroying the agricultural and construction sectors overnight. Nor can we allow the current caste system to persist, where a significant portion of the workforce exists outside the protection of the law.

The only rational path forward—the only path that restores the rule of law, protects American workers, and generates economic growth—is "Earned Legalization."

This concept is distinct from the "blanket amnesty" of political caricature. It is a rigorous, punitive, and restorative process designed to bring people out of the shadows while acknowledging their initial violation of immigration statutes. As outlined by the Center for American Progress and bipartisan legislative proposals, earned legalization operates as a plea bargain with the state. It offers a path to status, but that path is steep.

The applicant must undergo comprehensive criminal and national security background checks to ensure they pose no threat to public safety. They must demonstrate continuous presence in the country and a history of employment. They must pay any back taxes owed to the U.S. Treasury. And, crucially, they must pay a significant fine—proposals have ranged from $1,000 to over $7,000 per applicant.

This is not a reward; it is a reckoning. It forces the undocumented individual to settle their account with the government. But in exchange for this penalty, it offers the one thing that transforms the economics of labor: legal standing.

The moment a worker achieves legal status, the entire architecture of exploitation I have described begins to crumble. The "paper chains" of Chapter 39 are unlocked. A legalized worker can walk into a Department of Labor office and file a wage theft complaint without fear of deportation. They can organize a union. They can leave an abusive employer and take their skills to a competitor. They acquire the "reservation wage"—the ability to say "no"—which is the fundamental prerequisite for a functioning labor market.

The economic impact of this transformation is not a matter of speculation. We have the data. The Congressional Budget Office (CBO), the nonpartisan scorekeeper of the federal government, analyzed the impact of comprehensive immigration reform in 2013. Their findings provide the definitive economic case for legalization.

The CBO projected that bringing the shadow workforce into the legal economy would increase the nation's Gross Domestic Product by 3.3 percent within ten years and 5.3 percent within twenty years. This is not a marginal increase; it represents trillions of dollars in new economic activity. It is the kind of growth that politicians promise but rarely deliver.

How does legalization generate such wealth? It unleashes the "virtuous cycle" discussed in Chapter 13. When workers gain status, their wages rise—historically by roughly 25 percent. This wage increase is not inflationary; it is a correction of the market distortion caused by exploitation. These higher wages translate immediately into higher consumption. Legalized families buy homes, purchase cars, and invest in education. They circulate money through the local economy, creating demand that supports businesses and creates jobs.

The CBO estimated that this surge in economic activity would support the creation of an average of 121,000 additional jobs every year for a decade. Far from "stealing" jobs from native-born Americans, legalized immigrants create them through their consumption and investment.

But the most compelling argument for the fiscal conservative is the impact on the deficit. The CBO found that comprehensive reform would reduce the federal budget deficit by nearly $900 billion over twenty years.

This deficit reduction is driven by the tax code. Currently, the "Tax Gap"—the difference between taxes owed and taxes collected—is fueled by the cash economy. Billions of dollars in wages are paid under the table to avoid payroll taxes. Legalization closes this gap. When workers have legal status, they demand W-2 forms. Employers are forced to withhold income tax and pay their share of Social Security and Medicare taxes.

The CBO calculated that for every dollar the government might spend on services for legalized immigrants, it would collect nearly two dollars in new tax revenue. It is a massive revenue generator. It shores up the Social Security Trust Fund, which is currently strained by an aging native population, by bringing millions of young, working-age contributors onto the books.

Furthermore, legalization ends the "Competitive Disadvantage" discussed in Chapter 34. Currently, honest businesses are being slaughtered by competitors who cheat. A construction contractor who pays his crew in cash and skips workers' compensation insurance can underbid a law-abiding rival by 30 percent. This rewards criminality and drives ethical firms out of the market.

Legalization levels the playing field. If every worker has legal status, every employer must follow the same rules. The "illegality discount" vanishes. Employers are forced to compete on efficiency, quality, and innovation rather than on who can be the most ruthless tax evader. This strengthens the entire economy by ensuring that capital flows to the best businesses, not the most corrupt ones.

Opponents often argue that legalization undermines the "Rule of Law." This argument relies on a shallow understanding of what the rule of law actually means. A system that permits eleven million people to live in a state of permanent legal violation, while rewarding the employers who hire them, is the antithesis of the rule of law. It is a state of "Rule by Loophole."

Earned legalization restores the rule of law by ending the black market. It brings a chaotic, unregulated population under the sovereignty of the state. It allows the government to know who is here, where they live, and what they do. It replaces the anarchy of the shadow economy with the order of the legal system.

The "moral hazard" argument—that legalization encourages future illegal immigration—is also flawed. The primary driver of illegal immigration is the availability of jobs. As long as employers can hire undocumented workers with impunity and pay them sub-market wages, the magnet remains. Legalization, paired with mandatory E-Verify and vigorous enforcement of labor standards (the "Labor Police" of Chapter 45), breaks this magnet. By eliminating the "discount" of illegal labor, we reduce the demand for it.

We must also confront the human capital argument. As noted in Chapter 40, we are currently destroying the potential of 5.9 million U.S. citizen children by keeping their parents in a state of terror. Legalization ends the toxic stress that stunts their development. It allows parents to earn better wages, moving families out of poverty and off social assistance. It turns a generation of "at-risk" youth into a generation of productive citizens. The return on investment for stabilizing these families is incalculable.

Historically, the United States has benefited every time it has expanded the circle of inclusion. The legalization program of 1986, flawed as it was in enforcement, helped millions of workers move into the middle class. Their children are now doctors, soldiers, and business owners. Today, we have the opportunity to repeat that success on a larger scale, but with the wisdom of hindsight to ensure that enforcement mechanisms are actually funded.

The choice is not between a "perfect" America without illegal immigrants and the current reality. That choice does not exist. The choice is between maintaining a permanent caste of exploitable serfs who drag down wages and degrade the rule of law, or integrating that population into the nation as rights-bearing, tax-paying, law-abiding members.

Earned legalization is the economic bridge out of the plantation. It is the recognition that the labor of these millions is essential, and that the only way to treat essential labor is with essential rights. It acknowledges that the undocumented are already here, already working, and already part of the fabric of American life. The only question is whether we want them to be part of the American Dream, or victims of the American Nightmare.

By choosing legalization, we do not surrender our borders. We reclaim our economy. We assert that in the United States, there is no such thing as a second-class human being. We declare that the market must serve the law, not the other way around. And we prove, finally, that freedom pays for itself.

Chapter 50: The Moral Mandate

We have reached the end of the ledger. Over the course of forty-nine chapters, we have traced the anatomy of a crime that is committed in the open, subsidized by the taxpayer, and woven into the fabric of our daily lives. We have examined the digital auctions that procure human beings, the debt contracts that bind them, and the legal loopholes that strip them of their humanity. We have followed the dollar from the smuggler's pocket to the corporate balance sheet, and we have counted the cost in the broken bodies of workers and the traumatized minds of children.

The evidence is in. The receipts have been tallied. We can no longer claim the privilege of ignorance.

For decades, the American conversation about immigration and labor has been dominated by the language of pragmatism. We talk about "labor shortages" and "border security." We debate the fiscal impact of visas and the logistics of deportation. We hide behind the sterile terminology of economics and law enforcement, treating millions of human beings as if they were variables in an equation to be balanced.

But the crisis we face is not, at its core, a crisis of logistics or economics. It is a crisis of the soul.

The system I have documented—the modern plantation economy—is a moral catastrophe. It is a betrayal of the fundamental promise of the American experiment. When Thomas Jefferson wrote that "all men are created equal," he set a standard that the nation has struggled to meet for two and a half centuries. We fought a Civil War to purge the sin of chattel slavery. We marched across the Edmund Pettus Bridge to dismantle Jim Crow. At every pivot point in our history, we have been forced to decide whether the phrase "We the People" is an exclusive club or a universal declaration.

Today, we are failing that test. By maintaining a caste of eleven million people who exist outside the protection of the law, we have created a permanent "separate but unequal" society. We have accepted the premise that a person's geography determines their human rights. We have decided that it is acceptable to consume the labor of a human being while rejecting their personhood.

This is not just a policy failure; it is a corruption of our national character. A society that relies on the exploitation of the vulnerable to sustain its standard of living is a society that is rotting from the inside. We cannot be a "nation of laws" when our economy relies on the systematic violation of labor law. We cannot be the "land of the free" when our fields and factories are populated by the unfree.

The defenders of the status quo will tell you that this system is inevitable. They will argue, as the defenders of slavery argued before them, that the "laws of economics" demand cheap labor. They will say that the world is a harsh place, and that we cannot save everyone.

But as I have demonstrated, this cynicism is factually wrong. The "laws of economics" do not demand exploitation; they demand efficiency, and exploitation is profoundly inefficient. It wastes human potential, destroys social capital, and generates massive hidden costs. The trillion-dollar price tag of child poverty and the billions lost to the tax gap prove that cruelty is the most expensive policy of all.

We are not bound to this path by necessity. We are bound to it by choice.

The choice before us is whether to continue down the road of apartheid—a road where we build higher walls, hire more guards, and construct ever more elaborate legal fictions to justify the theft of labor—or to choose the path of abolition.

Abolition, in the twenty-first century, does not mean a war. It means a legal and moral reconstruction. It means extending the canopy of the Constitution to cover every person who labors on American soil. It means recognizing that the right to be paid, the right to be safe, and the right to walk away from abuse are not privileges of citizenship; they are rights of personhood.

The blueprint for this reconstruction already exists. We have seen it in the tomato fields of Florida, where the Fair Food Program proved that the market can be harnessed to enforce dignity. We have seen it in Minnesota, where the law finally called wage theft by its true name. We have seen it in the companies that have chosen to invest in refugees rather than exploit the undocumented.

We know what works. The question is whether we have the will to scale it.

This moral mandate requires us to reject the false binary of "us" versus "them." The history of American labor is a history of division. The Irish were pitted against the Italians; the white worker was pitted against the Black worker. Today, the native-born worker is told that the undocumented immigrant is their enemy.

But the true enemy of the American worker is the degradation of work itself. When we allow *any* worker to be exploited, we degrade the value of *all* labor. When we permit a roofer to be treated like disposable equipment, we lower the floor for every carpenter and electrician. The fight for the rights of the undocumented is not charity; it is self-defense. Liberty is not a finite resource to be hoarded; it is an ecosystem that collapses if it is not shared.

We must also confront the complicity of the consumer. We are the beneficiaries of this system. The cheap food, the clean hotel rooms, the manicured lawns—these are the dividends of exploitation. We have become addicted to prices that lie about their true cost.

Breaking this addiction requires a new kind of consumer consciousness. It requires us to look at the strawberry and ask not just "Is it organic?" but "Was the picker paid?" It requires us to demand the same transparency for labor that we demand for ingredients. It requires us to recognize that a bargain purchased with another person's suffering is not a deal; it is a theft.

But individual action is not enough. The scale of this injustice demands the power of the state. We need a government that acts as a shield for the vulnerable, not a hammer for the exploiter. We need to fund the Labor Police, pass the Supply Chain Transparency Act, and enact Comprehensive Immigration Reform not because it is politically expedient, but because it is right.

There will be a cost to this transition. Prices in some sectors may rise. Business models built on fraud will collapse. But this is the cost of healing. It is the cost of realigning our economy with our values. It is the down payment on a future where American prosperity is built on innovation and productivity, not on the grim arithmetic of the sweatshop.

Imagine that future for a moment. Imagine an America where every worker on a construction site wears a safety harness and carries a union card. Imagine an agricultural sector where farmworkers are respected professionals, earning wages that support families, protected by the same laws as the office worker. Imagine a society where the child of an immigrant goes to school without fear, their mind free to learn, their potential unleashed to cure diseases or build starships.

This future is possible. It is within our grasp. But it requires us to stop looking away.

For too long, we have lived with a cognitive dissonance, celebrating the "nation of immigrants" while terrorizing the actual immigrants in our midst. We have tolerated a "shadow world" beneath the surface of our democracy. But shadows cannot sustain a republic. They rot the foundation.

The time has come to bring the shadow world into the light. The time has come to declare that in the United States of America, labor cannot be coerced, wages cannot be stolen, and human beings cannot be illegal.

We are defined not by the ideals we profess, but by the reality we tolerate. As long as we tolerate modern slavery in our fields and factories, we are not free. The chains that bind the undocumented worker bind us, too—to a lie, to a crime, and to a past we promised to leave behind.

The final chapter of this story has not yet been written. It will be written by the choices we make now. Will we be the generation that perfected the machinery of exploitation, or the generation that finally dismantled it?

The moral mandate is clear. The economic case is undeniable. The tools are in our hands.

Let us begin.

Selected Bibliography

American Immigration Council. "U.S. Citizen Children Impacted by Immigration Enforcement." Washington, D.C.: American Immigration Council, March 2017 & June 2021.

America's Voice. "Quotes from Farmers About Immigrants." Accessed July 2025. americasvoice.org.

CBS News. "Bipartisan lawmakers re-up immigration bill that would offer path to legal status." *CBS News*, July 2025.

Center for American Progress. "A New Immigration System To Safeguard America's Security, Expand Economic Growth, and Make Us Stronger." Washington, D.C., July 6, 2025.

Center for American Progress. "The 6 Key Takeaways from the CBO Cost Estimate of S. 744." Washington, D.C., June 21, 2013.

Center for Construction Research and Training (CPWR) & Labor Occupational Health Program (LOHP). "Building a Stronger, More Diverse U.S. Construction Workforce." Silver Spring, MD: CPWR, 2010.

Chobani. "Refugee Support Batch." Accessed July 2025. chobani.com.

City of Hialeah. "Elements of Human Trafficking." Hialeah, FL City Government. Accessed July 2025.

Community Psychology. "The Effects of Deportation on Families and Communities." *Community Psychology*, 2018.

Costa, Daniel. "Immigration enforcement is funded at a much higher rate than labor standards enforcement—and the gap is widening." Washington, D.C.: Economic Policy Institute, June 20, 2019.

Costa, Daniel. "New report finds that immigration enforcement is funded at much higher levels than labor standards enforcement—and the gap is widening." Washington, D.C.: Economic Policy Institute, May 2022.

Crane, Andrew, et al. "The Business of Modern Slavery: A Review of the Business Models of Modern Slavery." *Journal of Management Studies*, 2022.

Cronkite News. "What is the true taxpayer cost of immigrants in the country illegally?" Phoenix, AZ: Arizona PBS, March 2025.

End Slavery Now. "Bonded Labor." Accessed July 2025. endslaverynow.org.

Fair Food Program. "State of the Program Report 2021." Sarasota, FL: Fair Food Standards Council, 2022.

Fisk, Catherine, & Michael J. Wishnie. "The Story of 'Hoffman Plastic Compounds v. NLRB'." In *Labor Law Stories*. New York: Foundation Press, 2005.

Fuchsberg Law Firm. "Undocumented Construction Workers' Right to a Safe Work Environment." Accessed July 2025.

Global Reporting & Media. "When Businesses Empower Refugees: A Look at Chobani's Leadership." U.S. Foundation, June 23, 2023.

Harmse, J.L., et al. "The impact of physical and ergonomic hazards on poultry abattoir processing workers." *International Journal of Environmental Research and Public Health*, 2016.

Harvard T.H. Chan School of Public Health. "How childhood trauma can cause long-term health problems." Boston, MA: Harvard University, 2019.

Holzer, Harry J. "The Economic Costs of Child Poverty." Washington, D.C.: Urban Institute, 2007.

Holzer, Harry J., et al. "The Economic Costs of Poverty in the United States." Washington, D.C.: Center for American Progress, 2007.

Hope for Justice. "How much money is made by human trafficking and modern slavery?" Manchester, UK: Hope for Justice, March 2024.

International Labour Organization (ILO). "Profits and Poverty: The Economics of Forced Labour." Geneva: ILO, 2014.

Jurispro. "Grooming: The Unseen Weapon of Human Trafficking." *Jurispro*, April 7, 2025.

Kaiser Family Foundation. "Less than 1% of Total Medicaid Spending Goes to Emergency Care for Noncitizen Immigrants." San Francisco, CA: KFF, September 2024.

Kirchner, Julie. Testimony before the House Budget Committee. Washington, D.C.: U.S. House of Representatives, May 8, 2024.

League of United Latin American Citizens (LULAC). "A New Wave of Hate." Accessed July 2025. lulac.org.

Littler Mendelson P.C. "Wage Theft as a Crime: States Escalate Enforcement with Criminal Prosecution." *Littler ASAP*, June 2025.

Minneapolis Federal Reserve. "You can't tax what you can't see: The underground economy and its impact on the nation." *The Region*, 1994.

Minnesota Department of Labor and Industry. "Minnesota's wage theft law." St. Paul, MN. Accessed July 2025.

National Employment Law Project (NELP) & National Immigration Law Center. "Impact of Hoffman Plastic Compounds v. NLRB on the Rights of Undocumented Workers." New York: NELP, April 2016.

National Immigration Forum. "Fact Sheet: Undocumented Immigrants and Federal Health Care Benefits." Washington, D.C., Accessed July 2025.

Newsweek. "Mass Deportations Could Devastate These Small Businesses." *Newsweek*, July 2025.

Nilan Johnson Lewis PA. "Sentence Handed Down in Minnesota's First Felony Conviction for Criminal Wage Theft." Minneapolis, MN, June 2025.

Nowrasteh, Alex. "The Economic Effects of Immigration." Testimony before the U.S. House of Representatives, January 11, 2024.

Number Analytics. "Navigating Farm Labor Contractors in Agricultural Law." Accessed July 2025. numberanalytics.com.

Our Rescue. "The Economics of Human Trafficking." Accessed July 2025. ourrescue.org.

Owen, C., et al. "Human Trafficking and Labor Exploitation in United States Fruit and Vegetable Production." Fairfax, VA: Terrorism, Transnational Crime and Corruption Center (TraCCC), George Mason University, 2022.

PBS. "Africans in America, Part 4: Conditions of antebellum slavery." Accessed July 2025. pbs.org.

PBS. "Slavery by Another Name: Peonage." Accessed July 2025. pbs.org.

Peri, Giovanni. "Do immigrant workers depress the wages of native workers?" *IZA World of Labor*, 2014.

Polaris Project. "Human Trafficking and Social Media." Washington, D.C. Accessed November 2025.

Polaris Project. "Human Trafficking and the Transportation Industry." Washington, D.C. Accessed November 2025.

Polaris Project. "Polaris Analysis of 2021 Data from the National Human Trafficking Hotline." Washington, D.C., July 2022.

Rank, Mark R., & Michael McLaughlin. "Estimating the Economic Cost of Childhood Poverty in the United States." *Social Work Research*, 2018.

Respect International. "Shady business: Uncovering the business model of labour exploitation." May 2020.

Sanders, Bernie. "The Stop Bad Employers by Zeroing Out Subsidies (BEZOS) Act." U.S. Senate, 2018.

Stanford Graduate School of Business. "Mapping the Maze: Where the IRS Could Find Billions in Unpaid Taxes." Stanford, CA, 2023.

Stanford News. "Study uncovers hundreds of billions in missing revenue from U.S. 'tax gap'." Stanford, CA, April 2025.

Texas Department of Insurance. "Safety tips for poultry processing plants." Austin, TX. Accessed July 2025.

Tyson Foods. "Tyson Foods Strengthens its Commitment to Immigrant Team Members with $1.5M Investment." Springdale, AR: Tyson Foods, November 15, 2022.

United Nations Office on Drugs and Crime (UNODC). "Global Report on Trafficking in Persons 2020." Vienna: UNODC, 2021.

University of Michigan. "Undocumented Construction Workers in the U.S." Ann Arbor, MI, May 28, 2024.

U.S. Department of Agriculture, Food Safety and Inspection Service (FSIS). "PULSE Poultry Study." Washington, D.C.: USDA, 2019.

U.S. Department of Labor. "DOL's Approach to Combating Human Trafficking." Washington, D.C. Accessed July 2025.

U.S. Department of State. "Online Recruitment of Vulnerable Populations for Forced Labor." Washington, D.C.: Bureau of Democracy, Human Rights, and Labor, March 2024.

U.S. Department of State. "What Is Trafficking in Persons?" Washington, D.C. Accessed July 2025.

Voxy. "WDI Launches English Language Training Program for Refugee Employees at Chobani." New York: Voxy, July 24, 2019.

Yale & Slavery Research Project. "John C. Calhoun." New Haven, CT: Yale University. Accessed July 2025.